To mike + Verna
Happy Trails,
always,
Judy Frog-

# Mules Across the Great Wide Open

B. Shields '94

**A true western
adventure by**
## Jody Foss

**with illustrations by**
## Bonnie Shields

Mules Across the Great Wide Open
A true Western Adventure
by Jody Foss
illustrated by Bonnie Shields

Published by: Mules Across America
Box 225, Tomales, California, 94971 U.S.A.
Publishing consultant: Stoneydale Press
205 Main Street, Drawer B, Stevensville, Montana 59870

*First Printing, April 1995*
*Second Printing, November 1995*

Library of Congress Catalog Card Number: 94-096517

ISBN : Softcover: 0-9643413-0-1
Hardcover: 0-9643413-1-X

Library of Congress Cataloging in Publication Data

Foss, Jody A.
    Mules across the great wide open : a true Western adventure / by Jody Foss ; with illustrations by Bonnie Shields.
        p. cm
    Preassigned LCCN: 94-096517
    ISBN 0-9643413-0-1 (softcover)
    ISBN 0-9643413-1-X (hardcover)

    1. West (U.S.)--Description and travel. 2. West (U.S.)--History--1945- 3. Foss, Jody A. 4. Women travelers--West(U.S) 5. Oral history. I. Shields, Bonnie, ill. II. Title.

F595.3.F67 1995                          917.804'33
                                         QBI94-2380

PRINTED IN THE U.S.A.

*Robert Wuthrich, Henrys Lake, Idaho, 1976*
*Photo by Debbie Foss*

Happy Trails to You.
Hope they cross mine
again next summer.
. Be always welcome
in my Camp.
I love my adventurous
Jody too – Robert

# Acknowledgements

Special thanks to the following people,
who helped make this a book:

Don and Marilynn Foss, Dale Burk of Stoneydale Press,
Stevensville, Montana, for editing, proofreading, typeset-
ting, layout and consulting; Charlie Parker, Dan Erickson,
Fran Hentz, Mrs. Nell Huang, and Jan Williamson for
proofreading; Debbie Foss and John Najar for the beautiful
photographs; Robert Wuthrich for the cover photograph;
Daniela Gayle, cover designer, Sausalito, California; Thea
Schrack, photo hand-tinter, San Francisco, California;
Solzer and Hail, San Francisco; Diane Gordinier, photo
retoucher, Santa Rosa, California; Photoworks, Santa
Rosa; Chromographics, Santa Rosa; The Lab, Santa Rosa;
Bonnie Shields, Sandpoint, Idaho; Keith Matthews, Mac
Guru, Marshall, California; the patient staff of Kinko's,
Petaluma, California.

And to all my friends and family who encouraged me
endlessly.

*Jesse and Sadie on Babe, Mt. Baker, WA, 1918*

This book is dedicated to Grandma Sadie Foss, a true lover of Nature.

And to my old white mule, Sarah Jane, who carries my pack to paradise.

# Table of Contents

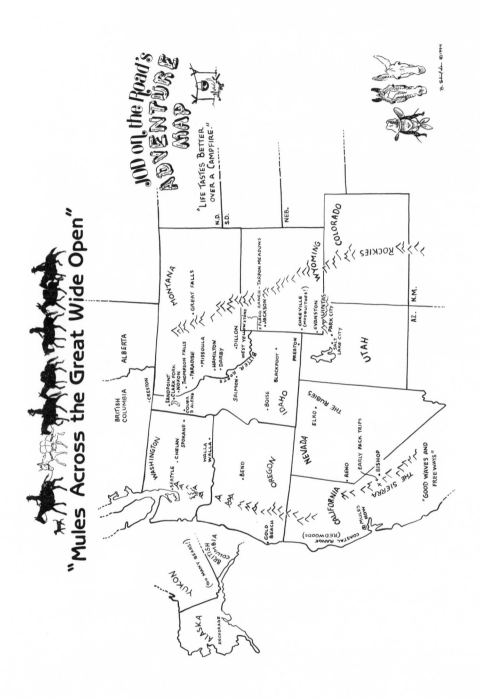

*Debbie Foss*

*Have you ever wondered
what it would be like to
ride off into the sunset?*

## *For The Love Of A High Country Trail*
## *Montrose, California. 1959*

This all started for me when I was a five year old with very short bangs, an innate love for all animals, and a nose for adventure. I found the half-acre hillside that was our backyard enough ground for the early years, spending the hours before dinner with my big blue eyes faceted on the tiny homestead I built at the base of Mom's roses.

The tiny creek, a tributary of the faucet runoff from the garden hose, flowed in front of the stick cabin I built of twig lumber, gathered from bushes that lined the yard. The path to the two-inch tall cabin was carefully paved with sand and trimmed with pebbles. And of course, there was a toothpick corral out in back of the cabin, on the edge of the roses' grand canal. That is where my first horse lived. His name was Sham. He was the living, invisible miniature version of the plastic stallion that slipped into my hands on my fifth birthday, and spent his days on the little white shelf in my bedroom, permanently prancing.

"Jody, Jody, Jody! Where are you, hon?" My mother yelled out the back door. I knew that soon Dad would be home from work; I could hear the sound of his engine from way past the corner where the school bus stopped.

"Go find her, will you, Deb?" She shouted out to the back yard.

"She's right there, Mom!" Debbie yelled from the upstairs bedroom window. I could see her through the screen. She was two and a half years older than me, and already in the second grade. Her bangs were equally as short; the mothers had lined my sister and I, Steffie, Jan and Suzie up on the break water wall on Balboa Island, cutting our bangs all at once, as if the five of us had one continuous forehead.

Debbie's eyes were golden brown, the color of horse chestnuts. Her teeth were large and white, she had a beauty mark she was ashamed of, and was always polite to adults in almost all situations, which impressed me greatly. She was equally as angelic as I was trouble, and I asked her questions incessantly from the time I first could talk. Everyone loved Deb; the teachers, my parent's friends, her classmates. She thought up adventurous schemes and I carried them out, much to her delight.

"Where? I can't see her!" Mom was annoyed. I could hear it in her voice, and could smell the garlic toast that had taken to flames, too close to the broiler. She turned and raced back into the smoking kitchen. Deb looked down at me, from the screened window.

"You burned the garlic toast, Jod!" She was smiling at me, through the window screen. I could hear Dad's car out in front of the garage door.

I took one last look at the cabin next to the creek with the horse in the backyard, picked a finger full of tender grass, and dropped it in the tiny feeding box in front of Sham. Usually, at night, my imaginary horse would jump the toothpick fence and race around the rose bushes, leaping over the creek with grace. I could hear the sound of his hooves on the brick path outside my window as I lay in bed, waiting for sleep.

We sat down to another beautiful well balanced dinner, something right out of Sunset Magazine. The table was set with matching napkin rings and place mats. Mom had dressed in a burnt orange felt shirt, that had huge olive green daisies sewn to it. Her outfit matched the place mats and the napkin rings, and this was not uncommon. Her hair was short too, but much shorter than ours, and jet black, with spit curls under each ear that stayed there with the help of a little hair spray. That night, her lipstick was a bright orange, and matched the napkins. Her gold pendant collection hung heavily from her wrist; a charm bracelet that represented everything special to her in fourteen karat gold. She was a beauty, there was no doubt about that, and she bubbled over with life, like a pan of water at a rolling boil. She looked admiringly at Dad as he loosened his tie.

The centerpiece would change with the table settings and my mom's outfit. There was no shortage of dried flowers and decorations in our house, and the rooms were often theme oriented, with long thin candles that color coordinated with everything else, tastefully placed on tables and mantles.

"How was your day, Donzie?" she asked him, smiling, sliding her spatula under the filet of sole with authority. It was stuck on the broiler pan.

"Great garlic toast, Mare!" he answered as he crunched into the buttery outside crust. Dad loved the heels of the sourdough. He was a young businessman in the City of Angels in the late Fifties with two daughters and a color coordinated wife.

He took another bite and we sat in silence while Harry Belafonte sang "Yellow Ribbons." Debbie and I joined in.

"And if I live to be one hundred," we wailed, "I will never know from where...." we continued, "came those ribbons, lovely ribbons, scarlet ribbons, for her hair." Mom and Dad clapped and we started dinner.

"Guess what, girls! We are going to the mountains!" he said as he wiped off his chin with the bright orange napkin. Mom tried to look thrilled, and I watched as her expression turned to one of panic.

"The mountains?! For how long?" she asked my dad.

She was already thinking about the menu. She would call Nancy Schmidt in the morning and talk over what they would bring.

Mom would have preferred to spend two weeks on a beach blanket across from the Fun Zone on Balboa Island, but when she married my father, the mountains were part of the package. They spent half their honeymoon in Carmel, perched on the edge of the Pacific in a stone cabin, and the other half in the High Sierras, searching the high country for the perfect fishing lake. Dad could have stayed up there forever. It was there that the world made sense to him.

"Yippee!" I yelled. I pushed back my half eaten dinner and knocked over a candle. In no time, the olive green place mat under my mom's plate was on fire, the burlap burning fast. "Yippee!" I yelled again, as I darted away from the table and galloped around the dining room. Dad dashed the burning mat with his tumbler of ice water.

I announced to the tiny Sham in the morning that he would be on his own for two weeks, and that the creek might get a little low unless we could get our dog training neighbors, the Jahelkas, to water for us. We would leave in two days. Mom spent several hours a day on the phone with the other mothers, arranging who would bring what. My Dad and Uncle Bill, Uncle John and Uncle Kenny cared more about the fishing equipment, the full bar, the first aid kit and the big tents we would take to keep the rain out of our ears.

We left Montrose as the last rays of the afternoon sun worked its way across the rugged San Gabriel Mountains, packing the little black Volkswagen with all the gear and putting the rest on top, on the ski rack. We raced up the Angeles Crest Highway, singing our repertoire of Mom and Dad's college songs and ones Deb had learned in Girl Scouts. I was to stay in the back, in the cubby hole, as Dad called it, behind the back seat. Mom poured a cup of coffee from the Thermos for Dad and the windows steamed up.

"Watch my crotch!" he said to her under his breath.

I looked out the back window upside down and imagined how lonely Sham would be in the miniature homestead without me, and how low the creek would be, maybe even dry, when I returned to my place under the rose bush.

Dad had told me all about the mule train that would carry our stuff up to the edge of the highest lake we could find. I closed my eyes and listened to my sister and my parents sing, "We'll Build a Bungalow Big Enough For Two" as the tiny round car crawled over the Angeles Crest in third gear. We hit the Mohave Desert and raced up the East side of the lower Sierra Range. I watched as the full moon lit the top of Mount Whitney, and fell asleep back there in the cubby hole, dreaming of tomorrow, and the real live horse that would carry me into the high country.

Mom and Dad drove along in silence, trying to think of things they had forgotten to pack. They could always go to the store in Bishop.

I woke up as the Volkswagen shifted down into low gear, just as the big neon bear on the Travel Lodge sign winked sleepily down at me. I carried my own sleeping bag up the stairs without opening my eyes, pretending I was still asleep. Mom and Dad would share the double bed and Deb and I would sleep in our bags on the floor. All the other families were there already. We were late. The Sierras were a deep blue velvet color in the darkness, a blue shadow behind the bright neon of the Travel Lodge sign.

At around four o'clock in the morning, I heard Uncle Bill Schmidt.

"YAAAK! YAAAK!" he screeched. He followed this wake up call with a short in and out whistle.

"YAAAK!" I could hear him approaching our room, as he walked up the aisle of the balcony. I could hardly contain myself. I was going on a pack trip! I wriggled out of my sleeping bag and rolled it up, in one continuous motion.

"Where's my toothbrush, Deb?" I asked loudly. She always knew the answers.

"You better keep track of it Jody, because where we're going, there are no stores." She scowled sleepily at the mirror, forcing a comb through her tangled light brown hair. She was wearing her new banana yellow camping jacket, a little nylon windbreaker with double pockets and a Yosemite emblem sewn on the sleeve. She reached into her pocket, feeling for the Swiss Army knife, her chocolate bar, and her mittens.

"Here it is, Jod!" Mom whispered. She was trying to be quiet, to set a good example. You don't yell at the top of your lungs in the Travel Lodge at four in the morning.

She handed me the toothbrush. "How did it get on the floor?" she asked me, another one of those questions that had no good answer. I smiled, as Uncle Bill repeated the wake up whistle.

"What about him?" I asked Mom. "He isn't whispering." We always asked each other questions that had no logical answer. The toothbrush had just ended up on the floor, and Uncle Bill was just

Uncle Bill.

Uncle Bill had worked as a firefighter and a mule packer in Yosemite National Park when he was twenty years old, and had hiked the high country ever since then, fishing every stream he could. My Dad and Uncle Bill were adventurers, and avid fishermen, and taught me all about baiting the hook, casting the line, and waiting for a bite. They enjoyed eating the beautiful rainbow and brown trout they caught, but most of all they loved the peaceful serenity they found on the edge of a rushing high country stream.

By four-thirty we were in the cars, heading for the pack station. Bishop sits at the base of the mountains, and the pack station was three miles up a steep hill on a dirt road, above a little lake. I rode along in the cubby hole in silence for once, unable to think of anything but the horse I would ride, and the big gentle mules that would carry our supplies for us. I reached in my pocket and wrapped my fingers around the Hershey bar I had stashed away there.

It was daybreak at the old corral, and the head packer, a thin dark haired man in a blue plaid cowboy shirt tried to organize everything we had brought into the wooden pack boxes, two for each mule. He had a wooden leg, and tapped it against a box, scratching his head.

"I don't see the kitchen sink! Did you leave it at home?" He laughed a little and said to my Dad and Bill, "You'll need a few more mules."

He had on a dusty black cowboy hat that looked like he never took it off, even in bed. He looked at the fifteen of us, unloading everything we had decided we couldn't live without, on to the old wooden loading dock. The sleeping bags, the tents, the canvas tarps, all the sacks and boxes of food for fifteen days; books, lanterns, duffles of clothes, fishing poles and first aid equipment. We all stood by, brimming over with anticipation.

It took six packers two hours to get all of our stuff onto twelve mules. I sat and watched, in awe, with my hands in my pockets, melting the Hershey bar. The big dark brown mules stood still as statues, majestic and patient, while the wranglers hoisted a hundred and fifty pounds onto each mule, slinging wooden pack boxes and canvas bags over the wooden sawbuck saddles. Then they piled our sleeping bags and tents up on the top of the packs. I climbed to the top rail of the fence and watched as the packers threw the diamond hitch over the white canvas manty; in a few swift motions they turned a long cotton rope into a perfect diamond, securing each load this way.

An hour later the packers had all fifteen of us on saddle horses. We milled around the corral, testing out the steering, gently touching their manes, talking softly to them, until all the mules were packed and we were ready to ride up the trail into the wilderness.

"Look at your horse," Debbie said to me, pulling up next to me on her big blue eyed Appaloosa named Steel. "He looks like Sham."

He did, too. He was big and red and the head packer said he rode him himself the entire summer before. His name was Blaze. I waited, quietly, patiently. I had a feeling for this. Another fifteen minutes and the packers had checked our saddle cinches and adjusted our stirrups.

Then, almost like magic, the head wrangler somehow worked all those mules, all tied together, into one long line, and headed up the trail. The mules knew just what to do. We followed. This was the beginning of my life on the trail. I loved, from the very first, waking up by a river in the middle of nowhere.

The well worn Sierra trail stretched out before me. I had my canteen, my parka. Half the Hershey's was gone already. My horse, Blaze, didn't seem to like chocolate. I held onto the saddle horn and sat up there for hours, watching the mountain scenery. White granite boulders, huge and foreboding, hung over our heads, on both sides of the trail. The wrangler had told us it would take all day to get to the lake. I could see my mom's jet black hair, shining in the hot sun, several horses ahead.

After a lunch break we continued on, following the switchback trail through the pine trees, and up over the top of a high divide, above the timberline. I listened to the sound of Blaze's big hooves as he worked his way between the granite that seemed to be everywhere. The sun was bright, throwing boomerangs of light off the sheer cliffs above and below our pack train. I reached down and gave Blaze a loving pat on his neck.

"I have a horse at home," I told the big red gelding. He carefully chose his footing as his ears moved rapidly back and forth, responding to my voice. "He's only three inches tall though, and he lives under a rose bush in a toothpick corral." His head moved slowly from side to side. He was a gentle horse and listened to everything I said, never misplacing his footing. We came to a big rushing river that looked deep to me, and crossed it, one by one, in silence. The freezing water brushed against the cinches on the horses' and mules' bellies. I felt the water soak through my shoe, in the stirrup.

We reached our camping spot by the lake as the sun disappeared behind a ten thousand foot peak. There, the packer unloaded every single mule, as they waited patiently, tied to trees. The mothers immediately sprung into action, while the kids walked around in circles, stretching their legs, before running off to see the creek. I stood by Blaze, staring up at his big, gentle eyes.

"He's been up that trail a thousand times, little lady," the wrangler said to me as he undid a diamond hitch on a big red mule's

pack.

"How old is he?"

"Blaze? Oh, twelve or so. He's a good gelding, real good stock. Did you like riding him?" he asked me, looking down at me from under his beat up, trampled down, white felt cowboy hat. He had brilliant blue eyes, the color of the lake he had led us to.

I looked at him and said, "Oh yes. I loved riding him," and squirmed around the other side of Blaze, sliding under his neck.

"I would love to stay right here, with Blaze, forever," I said seriously to the man in the white hat.

"See how you feel in fifteen days!" he laughed, as the mule he was unpacking swatted at a fly with his long red tail.

Auntie Steve, a dear friend of my parents and my Godmother, had agreed to the fifteen day mountain trip, as long as the husbands agreed to build her a special wilderness bathroom.

"I'm sorry, but I need a little more than a shovel and a tree to hide behind," she had told them.

The construction of her bathroom was remarkable. Taking several hours to build, the dads considered it a work of art. They carefully hung a red and white striped canvas between the trees, boxing in an area for the toilet. A small seat was placed on top of some pine poles they had made into the throne. They had a small mirror, and carefully hung it on one wall. Auntie Steve came to the wilderness and brought a touch of luxury with her.

"Can you build me a bathtub?" she asked Uncle John and Dad as she walked towards them with cocktails. "Here's some hors d'oeuvres." She gracefully balanced water chestnuts wrapped in bacon on a soggy paper plate. Auntie Steve looked beautiful, even in her camping clothes.

The men were glad to build her a bathtub, too, which we all enjoyed. It was a big tin tub with a canvas tarp wrapped around it, with water boiled on the campfire mixed with the cold stream water, and was a perfect place to get squeaky clean after a long hard day of fishing and hiking in the mountains.

I watched as the packer tied all the riding horses together, and then tied all the big gentle mules to the long string of horses.

"I'll be back to pick you up in fifteen days!" he said to my father as he threw his leg over the saddle and gathered his reins. "Let's go," he said quietly to the long string, turning his black and white Paint horse up the hill and back to the trail.

"Goodbye, Blaze," I said softly. I stood there and watched them leave, listening to the bells as they faded behind the sound of the river. I stood there a long time, beside the well worn Sierra trail. The dust settled, and the handsome wrangler and his horse, the dude horses, and the twelve mules had disappeared from my high Sierra world.

I became familiar with boulder jumping, setting a hook and finding my own way back to camp. This was as close to Paradise as I had been in all my five years on the planet Earth. My family and friends around me, fresh trout in the pan, four mothers to keep everything rolling, and more stars than I had ever seen.

Julie, Sue, Steffie, Debbie and I dammed up a little pond, a natural punch bowl, in the creek that our camp bordered. This little dammed area, with its built up rocks and the slow intake of fresh stream water, was the perfect Fizzy bowl. With the wilderness as our playground and carbonated strawberry Fizzies flowing freely in the creek, fifteen days passed much too quickly. Mornings came early, with the familiar squawk from the Schmidt tent; that whistle that sounded like an old parrot on a pirate ship.

The trout always seemed to be up close and jumping, just as the early morning sun gradually appeared over the white granite ridge that protected us from the rest of the high country. Dad and I would get our warm gear on, grab our poles and food for lunch, and hike around to the dark side of the lake, moving quietly along the small foot trail that passed through a large meadow of skunk cabbage and cattails. The dark side, where morning came almost an hour later, was where I learned how to cast my line onto the quiet water, as a large dragonfly circled the place where my line broke into the lake.

It was at this place, sitting silently on the gigantic granite border of the lake, I learned how the high mountain sun feels on your skin, and how a day can pass, from lazy hour to lazy hour, ending with late night hot chocolate and stories around the campfire. The number of stars I could see, from the rocky cliffs above our camp, numbered into the Too Many to Count, and that was when I first noticed the stars you think you can see but can't be sure. The stars are there, but they are so far away they are almost invisible.

Dad and I sat high up on the rock late at night. He held on to me, with his arms wrapped tightly around my shoulders, as if to protect me from the black velvet vastness of the dark Sierra sky and too many falling stars.

"Where do the stars fall to, Daddy?" I asked him, looking out from beneath the hood of my red parka.

"They don't fall," he told me, as we watched the sky, alive with light. "They are just the same stars, racing around the Earth. Now here they come, around again," he said with a laugh.

By the time the wrangler returned, we had almost forgotten about going back, except for the Moms who had started talking about the comforts of home on the tenth day out. The rest of us would have eventually forgotten about our old lives, settling into a steady diet of trout and berries, at least until the winter snows brought us to our senses. After all, we were from the City of Angels, and we were all very fond of nice weather.

The horses and mules could be heard from a mile away, with their bells echoing off the granite. The Mothers were moving fast. Though all the food was gone, save half a jar of peanut butter and some pancake mix, there was still plenty of gear to pack out on the mule string. The sound of the bells got louder and louder as they headed towards our camp. Making sure that the fire had been drowned with eight buckets of that blessed fresh spring water, we left not even a tent stake behind.

After the last of the big brown mules picked its way over the white pine root across the trail and crossed the stream, the chipmunks arrived with their families, to set up camp and live happily for weeks on the bounty of our families' crumbs.

Heading back to our ranchette, I gazed out at the full moon from the small cubby hole of the Volkswagen. The lower Sierras, heading South by Mount Whitney, were shining in the glow of the whitest moon. I stared at the moon's sad face, leaning down over the mountains, as if he was sorry to see me go. I fell asleep to the sound of the shifting gears, dreaming of the big red horse that had carried me so close to Paradise.

I was never the same after that.

I loved the smell of my skin in the hot high country sun, after a skinny dip across the lake, for ten dollars on a dare. I loved the large, intelligent eyes of the big red mules, the smell of the leather and the horse I rode. I was incurably horse crazy, and it was going to take more than the fast ponies at the Griffith Park Pony Rides to satisfy me. I had left my heart back there by the mountain stream, off the high country trail. From that moment on, I spent my time dreaming of a horse and mule of my own.

B. Shields '94

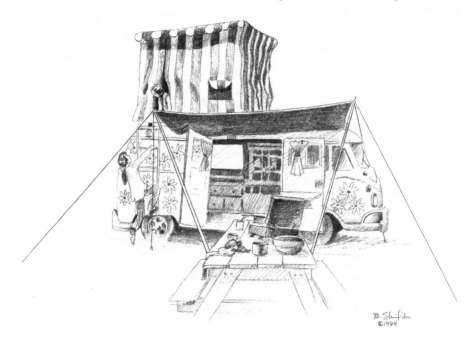

## *La Cañada, California, 1967: Shangri-la*

I watched the Christmas special on television starring Bob Hope in Vietnam. I cried, sitting there with my hand in the greasy popcorn bowl, warm in my flannel pajamas, as the cameras panned across the huge crowd of young men in dirty uniforms, sitting on the ground in front of Bob and his troupe; Christmas cheer, inches away from the war. They were very young, some of them only a few years older than I.

He went to Vietnam several years in a row during the war, as a morale booster, travelling on small planes with four or five beautiful women, bringing his routine with a tense smile to the soldiers. Each year I would write him and ask him the same question. I asked him why we had to fight the war, and he would write a letter back to me. He would say that the Shangri-la in which we lived was only free because of the young men who were willing to give their lives to the country so we could remain free. I never understood exactly what he meant, as the drama of the war unfolded before my eyes in black and white on the television, after dinner and before homework.

La Cañada was Shangri-la. Bob Hope was right about that. Aside from school, my life was a permanent vacation. My sister and I bathed in the luxury of my parents joie de vivre. From Capistrano Beach to the tennis courts of the Kona Kai Club, they were out to enjoy every moment of their lives together, and we got to come along for much of the fun.

The first thing they had built together, after returning from their honeymoon, was the party shack. It took up most of their tiny back yard and was like something off the set of South Pacific. With fish nets hanging from the thatched roof, a bamboo bar and speakers blaring Harry Belafonte, big tall tropical drinks were sipped from pineapples my mom dug out with a slotted spoon.

If we weren't on a pack trip in the high country, skiing in Mammoth, or hiking into volcanoes in Hawaii, we were galloping horses on the beach in Ensenada. Life at this point was one long picnic.

Instead of investing in stocks and bonds, my parents invested in their vacations. This always made sense to me. We were taught not to complain; they told us it ruins another person's time, and we were not to run around swimming pools. Mom thought that waiting a half hour after eating to swim was an old wive's tale. There were very few restrictions, as long as we stuck to the program, which was for the most part plenty to think about. There was always some holiday approaching, something to look forward to.

Dad and Mom had purchased a Volkswagen camper by this time, and in it we travelled the back roads of the West. Dad really liked the dirt roads. Mom, with her bag of tricks in her tiny camper kitchen, created some incredible meals in minutes on the Coleman stove, and we would eat on the tiny fold down table as the sun set over the ocean, behind a high peak, or over the desert, wherever our vagabonding had taken us.

Dad built a box rack on the top that served as our bedroom. It had a little ladder that led us into our own private red and white striped canvas tent on top of the van. Deb and I would lay awake for hours up there, listening to the sounds of the various birds and critters that lurked in the shadows of our campground. Dad liked most of all to drive a dirt road to the very end, just to make sure we had the best camping spot available. This often lasted until seven or eight at night, and he would say, "Just around the next bend, kids."

We were born to wander. I attribute my insatiable wanderlust to my parents, and the thousands of miles we drove in that oil-burning Volkswagen van. To show our appreciation, Debbie and I covered it with big plastic daisy stickers that welded themselves to the fading red paint job and remained there forever, fading in the hot California sun, long past the Summer of Love.

At school, things were getting pretty interesting, and I was certifiably boy crazy. I sat next to John Kautz in Math that year, and the smell of his after shave, Aramis, filled my little world and I could make no sense of the numbers game. I spent most of my time drawing horses along the border of the math problems, batting my eyelashes, thick with mascara, at John Kautz, as he excelled, receiving an "A" at the end of the year. I could not see the numbers on the blackboard, unable to see beyond this blue eyed, blond haired boy with whom I shared the table.

By this time my sister Debbie and I had ridden every saddle nag and stallion from Hansen Dam to Flintridge Riding Stables, and we had escaped to the High Sierras every year for two or three weeks, and each year I left a piece of my heart next to the high mountain stream. Eleven months was a long time to wait to rekindle my love for the rugged life under the stars, in the company of the gentle horses and pack mules I had grown to love.

My friend, Laurie Weed, was almost as horse crazy as I. She was tall and blonde, with an open smile, and long tan legs. Her parents, Bud and Carolyn, had a sail boat down in San Pedro Harbor. Laurie and her sister, Currie, had twin dinghies called the Pee Weed and the Wee Weed. The big sail boat was called the C. Weed, named after Carolyn.

"What do you want more than anything?" I asked her as we raced into the surf at Corona one afternoon. We were both running very fast across the sand, in the pink and orange striped bikinis her mom had picked up for us. She would buy several of the same thing, if it looked cute on Laurie.

She looked over at me, smiling, and said, "A horse," as she passed me, diving into the shallow surf and swimming off under the breaking waves. I followed her, and thought about what she had said.

Laurie had stayed overnight at my house, and we were

spending the day as we pleased, walking down Foothill Boulevard to Flintridge Riding Stables, with a stop by Jack in the Box for a nineteen cent taco. We were dressed in shorts; mine were lime green and hers were orange. We both had our Slicker Lip Gloss in the pocket of our surfer shirts, bright with lime green and orange stripes. Each of us had a St. Christopher on, a token from the boy we were going steady with. Usually our friend Muffi arranged these unions for us. The guy always wore cords or Levis, desert boots and button down shirts or T-shirts. Often, the St. Christopher was thrown across the school room in an act of courtship. We chased these boys relentlessly until they were ours, breaking up with them on a monthly basis, with no hard feelings.

We climbed the chain link fence that stood tall between us and the horses, one at a time dropping into the soft, freshly raked dirt. The place smelled wonderful to me. Every time I went riding I would avoid washing for as long as I could  because I loved the smell of horses on my hands.

"Look at this!" Laurie said to me, grabbing my shoulder and steering me towards a small pole corral at the back of the stable. A small sign said "For Sale" and a little  charcoal pony stared out at us expectantly from behind the bars.

"Isn't he cute?" she asked me, as she reached through and grabbed his light grey forelock. She scratched him on his forehead and around his ears. "He's so cute," she repeated, quietly, to herself.

"I think he is too. I wonder how much they want for him. Let's find out." I stood up on the bottom bar and looked in at the little grey pony. He was as wide as he was tall and looked smart enough. But, no matter how much we wanted him to be ours, we would still need roller skates to keep our feet from scraping the ground, and our legs were getting longer by the day.

This was a really cute pony, but no matter how much we wanted him, it wouldn't make him any taller. He was not our size. We both knew this, but we didn't talk about it. We walked up the bridle trail and back to my house. All the way there, as we walked the Saturday away, we talked about what we would do if we had our own pony.

"Mom!  Mom!" I screamed, heading towards the house at a dead gallop with Laurie close behind.

Mom was vacuuming. She had on a bright red sweater and black pants. Her lipstick matched the sweater. "Hi, girls," she said to us both. The vacuum drowned out everything I blurted out about the pony. She was listening to Trini Lopez, and he was competing with the vacuum.

"We'll walk over to Flintridge in the morning and the evening and feed him," I told her. The vacuum whined as it picked up the cat's plastic toy. Trini Lopez wailed and I kept at it. "We'll trade off! It can't be more than four miles. That's not a bad walk. And he's only two hundred dollars. We each have a hundred saved. You'll love him, Mom!" I smiled at her. She hadn't heard a word I had said about the pony.

Laurie's mom came down and picked her up. They were going to sail out to Catalina Island for the rest of the weekend.

At dinner, I told Mom and Dad all about Chap, the little pony.

"How tall is this pony?" my dad asked me.

"Not too tall," I shrugged.

"Short!" Debbie said. "He sounds too short! What're you gonna do, Jod, wear wheels?" She laughed, and put some sour cream on her baked potato.

After dinner, we watched Lassie. I had homework. There was to be a math test tomorrow. The phone rang, and mom pushed back from the table and went in to answer it.

"Hi Marilynn, this is Nancy." It was Nancy Tipton. Mom opened the fridge door and grabbed a strawberry from a green plastic basket.

"Hi Nancy. What's new?"

"Not much, really, Mare," Nancy answered. The Tiptons lived on a palm tree bordered street that made a straight line to the foothills, in a little ranchette of their own, with lots of nice eucalyptus and pines and plenty of room for a goat they called Katarina, a boxer named Nugget and a cat named Puff.

"Well, Jody and Laurie have decided they have to buy this little pony named Chap. He's down at Flintridge Riding Club and he's two hundred dollars. They say they'll walk each morning to feed him. That is at least a four mile walk! Give them two weeks and Carolyn and I will be driving them down there with alfalfa hay in our car trunks. And he sounds too short," my mother continued. "Every time we ask her how tall he is, she just smiles and shrugs." Mom was silent. She was picking seeds from the strawberry caught in between her teeth.

"He sounds fat and short," my mom said again, thoughtfully into the receiver.

"And the girls are sprouting like weeds!" Nancy said.

Mom and Nancy were both quiet for a moment. Mom was rearranging the cookbooks in the rack in front of her, pulling one out, The Good Housekeeping Cookbook.

"Nanc, I tried that BBQ rib recipe. It was a smashing success!" Mom said enthusiastically.

"Well, just a minute!" Nancy said. "The eight ponies running free up at Dad's in Apple Valley need permanent homes. They're running wild, and Grandpa doesn't want them up there any more. They're beautiful, too. Sarah and Star are the biggest and best trained of them all. They would be big enough for the girls."

Mom was silent, thinking.

"We'd give them to you, Mare, no charge, as long as you keep them in the family," she continued.

Mom smiled, and said, "What a wonderful offer, Nancy. The ponies need homes and the girls need ponies. I'll talk to Jody about it."

They both walked back to their dinner tables, quietly, thoughtfully, remembering the years they had spent together, young friends on spirited horses, galloping along the wash. They had been friends a long time, since they were fourteen.

We drove out to Apple Valley, with Kenny and Nancy Tipton, humming along in a rented truck, towing a two horse trailer. It was Mother's Day. Laurie and I could hardly speak, which was rare for us. Mom had made a big batch of Rancher Cookies and we filled up on those. It was a three hour drive that seemed like three days. Time stood still, and the air was heavy with anticipation.

As we drove up to the ranch, turning onto the bumpy dirt driveway of Grandpa Tipton's place, the ponies raced us along the wire. Two large red ponies, Sarah and Star, were in the front. Behind them were two smaller black ponies, Romeo and Juliet. Then there were two more, black and white. They were called Snip and

Snap. They were showing off, as if they knew we were coming for them. Their manes were long, their coats shiny and sleek. It was already warming up in the desert, and their winter coats were long since gone.

They were easy to catch, and jumped into the horse trailer in seconds flat. The rest of the herd stood by as we drove back down the bumpy dirt road, then galloped behind us, as far as they could go, stopped by the wire. Sarah and Star were crying out to the others, and they cried back. Soon the truck hit the highway, and their new lives had begun. We were so happy, they had to feel that.

Dad let us ride home in the horse trailer with the ponies, all the way back over the mountains to La Cañada. Dad was like that; he didn't always go by the book. We sat in the alfalfa, up on the feed boxes, as the ponies tasted the delicious hay, and started in to eat.

We were mesmerized. Ponies of our own! We looked at each other knowingly; we were the luckiest twelve year old girls in the whole world. The smell of the hay and the ponies filled the trailer.

"Can you believe how beautiful they are, Laur?" I asked her.

"No I can't," she answered. We couldn't take our eyes off them. They were the color of caramel, with cream colored manes. Star's mane was almost white, and very long and straight. Sarah's hair was frizzy compared to Stars, and she was a little shorter. They smelled like the desert, like sagebrush and juniper. Soon, we would be racing up the canyon to the place where the streams begin.

Everything was different after that.

## Across the Creek and Up the Canyon

Laurie lived right down the road from the Kruse place, and she had skipped over there on Friday and asked Mr. Kruse if we could keep Sarah and Star in his corral. We both knew it was empty; everyone in the neighborhood knew. He said yes right away, without hesitation.

"As long as you let my daughter Lindy ride once in a while," he told Laurie.

When Mrs. Kruse had died, leaving Mr. Kruse with the two children, a boy twelve and a girl seven, he had sold her horses, leaving the stalls and corral empty. The tack room, at one end of the red wooden building, contained too many memories for Mr. Kruse. His deceased wife's chaps hung on the wall in the corner, green and white leather ones with "Alice" written in big suede letters down each leg. The silver conch buttons were tarnished, and the spiders had built homes in the folds of the white leather.

We never touched these; we just looked at them through windows that needed cleaning. Mr. Kruse never went up there; hadn't since she died. No one went into this tack room. It remained a memorial to Mrs. Kruse for as long as we kept the ponies there. Liniments, ointments and salves, in old, greasy tins, lined the dirty shelves. Brushes to groom with, in every shape and size, were neatly arranged in another old cabinet. Feed store calendars, with pictures of parade queens on Palominos dressed in silver tack, hung crookedly on big rusty nails. And a picture of Alice and her big Palomino sat on the dusty window sill. The room was off limits to us. We just knew this; no one had to tell us to leave everything as it was.

This corral was on the edge of the wilderness. On the far reaches of our town, it sat there, in its barn red brilliance, the gateway to a quiet world of old pines, rushing creeks, formidable boulders, steep trails, and fire roads that crossed the San Gabriel Mountains, ending up at the edge of the Mohave Desert.

The corral area was large, with a big old sycamore shading most of it. The fence was all board, and we immediately white

washed it. We had two stalls which we cleaned daily, and a nice tack room of our own on the far end of the building. It was actually just a feed room, but it was much more to us than just a place to keep the ponies' hay and grain.

It was the fantasy ranch of our dreams, a home away from home where, on the backs of these wild ponies, we became the cowgirls we had always wanted to be. We had our own ponies, our own corral, our very own tack room and saddle pads. We had thousands of acres to explore and we disappeared into the canyon every chance we got, galloping up the small dirt trail that followed the stream up the draw to a waterfall. As the rest of our girlfriends became more and more interested and involved with the young men, Laurie and I lived in a world all our own, far away from the pressures of being thirteen. I was viewing the world from the back of my pony and it looked pretty good from there.

We painted the outside of the building, sprucing up the old red barn with new paint. We hung horse shoes, found under the big tree, above the doors of the two stalls and our tack room. We put yellow gingham curtains up in the window, and hung our bridles, halters, ropes and saddle pads on nails on the wooden wall. There were always two or three bales of hay in the corner. We framed a big autographed picture of Dale Evans and Roy Rogers and placed it above the door.

Two rats named Stuart and Stanley lived under the pine floor boards of our tack room, and approached us with interest. They soon figured out we wouldn't hurt them, so we could pick them up and carry them around. They were large black and white rats, certainly someone's lost pets. Stuart didn't stay for more than a year or so; we think he fell prey to the Kruse's cat. But Stanley stayed around for three years.

We built the rat a little wooden table, three inches wide and three inches tall. Then Jan, my best friend who lived right up the street from the corral, gave me a miniature cast iron stove to put by the hole to his bedroom. A tiny window, just like the big one directly above it, was trimmed with frilly yellow gingham curtains.

On school mornings, after we fed the ponies their alfalfa hay and sweet grain, we would dress for class in the tack room. Stanley would ride my tights all the way up my leg without running them.

We laughed so much over that black and white rat. He really liked the little home we had put together for him, always peeping his head out of his hole in the floorboards, checking the table for offerings of fruit and grain.

I made a mailbox in my dad's shop for Stanley. It was no larger than the rest of his furniture, and on it I printed Stanley Rat: 100 Pony Place, La Cañada, California, U.S.A.

After school and on the weekends, we rode Sarah and Star out across the creek and up the canyon, riding into our own private world, a magic world, where the years passed without a care. The little chestnut ponies carried us easily down the fern and pine trail leading up the canyon, and awaited our arrival after school with anticipation.

"Let's go down to the ring," Laurie shouted back to me, as she trotted up the trail on the pony Star. Star was always Laur's favorite. I can see her now, Twiggy cut bouncing up and down, blonde bangs over her eyes, racing down the trail; long brown legs wrapped tightly around the little pony.

"O.K. Yee Ha!" I yelled out. The cry echoed off the narrow walls of the canyon. The ponies were sure footed, and could trot gracefully down rocky trails and roads without missing a step. We grasped their long white manes in our fists, wrapping their long, thick hair around our hands. We never had saddles, only saddle pads, but usually we rode the ponies bareback.

"Let's go see Mrs. Crapo!" I said to Laurie, on my back next to the little stream, with Sarah grazing next to me. She nibbled the grass all around my bare feet, and was very careful not to catch my toes in her teeth.

We liked the ride to the Crapo's cabin. It was a narrow trail, rocky, with brush and trees hanging over it on both sides. It opened up into the lower reaches of the Crapo's yard. Large sycamores and oaks shaded the spacious log cabin. There was a beautiful waterfall, surrounded by deep dark ferns, just up the trail above their house. We tied our ponies to the trees out in front, already smelling the fresh cookies she had just pulled out of her oven.

Mrs. Crapo was big and round, with thick ankles and a kind heart, lonely for children. We rode into her life one Saturday morning, when we followed the trail into her yard. She lived there with her long, stringy old husband, Asa, who seemed ancient to me. They lived there for years, as caretakers of the canyon. Squirrels, chipmunks, raccoons and skunks lived comfortable lives at their doorstep, and little animals and all children were welcome to spend time in their private paradise. Laurie and I, after riding for two or three hours, found ourselves in Agatha's kitchen, washing our hands, and then partaking in whatever delicious treat she had just baked. Squirrels watched us with envy from the box of geraniums, next to the big window, as we savored every bite of her cookies. Always, she sent us off with something for later, wrapped in wax paper and held together with a rubber band. They never asked us about our lives outside of the canyon.

Our parents never saw us much after that. Once these sweet, furry, four-legged babysitters showed up on the scene, we had plenty to keep us busy. They had agreed we could have the ponies, as long as Laurie and I picked up the bills. This was the best thing they could have ever done for us, because we started our own business, calling it "La Cañada's Birthday Ponies". Laurie and I were both the budding young daughters of ad men, and we both knew the value of advertising. Our fliers, carefully produced with ink pens and colored paper, were all over town. From laundromat bulletin boards to the local paper, we advertised our pony ride service.

The Honolulu Days parade took place every year, in Montrose. We took the opportunity to spread flyers all over town, with Lindy Kruse and her friends, shy and skinny eight year olds, handing them out along the parade route. The flyer read, "Having a Party? Call La Cañada's Birthday Ponies!" and had our phone numbers at the bottom, written in bold shadow letters. The little girls passed these out of baskets they carried, as Laurie and I, dressed in matching lavender outfits we got at Pam's, rode our ponies proudly, our growing legs hanging a foot from the ground. We were covered in lavender satin ribbons and flowers.

Our dads had rented a small trailer, more suitable for hauling tables and chairs than ponies, and the ponies rode in it to the parade.

Our phones rang off the hook, and we booked our weekends with parties, always having plenty of money to pay for the ponies' feed, shoeing, tack, shots and anything we couldn't resist at the feed store. That was my first job. Laurie and I were our own bosses, and we were making money having fun.

The birthday parties arrived in big station wagons, usually with one mom in charge of twenty-four or so party goers, between the ages of three and nine or ten. Laurie and I had the ponies dressed in matching navy blue saddle pads, trimmed in Swiss ribbon, with balloons tied to their long white tails. We were usually ready and waiting when the party arrived.

"Walk!" the mother in charge yelled as the children streamed excitedly towards the ponies. In an hour, we would give each child at least two rides, and the birthday boy or girl an extra ride. We then took the party into the tack room, making them stand quietly in front of Stanley the Rat's hole. Before too long, Stanley would peek his head out of the hole at the eager, curious children. We never let them pick him up, because that would have been too much for him. They would stand and stare in disbelief as he carefully came up from his hole, and gracefully ate the single grape, or a piece of cookie we had placed on his little wooden table.

Out beyond the last of suburbia, in the high chaparral, I grew from a child to a young woman, with my feet never touching the ground.

*I soar as if on the wings of eagles*
*Across the mountains, all around me, the smell of pines*
*and open air.*
*Below me, my beloved earth.*
*The sky, the cold morning,*
*the rushing rapids on the river.*
*This is my home.*
*I soar from one mountain to the next.*
*It's morning, my favorite time.*
*The quiet is music to my ears,*
*the spirits surround me, touch me,*
*hold me in their arms like a small child.*
*Each wild flower, each tree,*
*each cloud, are creations of beauty,*
*And I soar, as if on the wings of eagles.*
*I am here forever, I am here for awhile.*
*All day and night, the spirit smiles on me,*
*amused, watching me grow.*
*This is why I am here.*
*The tiny yellow wild flower on the trail.*
*This is my home.*
*I would like to put on my boots and walk from shore*
*to shore.*
      *Jody 1972*

## Dangers of a Liberal Arts Education

I had just started another semester at Whitworth College, "behind the pine cone curtain", as we called it, and had changed my major three times in two years. I was living in an old chicken coop I fixed up, moving off the campus when they banned dogs. We organized the "Poop in the Loop Group", and they still banned dogs, so my brindle Lab puppy, Robin, and I moved to the coop. It was an old abandoned chicken shack with a feed bin and a big pane window. I made it my own.

There was no electricity going out to the coop from Albert's house. I used the bathroom in the house, and paid thirty-five dollars a month for the rent. I had three little gas lanterns and a wood stove. The bed was built high in the far corner, and the feed bin I used as my dresser. In two weeks the place had been transformed from a former chicken house into a very small cozy cabin, varnished and smelling sweet. Nobody could believe it.

On really cold mornings, my hair would be frozen to my pillow, and Albert would come out and tap on it, to wake me up for class. It was easy to go to bed with wet hair, when the little wood stove had the temperature well into the eighties in the evenings. It was a very cozy place with the fire going. But once it went out, the place felt a lot like the chicken coop it was. No amount of fixing could change that, it seemed. Snow storms still managed to find their way to my bed, and I would often wake up with a snow drift at my feet.

Attending Whitworth College was enlightening. My boyfriend Evan and I had driven up to Spokane in his convertible Jeep, dreamers looking for big wide valleys with little log cabins in them. We had taken five days to get there, driving through mountain towns, dreaming of living out in the sticks together until the cows came home.

Sleeping out under a dark blanket sky covered with diamonds, Evan and I lay on our backs, in our sleeping bags, on the edge of a

northern Idaho lake called Coeur d'Alene. The stars were dancing on the water, which sparkled like the silver suit of a baton twirler in a parade.

"I can't believe there are so many stars," I said to him. I reached over and stuck my hand in his sleeping bag.

"Your hand is freezing, Jod!"

"The air is cold out there! My nose is about frozen!" I kept my hand under his back. It was warm.

"I wonder what Whitworth will be like," he said, thoughtfully, to the sky above him. We were both stretched out, on the edge of the giant mirror of a lake.

"I don't know, but I sure hope I like it. Dad is paying big bucks for this," I added, "and I don't even know why I am going. I am the absolute opposite of career oriented. To tell you the truth, I keep thinking about this life, on a mule, with just my saddle bags and the trail before me to worry about. But a real job someday? I just can't see it somehow."

We both lay there, in silence, thinking. My hand was warm in his hand, buried deep in his sleeping bag.

"I just want to run the rivers, Jod," he said quietly. We fell asleep like that.

We arrived in Spokane, heading west, through the ponderosa pines and brush the color of wheat. The Spokane River goes winding through the valley, on the edge of pine covered forests that stretch to Alaska. Spokane spread out below us, her red bricks glowing warmly in the afternoon sun.

"Kind of on the edge of the wilderness up here," I yelled to him, as we raced down the Interstate, through downtown, exiting at the Whitworth College sign.

"Well, this is a pretty official looking sign," Evan said. He put on a tape. We drove slowly up Division Street, one of those four lane streets that has every franchise and car dealer you can name. The sunset had turned the sky bright orange. I held back the tears as we turned onto the street with the college entrance; cement pillars next to a large wooden and stone sign.

This was it. My high school boyfriend was dropping me off at a strange college and leaving me there.

"Evan, get me out of here!" I said to him, as we pulled into a parking place in front of a big brick red dorm.

We sat in silence in the Jeep and watched a girl skipping across the beautiful tree studded campus. Autumn had painted the trees deep red and yellow; they held onto their leaves for Orientation Day, fending off the approaching freeze, and ultimately, Winter. The girl had on anklets, clean white tennis shoes, short bangs, cut to the middle of her forehead, and a T-shirt with "Jesus Loves You" printed on the front, surrounded by a daisy border.

As she skipped by, she saw us sitting there in the Jeep, and said, "Smile, you guys, Jesus LOVES you!"

I turned to him, grabbing the sleeve of his well worn Levi jacket. Evan was everything to me. He was a river runner, who ran the Salmon fearlessly. He could ski the toughest slopes at Mammoth. He wrote poetry and played the piano. But the winds of change were blowing. I knew he was heading back to California to attend school down there, and I had to let him go.

"Maybe we can find another campus, somewhere up here. That way Dad and Mom won't take it so hard when I tell them I changed my mind."

I grabbed his hand, wrapping the fingers of my other hand around the beautiful silver and turquoise piece he had brought me from Sun Valley, Idaho, last summer, when he was coming back from a run down the Salmon. I never took it off; it hung around my neck on a piece of leather.

"Let's go. Let's go check out Evergreen, and Moscow, and Seattle. Let's go find a different college!"

We drove the little Jeep to Seattle, Olympia, and Ellensburg. I didn't find a school that looked better to me.

"I wish we were going Back to the Land instead of Back to School," I said to Evan as he unloaded my belongings in front of the dorm.

"Raising bees and mules," he said softly and smiled.

He didn't want to stay for the orientation in the auditorium. It was time to say goodbye.

I took one good long look at him, and then hugged him close to me. I kissed him goodbye; one long kiss. I heard a girl upstairs, in one of the windows, laughing, calling to her friend to come see us. I watched as the Jeep disappeared down the road in front of the dorm, until it was out of sight. Evan looked back and waved to me, his blond curls shining in the late afternoon sun, and shifted into third and onto the highway back to California. The pine cone curtain closed behind him.

By the time Thanksgiving rolled around, there was distance between Evan and I, since Whitworth had already provided me with new young men to captivate my interest. Our lives went separate ways, but we never forgot the dream we had dreamed, as we drove through those high mountain valleys in Idaho and Montana. We could have settled down in one of those little cabins we passed, up some lonesome valley in the middle of nowhere, and stayed forever, with our cordwood on the front porch and our own packstring in the pasture.

Somehow, I would slip under the barb wire of expectations, and gallop off, unfettered and free. Mom and Dad had taught me how to enjoy life, how to ride a horse, and how to get the most out of a three week vacation. I was clear on these things. But when it came to career plans, I would laugh and say, "Oh, I don't know, maybe I'll homestead and raise mules."

The first question out of any inquiring relative was always, "What are you going to do?" Such an answer got a laugh out of everybody, as they nervously edged away towards the hors d'oeuvres table. How could I tell them I wanted nothing more than a good mule and the rest of life to ride him?

Whitworth College only made this question more difficult to answer, once I looked at all the choices. They were endless. I watched all of us, confused, tired from years of the war, clutching the classics, walking in boots across campus through the silent snow. I read all the great American authors. Laughing out loud at the antics of Mark Twain and the clever Thoreau, I stoked the wood stove and kept the kerosene lamps burning in the chicken coop until three in the morning sometimes, as the Spokane winter wailed outside and the snow piled high against the old wooden door.

As I read my books at night in the coop, in front of the wood stove with the fire blazing, I became sure of one thing. I knew it was up to me to take steps in the right direction towards a life of adventure. This required leaping faithfully towards the unknown.

Sitting in Phil Eaton's American Literature class on a snowy

Thursday, I listened to him as he spoke excitedly about Mark Twain. His eyes had a sparkle to them, and they flashed brightly. He loved his work, this was obvious to me. He was a very inspiring and attractive young professor and we all worshipped the ground he walked on.

He stood in front of the class and said, "This summer, one of your classmates has decided to live an adventure. Jody plans to ride a horse from Salt Lake City to Spokane, across three states."

I could feel my skin turning red. Randy Starr turned and stared at me. I turned even redder. I had been crazy about him since Orientation Day. He was leaning towards the small blonde beauties, and I was quite the opposite. The food in the cafeteria had done a lot more than just nourish me. I knew in my heart Randy liked the kind of cowgirls he could really swing, swing right off the dance floor and into the air if he wanted to. He did give me enough attention to make it difficult to concentrate on my studies.

It was clear to me that nothing else would fall into place until I had lived the vagabond life I longed for; living in the pages of my own adventure story. I had one eye on the books, and the other on the open road.

I walked downtown, which was a good four miles from the campus. I walked for miles around the brick city, eventually ending up down by the Spokane River. It ran right through the middle of town, powerful and clean, working its way to the Columbia.

Sitting on the bank, throwing sticks for Robin, I looked up and saw a man with jet black hair and eyes that held the wisdom of all ages. His shirt was a plaid flannel one, with the sleeves rolled up on his strong arms. As he approached me, he put up his hand in a friendly gesture and then he smiled; his whole face smiled.

"What are you doing here, little lady?" he said quietly.

"Giving the dog a little swim. She loves to chase sticks in this river. Any river, for that matter." I grabbed the stick as she brought it up to me, dropping it on my shoes.

He pulled out a package of tobacco and rolled himself a smoke. I looked at the deep lines in his hands, like a million ancient canyons of sandstone. He had rolled a million such cigarettes. I sat quietly and Robin came up on the bank, shaking the water off her coat.

"I come down here every day, to the river's edge," he said to me. He was looking out at the water.

"I wish I could, but I get down here every chance I get," I answered as I threw the stick again for Rob.

"I used to live in Nome, Alaska," he said to me, looking me right in the eye. "My people still live there. They ride snowmobiles now, and don't keep a team of dogs anymore. All my cousins, my aunts and my uncles; they are all still there. I haven't been back since 1955," he continued. "Now this is my home. Spokane. Never been anywhere but Nome and Spokane."

We sat quietly while he smoked his cigarette. He had a cowboy belt on, the kind with all the fancy leather tooling, and a real nice belt buckle. It was silver with a bucking horse in the middle, tossing a cowboy high in the air.

"My best friend died," he told me. "She was an Appaloosa named Ready. She was the swiftest horse I have ever had the pleasure to ride. I had her for thirty years, and we rode all this prairie land, all the way to the Coeur d'Alenes. We rode on some of the trails I helped to build. You see, I worked on the trail crew for years, in the Colville Forest and the Coeur d'Alene. I knew all the trails, every one of 'em. Ready carried me all over the mountains and across the rivers and never complained, never once." He stopped and looked down at the sand.

"I loved that horse, and when she died, I took to drinking, and I never stopped. It didn't ever mix well with my blood and made me crazy. I missed the horse so much and my own legs couldn't carry me into the mountains anymore." He looked at me and smiled, his teeth stained from the tobacco. "Ever done much riding, little lady?"

"I had the best ponies growing up," I told him. "But when I left home they went to stay with younger girls in Oregon."

"My horse made my life worth livin'. Otherwise I was just a lonely old man. Now the soul is willing but the flesh is not, if you know what I mean. Without Ready, the mountains will remain a memory and this river will be the closest I can get to God." He rolled another smoke and sat beside me for a long time. We were both quiet.

We walked up the beach together and up the forested trail to the street below the big cement bridge.

"Quit drinking here about a year and a half ago," he told me. We walked up the sidewalk to downtown, with Robin trotting ahead. "Mind if I walk you through my hotel?" he said, grinning from ear to ear. "The boys won't believe it."

We walked up to the old hotel, and in through the giant door. There were seven or eight old men in the lobby, watching a television in the corner. The walls were light green, and cast a dreary shadow on the stained curtains covering the windows. I shuddered. He held my hand and walked me through the lobby, around the old couches.

"There," he said, "I want them to see how good life gets after drinking."

We walked back outside and into the light on the street.

"I had better start back towards home," I told him.

He took off his cowboy belt with the silver buckle and rolled it up, handing it to me.

"This is a gift for you. I have had it most of my life," he said, seriously. "Wear it to keep your jeans up, and remember to always make your way to the mountains, as long as your legs will carry you there. Think of me sometime, will you?" he said, smiling.

Four years had passed since I had stood at the edge of the trail in the Sierras, vowing to never leave the trail, and I hadn't been back since. Everyone had grown up and left home, and the family pack trip was a thing of the past. The ponies Sarah and Star were living happily in Oregon, with other little girls combing and braiding their manes.

Knowing that backroads of fine clay awaited me in places I had never heard of, I headed towards an unknown world, one I was going to make up as I went along. I was twenty-one years old and itching for adventure. There was nothing I wanted more than to ride away; to make the outside my home, to travel ten or fifteen miles in a day on horseback, making camp by rivers and streams, in the shade of huge trees.

My sister Debbie was my first choice for a trail partner. Since she was living in Park City, we could start out there and ride up to Spokane. It would take us three months or more to ride from Utah to Washington.

As the wind blew through the countless cracks in my chicken coop, I put together a plan that included my sister, my dog, two horses and a mule we didn't have.

By Christmas I was determined to make this dream a reality.

"Hi, Deb! " I said to my sister as I gave her a hug, difficult in our down jackets. It was thirty degrees when I got there; Dad had come down and picked me up at the airport in Salt Lake City. Debbie lived right below the ski hill in Park City with her fiance, John, only steps from the chair lift.

Her place was warm. I could see the coals glowing orange in the fireplace. A storm was expected that night.

"Merry Christmas, Jod!" Deb looked at me and smiled. "What's this about a plan?"

"I'm going to ride across the West and I want you to be my partner, Deb. We can buy a couple horses and mules, pack our gear, and ride off into the sunset," I told her.

"But I'm getting married in June, Jod! You know the wedding is already planned. Yosemite Valley in June, remember? When are you planning to leave?" she asked me, her brow furrowed. I could tell she wanted to go with me. She took a quick, nervous bite of a Christmas cookie, a rum ball. The powder sugar left a white mustache over her lip. She laughed, blowing more of it into the air. I watched as the sugar landed on the glass table, like a light snow.

"I don't know, how about July Fourth, since it's the Bicentennial!"

"Mom will kill you for talking me into this," she said quietly, laughing. Her long, straight brown hair hung almost to her waist.

"No! You will be at your wedding and you will spend a month with your loving husband!" I laughed. "And remember, Deb, our family motto: 'A rolling Foss gathers no moss'."

Christmas in the little cabin came and went, and the heavens dropped two feet of fluffy white snow on Park City. As I carefully walked out to the road in the deep snow and said goodbye, Debbie hugged me, looking at me with those bright determined eyes she has, like horse chestnuts after rain.

"See you on the trail," she said.

B. Shields
©1994

## A Ride Through History

The next six months were spent preparing for something we could only remotely understand. We really had no idea what we were getting into. We needed horses and mules, saddles, halters, bridles, tents, sleeping bags, maps, and food for three months. We sent away for the Forest Service maps and split them up. Debbie would research the trail from Park City to West Yellowstone. She was to find out every spring, every cattle guard, every tasty meadow and river crossing. I traced the narrow trail from West Yellowstone to Spokane, our final destination.

When the maps were stretched out across our respective floors in the comfort of our homes, their colors did not show the deep clarity of the rivers, or the shale on Dead Horse Pass, or the majesty of the Tetons. They showed towns, with names like Dillon and Paradise.

The maps became symbols of our journey. Rivers and creeks, represented by the thinnest blue lines, meandered through the valleys. I followed them, with my eyes, as they worked their way towards the Colombia River from the Continental Divide.

Little did I know then how very important, how vital, these maps were to us. In only a few months, names like Hungry Horse Meadow and Bear Cub Camp would take on new meaning. We added up the squares on the maps between Park City and Spokane, and came up with over a thousand miles.

Mom called Debbie to talk about wedding plans, and Debbie called me with plans for our trip. By this time, February of 1976, John Najar had decided to accompany us on the adventure. John was a red-haired young man, with a tassel of curls some girls would kill for. His skin was fair, and he looked out at the world through gentle eyes. He was adventurous and willing, and Peter's little brother.

Peter and Deb were friends when Deb first moved to town, and they all lived uptown in an old miner's hotel called the Imperial, which sat on the main street of Park City at the top of the hill. It was a big, creaky, run down place with four stories. The ceilings were so high in all the apartments, the spiders and flies had a heyday, and multiplied without interruption.

John and Peter had grown up in Egypt, Paris, and finally, Washington D.C. Just matter of factly one day he had said, "Can I go too?" to my sister in the ski repair shop. Deb said yes.

Meanwhile, up in Spokane, I was busy looking for sponsors to help make our ride a reality. I dressed up in red, white and blue and hit the streets of Spokane in search of sponsors, to help cover the cost of the trip. This took me downtown, to radio stations, Chamber of Commerce meetings, and to the homes of some very wealthy widows on the South hill.

Fearless daughter of the ad man, I headed into the chilly winds of the brick city, looking for the pot of gold at the end of the rainbow.

I could name drop Whitworth College, and the Bicentennial, and talk about our Ride Through History, and how I was getting college credit, and did so repeatedly for potential sponsors. In the hollow halls of a massive brick mansion, overlooking the river and the city, an old widow sat and listened, clutching the little Xerox booklet I had given her.

"My sister Deb is looking for horses and a mule to buy," I told her. "We're really starting from scratch. We're hoping to be ready to leave Utah around July fourth, you know, if everything works out." I watched as her eyes lit up; I could almost see the reflection of our pack train in them.

We were going to travel the old historic trails and routes from Utah to Washington, gathering the stories of the old timers we met on the way, in the towns we planned to pass through. We would be there to replenish our food supply, as well as to preserve some of these stories the old-timers told us on cassettes and in photographs. John Najar was an excellent photographer, so he'd take the pictures.

I finally ended up catching the interest of a very friendly disk jockey at KGA Country Radio. He agreed to pay me five hundred dollars to call in to the station, along the trail, whenever I could find a phone booth. He would broadcast his conversations with "Jod on the Road" over the air as part of his special summer programming. I would receive two hundred and fifty dollars to help with supplies, and two hundred and fifty dollars more upon arrival in Spokane. I was thrilled with this offer.

The phone was for me. "Hey, Jod, this is Deb." She sounded pretty happy about something. "I think I found you a horse, Jody. He's a big, young roman-nosed, pintail Appaloosa. He is a little spooky and loves to run. Hates the sound of raincoats I guess. They broke him to ride by running him up a stream!"

How old is he?" I managed to squeeze in.

"He's just four. The man who owns him is getting out of the horse business. His wife fell off their other horse and hit her head on the only rock in the entire field, dying instantly. The guy doesn't want these horses anymore. I guess just looking at them makes him think about his dead wife. He's three hundred dollars, Jod. What do you think?" Deb was real quiet on the other end.

"Perfect. Buy him!" I said excitedly into the receiver.

Deb and John Najar rented space in a big pasture next to the ski resort as the grasses started to pop through the snow. I had only seen our animals in pictures. I spent that semester anxious to be in Utah, getting to know our new four-legged friends. The ad in the paper said, "Mules and Horses for Sale: Good on the Trails". My sister called and a man named Dave Thompson answered.

"I've been running a pack station up in the Deschene, and I'm selling out," he told my sister. He had an accent, very Midwestern. He and his wife Sherry had come out West to Salt Lake from the hills of the Ohio River country. Dave took to the high country like he had always belonged there; a mountain man born a hundred years too late. He was a heavy equipment operator with a soft side, a big belly from too much bacon and eggs and white bread and coffee with four sugars. He chain smoked and liked his Wild Turkey.

Debbie said, "We're going to ride from here to Spokane, Washington. We think it will take us about three months, so we should get there before the snow flies! We're looking for some good animals to make the trip."

"Well, I have a really nice young mule named Sarah Jane for sale. You should come see her. She's a beauty, one in a million. She has a couple of years on the trail already, and knows how to ride, pack and drive! She's a  real sweetheart."

"We'll come out and see her this afternoon," Debbie said into the receiver.

Debbie and John jumped in Deb's pickup and headed out to the little town where Dave and Sherry lived, north of Salt Lake, in a patchwork of old fences, hay fields, and trailer houses. As Deb and John drove up, the first thing they saw was the white mule.

"Look at her!" Deb said to John as they parked the truck next to the corral. "She's so beautiful."

"She looks like the perfect size, too. Easy to pack," John said as he got out of the truck and walked towards the white mule in the corral.

She looked at them with big soft eyes. She was smart, they could tell that, the minute they set eyes on her. Her ears were forward, and she studied my sister and John. For a long time she stared at them, and then she started pawing the ground with her front foot. She was not a large mule, but she was strong and stocky. Her white mane was long and silky, and so was her tail. They could see a few black spots on her chest between her front legs, but they were covered with a layer of white hair, and were almost invisible.

"Look at the brand on her back hip," Deb said to John. They could barely make out the CW brand. It was covered in long white hair too.

After no more than a few minutes, Deb and John had decided to buy the mule. Her name was Sarah Jane, and she was the most beautiful mule in all the West, as far as they were concerned. She was the daughter of a pure white Appaloosa mare from a local Wasatch Ranch, and a donkey that lived nearby. Dave really hated to part with her; but he was thinning down his hay burners, and had given up his pack outfit already.

Sarah Jane would show us the ways of the trail.

After hearing all about the ride, Dave Thompson wanted to go with us, but couldn't exactly drop everything; Sherry and the kids depended on him to bring in the bacon. It had always been his dream to ride off into the sunset and keep going. As my sister, John and Dave talked, sitting out by the corral, the Utah sky filled with reds, yellows and purples, mixing together on the edges like a watercolor palette. The sun disappeared somewhere over Nevada.

Dave knew a lot about packing, and since we were greenhorns, he decided to ride with us, to help us get started. Dave could get away for a week or two, and said he'd go as far as Evanston, and then Sherry could come pick him up. He had a real nice mountain horse he was very fond of, and a little pack pony named Pet, who could carry any load, no matter how cumbersome, without a care. When the pack was off, he would just pick up a big rock and pack it on the light side to even it out.

Dave had a couple of other horses for sale, and Debbie ended up buying them all.

We had acquired our own packstring. We had Chief, the big red and white Paint Horse, stunning with his large red blotches of color, like continents. Red was a big chestnut Quarterhorse, and Deb and John liked his disposition. He thought things through before taking any action, and turned out to be the slowest of all our animals.

We bought another horse from Dave named Comanche, another very young green broke Appaloosa. And we had my horse, Dudley, the innocent bystander at a fateful accident; the pintailed, roman-nosed, brown and white horse I came to love so much.

Sarah Jane nudged Debbie with her nose, lovingly, and nodded her head up and down against Deb's outstretched hand. It was love at first sight, and it was, by far, the best four hundred dollars any of us had ever spent.

It was clear right away to us that she was a great deal more intelligent than the others, but we loved them all, and the spirited horses had their own way of learning the ways of the trail. We all had a lot to learn.

Later on, I changed my horse Dudley's name to Ranahan, cowboy slang for the best hand on the ranch. I called him Cowboy. He was especially athletic and handsome, a proud gelding with a wild side.

Debbie located a good local saddle builder over in Heber City, who custom built two sawbuck saddles for us, charging eighty dollars apiece for them. She made our pack bags, out of a strong, waterproof material. She sewed us little bags for our food. Yellow was full of breakfast things, red for lunch, blue for dinner.

We wrote long lists of things we thought we should take with us. We would need a leather repair kit. We would carry extra shoes, human and horse. We would carry a first aid kit, a snake bite kit, and a sewing kit, complete with a leather awl. We'd have books on the plants, the birds and the trees. We'd have books on the history, too. We would limit our clothes to what we could carry on the saddlebags. We'd each need a good sleeping bag. The list of things we needed seemed endless, but slowly and surely, things were gathered together, as the months flew by, and the adventure took shape, carrying itself forward on perpetual excitement as the summer drew near.

Mary Stone, a friend from school, sold me her old saddle. It was a little fiberglass tree low back saddle with very simple tooling and strong latigo straps. She charged me fifty dollars for it. The saddle sat there, at the edge of the converted feed bin in the chicken coop I called home, until that golden day I was waiting for, the day I would go to Salt Lake and meet my horse. I could hardly wait for the semester to end.

Time passed, and school came to a close, perfumed with the delightful smell of the jonquils surrounding every building on campus, calling to us all to come run away into the summer at hand. I headed towards Utah with my dog Robin and Mark Sloan, a friend of mine from school. We raced southward in his little Ford Courier. Robin rode in the back with our stuff. He had a little camper shell on his truck.

Markas and I worked on the grounds crew together at Whitworth. For hours, we would walk together through the forest behind the college. With our sticks for picking up trash and cans, we basked in the shadows and light filtering through the stately ponderosa pines behind the campus.

Markas was big and lovable, a good friend. One Christmas, I spent eight hours building a gingerbread house for him, mistakenly using flammable cotton for the snow surrounding the house. Complete with candles inside the cookie abode, the yellow cellophane windows glowed as if someone was home. I stood at his doorstep and lit the candle and the cabin went up in flames. The little clothing hanging on the clothesline disappeared in seconds, and the burning gingerbread smelled good. Markas just stood there and laughed as we watched it burn.

As we drove south towards Utah he said to me, "This trip you are taking could be the best thing yet, Jod." He was messing with the radio, settling on a clear Idaho Falls station. The sun settled down behind the endless fields of alfalfa and oat hay, as we raced southward in the little Ford.

"I know. I'm so excited to see my horse, Markas." I looked out the window and saw a man, on a very large, graceful black horse, galloping in the ditch along the highway. He had taken his hat off, and had it in his hand.

We made it to Park City the next day about noon. Spring was blooming up there in the canyons. The hills were bright green, and the cottonwoods and aspens glistened yellow and gold. Summer was buzzing in Park City, and the mountains beckoned. At such a high altitude, when winter finally bows her head to the warm months, everything seems to thaw in a hurry.

When I first saw my horse, he was far away, grazing with the other horses, up against the cottonwoods. He had a very beautiful, furry coat — white, light brown and dark brown all mixed together. His mane was thin, along with his wisp of a tail. But he had the most innocent, curious eyes, with an intelligent look to them. He stood still and looked at me, standing there like a toy horse, not moving a muscle. He snorted at me.

"Hey, Dudley. Mind if I call you Ranahan?" We stared at

each other. I walked over to him and let him sniff my hand. He snorted. I stood next to him, and gently slid myself up his big spotted side, jumping up onto his broad back. The other horses were watching us; so was Markas.

Ranahan felt so warm. I reached up, petting him slowly on the side of his neck. His coat was so beautiful, like a Navajo blanket; shades of brown and white. The darker brown was the color of cattails. The lighter browns were tinted with gold, like the color of wheat, just before harvest.

I had never stopped missing the ponies; life was not the same for me without them. I was so happy to be on the back of my very own horse. And he was a full size horse, too. Although he was barely four, he was tall. He stood there, like a statue.

I moved on up until I was comfortable and sat there, holding on to as much of his mane as I could get a hold of. He jumped forward, suddenly, and followed this first move with a twist. I sailed high in the air, and the world was upside down for an instant, before I hit the grass. I was bucked off, plain and simple, without a fight. I could hear my friend Markas laughing up by the gate. I sat in the vetch and clover, watching as my new horse ran gracefully back to his herd, kicking up his heels. Markas thought this was terrific.

It took little time to convince this fine young gelding that I was his girl. I brought peace offerings of grain and apples, and soon we were friends.

Dave the horseshoer had a mare named Molly. She was a dapple white and grey mare, with a little foal named Moon. He rode his Molly bareback, up the canyons, to the top of the pass, with his food for the day in a small navy blue pack he carried on his back.

"I'll show you the trail to the lake," Dave promised me the first day we met, down at the old corral. He had a great smile and I liked him instantly.

I spent the days that Spring in the aspen groves above Park City, winding my way up narrow canyon trails on my green broke gelding, following the creek, in the shadows of the tall stands of aspens. This is where I became acquainted with these animal friends of ours, learning their quirks and giving them time to learn ours.

David and I packed up some food, grabbed our sleeping bags and headed up the canyon trail. We rode along, silently, listening to

the music of the stream. The trail steepened, as we climbed towards the base of the tallest peak in the range.

After about a three hour ride we arrived at Summit Lake. The trail had led us up the steep hill above Park City, and over a ridge to a hidden emerald lake.

We picketed the horses out. I had brought a hobble, which I attached to my horse's front right leg. I tied the picket rope to a pipe that looked to me to be firmly rooted in the soil. Dave tied his mare nearby, and let the foal run free so she could graze.

His savvy Collie, Trampas, shook the water out of his long black and white coat, and lay down close by, waiting patiently for his dinner, never taking his eyes off Dave. The dog knew he had a little bag of dog food in his saddle bag.

The minute we got there, Dave had stripped down to his birthday suit and dove in the lake without a second thought. He kept on swimming, crossing the lake as Trampas carefully carried Dave's towel in his mouth, trotting gracefully, head up, around the lake to the other side. The dog was sitting there, with the towel, waiting for Dave's swim to end.

There was plenty of good meadow grass on the edge of our camp for the horses.

I built a fire and made some coffee. Just as I was taking a sip of the hot brew, I saw a mountain lion, from the corner of my eye. He was on his way past our camp, just sneaking by, not trying to alarm us or anything, but the horses didn't take his passage lightly. I don't remember ever seeing such wild, golden eyes before.

At this same moment, my horse Cowboy saw the cat, and took off running, taking the pipe with him, still attached to his leg by the hobble and the picket rope. As he disappeared out of sight, gone completely out of his mind with this pipe chasing him down the hill, we knew there was a chance we wouldn't see him like that again. There was the surreal clanging of the pipe, and then, silence. The mare had run a short distance and stopped, because the foal had stopped. Cowboy kept running.

I will never forget that sick feeling in my stomach, standing there listening to the clanging of the pipe I had tied him to as it hit the trees, swinging behind him. Trampas was on his feet, looking out into the blackness, whining, as worried as Dave and I. It was dark, and still the search began.

We walked down the trail after him, heading down the canyon. I felt so sick. My new horse! I was angry that I had made a bad choice, picketing him to that pipe. It might end up costing his life!

"No," I said to myself as I followed David and the dog down the dirt road, looking for a sign of my horse, "Cowboy won't die. That would be too awful."

I could only hope I was right. The road down the canyon was dark and steep. We weren't talking to each other. We were both trying to keep our minds from going to the dark places; what might have happened to the green broke Appy with the pipe hobbled to his leg. There was no moon. David was a dark shadow I followed down the rocky dirt road.

After several hours of searching, walking down the trail in the dark with the dog, we found the pipe wrapped around a tree, with the rope disappearing down the hillside. Dave looked at me and said, "You know, your horse may be at the end of this." I nodded, and swallowed hard.

He pulled on the rope, and there was the leather hobble, broken clean in half. No Cowboy! We could only hope he wasn't running on a broken leg. I never went to sleep that night.

Back at the ranch, Cowboy showed up around two a.m. without a scratch on him, breathing hard. He had run back to the corral, nine miles or more, in the black of the Utah night, down the highway. He woke up Michael and Dorry; they said they saw him standing out in the yard, next to the corrals, turning in excited circles, trying to get back in with the other horses. He was pretty jumpy, they said. They put him to bed. That was our first night out on the trail together. I walked home. Never again did I tie a horse's leg to anything.

"Tie to their head. The rope is closer to their brain that way," commented an old man who saw me walking down the highway the next morning with my sleeping bag under my arm.

## Off: Into the Sunset

*The journals from our adventure have lived through a lot.*
*Fires, floods and worse disasters did not destroy them. They hit the*
*wind in Montana, flying high above our pack train, and spread*
*across the dirt road when my saddlebag ripped, some pages sailing*
*high into the air before settling in the desert sagebrush and briars.*
*Much of it was written by campfire light, and under smoky*
*florescent lights in old-time Western cafes — the kind with the*
*homemade pie. The rest of it was written in the saddle as I rode*
*along. I was twenty-one, a rambling rose, saddling up and riding off*
*into the sunset, on the back of a green-broke Appaloosa.*

Park City, Utah. July 5, 1976

Today is the day we are leaving on our trip. I woke up in the
upstairs apartment in the Imperial, and walked out into the garden,
listening to the roosters welcoming in the morning.

"Tonight I will be sleeping in a pasture," I thought to myself.
I went to the propane stove in the corner of the sunny kitchen and
made a cup of coffee. I opened the refrigerator door and found the
milk on the top shelf.

"Last of the cold milk for awhile," I said aloud.

"What?" Deb answered. I didn't know she was there. She and
John Najar were standing in the door of the ancient loft room with
the high ceilings.

"I was just thinking about how cold the milk in the fridge will
seem to me in a few days. Want coffee?" I asked them. They looked
clean. They were dressed in jeans and T-shirts. Debbie's hair was
shining in the sun that filtered in on the kitchen area.

"By tonight this will be like a dream," I said to Deb. She
understood what I meant. We drank our coffee and the town outside
started to wake up. Park City was an old mining town with some of
the best skiing in the West, or in the world for that matter. In the
summer, the aspens filled the canyons with a bright gold light, and

the trails ran up these canyons and over the mountains. This time we wouldn't bring the horses and the mule back to the old corral at night. We'd just keep going and ride on, all the way to Spokane.

The room looked inviting to me. I was just staying there while my sister's friends were away. The bed looked comfortable, while the morning sun reached that room and the street below, and the townspeople started to gather for the Independence Day Parade. I could hear the Park City High School band, way off in the distance, tuning up.

We gathered our saddle bags together and walked down the creaky stairs to the street. I will never forget the sound of the old Victorian door as it closed behind us. Deb turned to me and smiled. I looked up on the hills above the town and the sun was all the way up and down the canyons, casting a bright yellow glow on everything.

"We'd better hustle. It's time to get on and ride," Deb said to John and me. "Let's go get the animals. The parade starts in an hour."

We caught a ride down to the old corral. The mule and the horses had been fed early so they were all ready to go. We grabbed brushes off the dirty shelf in the old barn and dusted them off, put on the saddle blankets, the saddles, the saddlebags and the bridles.

"Dave Thompson will be a big help on this packing deal for the first couple weeks," Deb said to us, "even though he still packs rocks." We laughed. Dave had told us how to solve the problem of an uneven mule pack.

"Get off your horse and find a small rock," he told us as he adjusted his rodeo belt buckle and rolled a smoke. "Take the rock and put it inside the light pack." We had laughed when he told us this, thinking he was kidding, but he wasn't.

We had everything packed on Chief and Sarah. Our own saddlebags were a little too heavy; we'd have to get rid of some more gear over in Charleston.

"You gotta be careful not to overpack those saddlebags," he warned us. "Horses and mules shouldn't carry too much weight over their kidneys. So try to figure out what you can leave behind."

It has been a long road. We are finally ready to go; as ready as we'll ever be. Maybe there is no such thing as being totally ready for anything. All we can do now is tighten our cinches and get going. Sarah Jane is pawing at the ground, and a great billowing cloud of Utah dust fills the air. The horses stomp their hooves and test their ropes.

Debbie has packed enough health food to feed us for most of the journey, at least enough food to get us well into Montana. The peanut butter seems precarious in those little plastic tubes. So does the soy sauce and the tamari sauce and the honey tubes. Everything is separated into breakfast, lunch and dinner bags.

After the Independence Day Parade, we will just keep on riding up Main Street and onto the dirt road that leads us up over the hill towards Charleston. I hope we didn't forget anything.

And now I am riding away! My saddle bags are packed with everything I think I will need. A bandanna, my address book, pens and notebooks, a little camera, a tape recorder, a comb, some Skin Trip coconut lotion so I don't turn into a leather handbag by the time we get there. Band-Aids, hydrogen peroxide, gauze. Toothpaste. Dry socks, a canteen, a flashlight. Fruit leather and licorice, trail mix and Vitamin C. Two oranges, my wallet with my three hundred dollars, and some lip balm. What will I miss? It's time to go! Mom and Dad sent twenty more dollars. I have three hundred dollars for three months.

We rode up Park City's Main Street, as the high school marching band played their parade songs. The white mule's ears swung around to the beat of the drums, and then as we reached the dirt road at the end of the parade route, her ears pointed forward intently, in the direction of the road ahead.

Deb was on Comanche, John was riding Chief, and I was on Cowboy. Dave was riding his horse, Maddie, and was leading the pack pony, Pet. Her long white mane hung over her eyes, and her bags were packed evenly and stayed on all day. Deb was leading Sarah Jane. My dog, Robin, was really excited to finally be leaving; she has been anticipating our departure for weeks now. Goodbye to our friends! Things will never be the same for any of us.

Heber City, Utah
John Najar looks like a mountain man already; his long red hair under a leather hat, down vest and plaid shirt and jeans. He's

got nice big saddlebags filled with trail snacks. He has his raincoat, and another jacket tied to the back of his saddle, a book about edible plants and poisonous ones, a loaf of Home Pride and a jar of Jif peanut butter in his saddlebags. Two canteens and his camera bag are strapped to the saddlehorn.

Debbie sits tall in the saddle, like an Indian princess. Comanche's brown and white dapple coat looks so beautiful with her long brown hair. They are quite a pair.

"You only got married a month ago, Deb, and here you go, down the road with your sister and a trail map." I adjusted my saddlebags. They were uneven and kept falling off to one side. I retied the latigos around my Levi jacket.

"I just hope I make it back," she said and laughed. "I haven't opened all the presents yet," she said to me and smiled as I rode Cowboy beside her.

I can tell already, Sarah Jane is the one that knows what is going on. She is the only one who does; she has already spent two seasons on the trail. And besides that, she is a mule.

She is really something. I can tell, she wishes she could tell us a few things. She could tell us exactly how much weight to pack, since everyone we talk to tells us something different. At least we'll be going through the country the slow way, so we'll have time to think out our moves. We've got to just take it easy until we get used to the trail, all of us. If I know Deb, she'll be kicking us out of bed at five in the morning. Just as long as she makes the fire and the coffee! Ha! Then I will get up!

July 6

At the going away party last night in Charleston, Robin got into a fight with another dog, a Samoyed. She got hurt before I could get outside to break it up. Her leg is swollen, and she can't continue on with us. Dave will take her back and keep her with Trampas. I will miss her so much. She's my big, lovable pup, my best friend, and the trail won't be the same without her. She will have to join up with us up the road, hopefully in Evanston.

Wolf Creek, High Uintahs

We travelled twenty miles today, to our oat cache up on Wolf

Creek. As we rode today, we climbed higher and higher, up the narrow trail, leaving the cottonwoods and aspens for the pine forests. We are on our way to Wolf Creek Summit, ten miles more. We are making a lot better time than we expected.

It's very peaceful, riding along in the hot sun. There are flowers everywhere, as if the forest was carpeted with color, a blanket of blooms. I love it out here. The sound of the rushing river we are following up the canyon is mesmerizing, and drowns out the sound of our voices.

After Debbie's five grain gruel on the side of a mountain above Wolf Creek Pass, the horses were hobbled, all except for Cowboy.

"He's got that wild Appy look in his eyes," Dave said to me, as he headed out to look for the herd. "I wouldn't hobble him if I were you, Jod."

They all learned to use their hobbles to their advantage after the first night on the trail, and can travel with them. They keep their front legs together and jump forward, leaping off to greener pastures. I prefer to have my horse tied up, picketed out, so I know where he is when I wake up in the morning.

As the moon came up, the horses ran off, and Cowboy was running back and forth on the end of his picket line, sending the willows bending in the direction of the herd. He was nervous, being left behind. I was glad I had tied him. He really hates to be alone, without the other animals, and jumps around like crazy.

I will always remember this night. Dave, Deb and John, in the moonlight, walking through the sage, searching for horses. I feel at home at the edge of this river bank.

Ottoson Basin, High Uintas

Six days on the road. Below me, a green meadow and six beautiful animals eating their breakfast, which is always right there, at their feet. Ahead, over the rocky, High Uintas, over streams that run down to the Big Muddy, Wyoming awaits us. To my right, in the distance, more mountains.

Dave tied Sarah Jane to a big pine tree in our camp, "High enough," he told us, "so she can't wrap her leg in the rope."

He tied what he called a quick-release knot in the thick cotton lead rope and wrapped the end under itself where it looped around the tree.

"That way," he warned us, "if she gets to playing with the rope in the night you won't wake up to an empty tree."

He laughed and sat down on the log for a minute, pulling out a smoke.

"The most important thing to remember in packing a mule is....well, there are so many things," he laughed. "Where do I start? Can't just let you all pack rocks your whole lives!"

He laughed and scratched his head.

"Let's see. Blankets. Good saddle blankets and a good packsaddle that fits. You've got the ol' style sawbucks, and Deckers are better. They've got pads on 'em! The blankets should be thick and absorbent. Next I'd say, boxes or bags?" He stopped and looked directly at Deb.

"Now, you can use pack boxes to save your eggs and bread, but you'll be running your pretty legs into them all day long when your green-broke Appaloosa decides to shorten the distance between you, the tree and the mule with the pack boxes. That's when your shin rams into the box, and well, it smarts mightily."

Dave stood up and patted Sarah on her back.

"Make sure her blanket is clean. No burrs or stickers. Otherwise they'll be stickin' her all day long while you're enjoying the scenery."

He picked some burrs and a foxtail out of the thick, fluffy saddle pad.

"You got to make sure your pack bags are the same weight, between forty and eighty pounds apiece. Everybody has his own idea of what is maximum weight for a mule to carry. But, tell me, do they ever ask the mule?"

Sarah pawed the ground in response.

"The rest is easy," Dave told us.

The high mountain wind came roaring through camp, out of nowhere, unexpectedly. The tarp flew up in the air and landed over by Cowboy, much to his dismay. His eyes turned to saucers and he did his panic dance on the confining picket rope.

Dave tested the weight of the two pack bags, lifting each one several times. "We should have brought a scale," he admitted.

"Anyway, you girls will be strong after lifting these pack bags every day!" He thought this was funny.

"I can't wait until our packs are lighter," I said to Deb.

"Me, too. Think how Sarah must be wishing that!"

Dave stood up, put the nylon pack bags on the sawbuck saddle and continued. "It's real important to pack your soft stuff next to the mule. Otherwise, she'll be walking all day with a coffee pot poking her in the ribs!"

He threw the manty over the load, after picking up two sleeping bags and a tent and placing them carefully and evenly on top of the packed bags. Tucking the manty in, underneath the pack bags, he was ready to throw his Diamond Hitch.

"Throw the Diamond Hitch like this!" he said, as he looped the rope over the load, tightening an extra cinch under Sarah Jane and then tightening the loop. He twisted the rope on top of the pack and continued leading it around the packs with finesse, tying a perfect Diamond Hitch in minutes.

"I'll have to see that a bunch of times to get it," I said to Debbie under my breath.

"I hope we get it down before Dave leaves us to go back home," Deb added seriously.

Sarah Jane stood there, standing quietly on three legs, while she drifted off to sleep. The lesson had taken too long, as far as she was concerned. And still, I'm sure she was glad Dave was teaching us what he could.

Dave taught us all about cowboy coffee, too.

"Just take some grounds and dump 'em in the coffee pot and let her boil. Then move it over, but watch the campfire — the handle will be hot. A single sock makes a good hot pad. Set the pot off to the side, let her simmer and you've got cowboy coffee!"

There are mountains in every direction. This is an interesting range, the Uintahs, stretching east to west, from the Wasatch to Wyoming. The high country is some of the most rugged, with eleven thousand foot peaks rising to the heavens. The sunset is pink, blue and yellow, with the black silhouettes of lightning charred trees between me and the night.

Soon, a full moon will rise and light up my page. My

flashlight is already dead and I'm glad. I won't change my mind about that until the moon changes, and by then we'll be to Evanston.

I climbed high above our camp in Ottoson Basin to look down at the world at my feet. High mountain pasture stretching all the way from half way up the slope, down through a moist, rich meadow to a creek, and up the other side in the direction of the trail. There's a campfire lighting up a big area around the camp. It is far below me; I sit perched on the edge of a rock half way up the mountain. The horses and Sarah Jane look contented as they dig into the thick meadow grass. Debbie and John are making tea, I can see them from up here. I think I will run down and get a cup, with some honey in it.

I love waking up in the middle of nowhere, living out here in the deep silence, under the stars. An elk bellowed, and the sound echoed over the valley, a sorrowful, lonely sound.

A black moose went lumbering right by us today, and the packtrain spooked and got away. I chased Chief on Cowboy. Sarah, carrying the other half of our lives, galloped by me, chasing Chief. Their long cotton picket ropes flew wildly behind them and kept them running.

"Let's turn around and go back the other way," Dave suggested. "They won't want to get too far from the rest of us."

Sure enough, once we stopped chasing after them and turned around, heading back towards Wyoming, they followed us. The main concern for these animals seems to be to stay together. This will be a great help to us.

When Sarah the mule first saw the moose, she just stopped and stood there, as still as a white marble statue, her ears forward like beacons of the trail. She thinks twice before she makes a flighty move any direction. Cowboy almost dumped me, but I might as well be attached with glue to my saddle, because nothing can get me off his back, at least not so far.

My new life is a mountain trail and noisy mountain streams with sweet flowers on high rocky passes. There is every color of the spectrum. I love the lupine and the Indian paint brush.

There's lots of water up here, and plenty of graze.

We are at a Dude Ranch, to pick up some more grain before

going on. We have only been out a few days, and already I feel like I am used to the life. We have been loving every minute, except a few, like when Deb's horse ran away, and the time Cowboy got stung by a bee.

This ranch was a welcome sight. The main lodge is a huge cabin made out of long, wide yellow logs. The chimney is built from huge river stones. There are curtains in all the windows; the kind with frills on the bottom. There is a corral full of horses next to the huge barn behind the lodge. All the trees around this place are ancient, and the Deschene River is wide and fast moving.

We were sitting in the cafe, listening to Willie Nelson on the jukebox. We put the horses in a meadow, just outside the window of the log cabin. Everything smelled like bacon and maple syrup and coffee; like a good dude ranch kitchen should.

The kid behind me never touched his breakfast. I turned around and ate right off his plate! I had at least ten cups of coffee. Then beans, for breakfast? A piece of fried chicken and a Coke!

I had a Dude Ranch bellyache that wouldn't quit. We rode off for Granddaddy Lakes. We camped last night at nine thousand feet. It was such a relief to me to be back in the wilderness again.

Here I sit, half laying down, in my sleeping bag with my back propped up against a big log. On my head, a bandanna. I'm in a pair of jeans that need to see a laundromat. I have on an old corduroy shirt, a dark green one, that Albert gave me before I left, and my down vest. It keeps me really warm at times like this.

My hands look like a horseshoer's. They are already looking older than Mom's. I could scrub them with my toothbrush, but I think I'll wait until Evanston and buy a nail brush.

Lake Fork Creek

We came today from Ottoson Basin all the way down to Lake Fork Creek, a big fast moving river that brought back memories of the Sierras. We started on our trail north, then, passing through a wooded canyon, right at the edge of the creek. We stopped and rested the animals next to a big flat rock, smooth and slippery. We laid around on the ground in the sun, sunning ourselves like young bears.

Dave Thompson will be leaving us tomorrow morning, riding

back to Park City with Pet and Maddie. We have a lot to thank him for. He and Deb stayed up talking almost all of last night, by the campfire.

Sometimes we get the feeling we could stay forever in the saddle, passing from ridge to ridge. This is one of those times. We came off the pass into this camp, and almost like magic, we were greeted by a pile of firewood, all cut and neatly stacked, next to an old campfire ring. This camp has probably been here for hundreds of years, welcoming people who crossed the pass. The huge trees arch over the camp like protective arms. It is everything we could ever hope for, after our rough climb from ten thousand feet.

Chief lost a shoe up on the pass, and now John is working at tacking on another one. Debbie is drinking a hot cup of tea and the last of the golds disappear from the walls of rock surrounding the lake. This is our nicest camp so far.

Deb had heard from a ranger that Red Knob Pass was "treacherous", and "hard for stock". We saw old horse droppings on the trail, and decided to go for it.

"I wonder if that horse made it," I said to Debbie, as Cowboy stood, frozen, his eyes wide, his legs stiff as fenceposts. I patted him gently on the neck. I think he knew I was terrified.

Debbie was skeptical, but considered it a better route than heading east through the Primitive Area. If we went to Smith's Fork, we would be four days off our schedule. Why did we ever think we could stick to an itinerary? How ridiculous. Some things, like plans, are hard to let go of.

We agreed to make a go at the pass, although we were all scared. I reached down and stroked Cowboy's warm neck and said, "Easy, Boy," both of us looking with a raised eyebrow at the straight down and steep hill directly below us off the shale trail. As long as it was a trail, I knew Cowboy could do it.

We climbed higher and higher, from deep green forests, quiet and dark, to the tundra, covered with miniature flowers and trees. We were following the little rock markers. They really help us find our way on these trails.

"I'm going back," Deb said when she first saw the pass. She started to turn Comanche around; I guess she was serious about not taking a chance. John looked nervous, unsure. I knew we would make it. It seems to me, if we just watch the white mule, she will tell us if it's possible or not. Sarah Jane is really sensible, and thinks before she moves. We trust her judgment.

I spotted the beginning of the trail. It was a long switchback, up through a solid wall of rock. We followed each other up and over, silently, the only sound that of the animals' hooves on the trail; me and Cowboy, John and Chief, Deb and Comanche. Sarah followed us, walking on her own. One by one we made it to the top.

On both sides of the pass, there are giant red rocky ridges, running along infinitely. To the south, I could see the Utah low country, and on the other side was big Wyoming, stretching out below us. We looked around up on top, and found lakes hidden up there at the base of the highest mountains.

Sure enough, Chief threw a shoe up there. John cut his finger twice while trying to get a spare shoe to the correct shape. He'll tack it on in the morning.

> Campfire, my friend, throw light on my page.
> Moon, spirit my heart!
> Tonight is a night after a day after a night.
> As I look back through my life
> I will remember this campfire light.

Each day on the trail, I feel closer and closer to my horse Cowboy. I talk quietly to him, and he listens. When I am nervous, so is he; I guess he can feel my pulse pick up when he's jumpy on the trail. Funny how it works that way. He is a beautiful horse, with his Appaloosa spots, his big knowing eyes, and so very smooth to ride.

He has a really nice running walk, not a trot and not a walk. He really goes. I often ride off, by myself, on the ridge, heading towards the state of Wyoming.

Only a week on the trail, and so much has happened. It's as if we are in a different time frame now. Evanston seems far away. I wish we hadn't told people a definite date we'd be riding in. The country is so much bigger than we ever imagined. Twenty miles and the day is over, and we're looking for camp.

Now we are camped at Little Lyman Lake, about twenty miles

from the Wyoming border. Tomorrow is my twenty-second birthday. We are still over forty miles from Evanston, and I have given up the idea of dancing my birthday away on some little dance floor in town. I may be dancing out in the sagebrush, under this full moon light.

We made about twenty miles today, staying on a jeep trail because of Chief's foot. His hoof looks bad. I hope Dave Goble can fix it in Evanston. Meanwhile, we have to stick to easy ground. Today was a long and very hard day. I have been walking; packing my saddlebags on my saddle to save my horse's back. He is still young and I want him to know I can walk too. He likes it when I walk. I can hold his reins in one hand. He watches me and we walk in rhythm together down the trail.

The mountains here are rugged peaks above the timberline, where the trees do not grow. The mule walks up these trails as if she's been on them before. I think maybe she has, since she used to work for an outfitter over in the Deschene. She walks evenly, slowly but steadily up the trail, keeping her eyes and ears on everything around her. She stops and stretches her neck to search the woods where the sound is coming from, and she spots the deer or coyote from a long distance, and the horses take the cue from her, finally seeing the wildlife themselves. Then the dog stops and listens, and finally, we can spot the animal they have been looking at.

The horseflies are huge, and my poor horse doesn't hardly have a tail, and can't defend himself. I tell him it is nothing to worry about; a lot of Appaloosa horses have "pintails". Once the fly bites Cowboy, I'm on a wild ride through horse fly-infested meadows. They won't leave him alone. The other horses are able to whip the flies with their long tails. Not Cowboy.

I hate to admit it, but we lost Wyoming. It is not an easy state to lose; it stretches from Idaho to South Dakota. John's compass is indecisive, and somehow we got turned around up there on top, and came down the wrong draw, trying to get to Evanston by my birthday. We followed Deb and Comanche down to this sheepherder's camp, stopping the animals next to the pines and tying them up. We could smell the wood smoke from the camp.

The sheepherders were from the Pyrenees, very strong Basque men, ruddy, tall and square. They had two creamy-white buckskin mares and two chestnut geldings picketed in a rich meadow, dotted with wild flowers of all colors.

Perched in this flat, out in the middle of nowhere, was a sheepherder's wagon with rubber tires, an aluminum roof, and a little smokestack for the wood stove sticking out up on top. We walked slowly towards the wagon. The smiles of the sheepherders made us feel more than welcome; maybe a little uneasy.

"Sit down, have a cup of coffee with us. You look like you have been travelling, where are you going?" His accent was heavy. He looked at us with blue eyes; white blue, the color of a swimming pool. These men were not used to company and were glad to have it.

"We're heading to Wyoming," Debbie said to them as she reached for the coffee cup. I could see the steam rising off the top. "And then on to Spokane, Washington," she said casually. They smiled at her with big enthusiastic smiles.

"Washington is almost to Canada," the sheepherder said. "You are going there by when, by next year?" he laughed. His clear eyes were warm and friendly. We all sat in front of the little wagon, on stumps they had set up for chairs.

B. Shields
© 1994

I spotted the brass spittoon and shuddered. It was sitting on the ground next to my stump.

"Where's Wyoming?" John asked them. He had his Jif and Home Pride Wheat bread out of his saddlebag, and was opening up his Swiss Army knife, ready to dig into the peanut butter.

The sheepherders thought John's question was very funny. They stirred their coffees, holding old silver-plated spoons with ruddy, fat hands, that felt like roots from the earth. They both had held them out to us when we arrived in their camp. They had been up there three months, going out once a month for a day, to resupply.

"Where's Wyoming?" I asked one of them, repeating John's question. They howled. They thought it was very funny that we had lost Wyoming. The shorter of the two, in his greasy undershirt, turned gracefully towards the north.

"There....is Wyoming," he said, as he raised both his arms, spreading them out like wings.

"We were never lost, just confused," I told them, as we put our cups back into our saddlebags and prepared to head down towards the flatness below us. They followed us out to the horses, looking at Comanche's ankle, which is obviously bothering him. He keeps knocking it with his other hoof, and the swelling is not going down. He has a real problem, and if it doesn't get better, Deb might have to walk to Spokane.

"I offer you my buckskin mare, for a french kiss from both of you girls, and a hundred dollars," the older sheepherder said to Debbie. I could tell he was serious.

Debbie smiled at him and said, "That's okay. I like to walk."

As we rode down the dirt road, away from their high meadow sheep camp, I took a good look at the hefty buckskin we had turned down.

"Maybe we should have gone for it, Deb," I said to her, as she led Comanche past Cowboy on the trail.

"Are you crazy? I would walk to Alaska before I would kiss that old sheepherder. Yuck!" She was leading her horse down the draw towards Wyoming.

Later on, up the road, we would not have turned that offer down. We knew that Comanche would have to return to Park City;

he couldn't make it the rest of the way. There wasn't enough money for my sister to buy another horse. She'd have to walk.

"Maybe I'll lose some weight," she said to me. I think she is being an incredibly good sport about this. I will let her ride Cowboy when she wants. She will lead Sarah Jane. I wish we had the money to buy another horse. I keep thinking about that hefty buckskin.

July 15

A bronc bustin' birthday.

Today we got off to an early start. Debbie is always the first one up. If it wasn't for her, the coffee wouldn't be made until nine or ten. She has been the alarm clock on this trip so far. We were on the road by eight this morning; our earliest start yet. We ate a little bit of wheat bread that a man gave us yesterday, and started out on the road to Evanston. We have a long day ahead. It's a hot dirt road, through the aspen and young pine.

A man in a Volkswagen bus came by and gave us some smoked trout, but later on, as we crossed a big lonely meadow, it dropped out of my saddlebag and we hadn't eaten more than a bite of it. Up in that meadow, which was on top of a ridge that ran down towards Wyoming, I saw a horse, way off in the distance. It was a large, dark animal, and I thought it was loose. I galloped up on Cowboy, and there, in the grass, was a strange man, lying next to the horse. He was a sheepherder. His eyes were giving him trouble and wouldn't cooperate as he tried to focus on me. Half of his face was severely scarred. I had arrived quietly on a tawny Appaloosa, and had caught him off guard; we had surprised him. He was reading, and didn't notice his horse's alarmed posture. The book was an old copy of "White Fang". He told me he had herded sheep alone for the past forty years.

"Don't you wonder why my face looks like this?" he asked, seriously. He put down his book and looked up at me. His features were about half there. I shuddered, but he didn't see me, I don't think.

"No, I hadn't," I lied.

"Prairie fire. When I was a kid. No one knew I was out in the field. The fire got me. And I have been up here ever since." He paused and looked down at the grass he was stretched out on. "Ain't no mirrors in the high country," he said.

I was speechless. I just stood there, with my hand on my horse's nose. I could feel the heat from his breath on my hand. My heart was beating fast.

Horseflies won't leave us alone. We made our way down to another sheep camp. We followed an almost invisible trail down over the hills, through some rich meadows and, lo and behold, there was Wyoming.

## *The Day We Met the Wagon Train*

We rode into Evanston. We could see it, way off in the distance, for two days before we ever got there, so there was a lot of anticipation. We all longed for town, for different reasons.

"I want to take a shower!" Deb said to me, smiling from braid to braid.

"I want a huge plate of spaghetti, and then dessert, in a cafe called the Wagon Wheel or the Cowboy Cafe. I'm sure there will be one in Evanston," John said, reaching down and opening his saddle bag, looking for a peanut butter sandwich he had made earlier. Sometimes the sun would rise and set behind that bushy red hair of his, and it would glow like a soft auburn halo.

I could tell the horses and the mule were ready for a break as well. They were looking forward to the grain we promised to buy for them. They have been out of grain for three days; they like to have it in the morning, just like we do. They walked at a fast gait towards town, and the little dots started to look like buildings. I watched as a big pickup passed us, turned around and slowed to a stop behind us. A man in a Western style suit jumped out of the truck and walked up to us saying, "Excuse me, could you stop a minute?"

"I'm the Country Gentleman, of KEVA Radio in town. Where are you riding from?" He looked straight at Debbie. "I'd like to interview you for the station."

"Sure," my sister told him.

"You won't believe this, but there is a wagon train coming into the fairgrounds this afternoon. They are coming in from St. Joe, Missouri! All the way from Missouri, in covered wagons. Can you believe that?" He stared at Debbie, smiling. He smelled of Old Spice and spearmint gum.

"So we'll all be out at the fairgrounds together," Debbie added.

"Yep. In fact, I just drove out and told the wagonmaster about you and your pack train. He would like to invite you to their camp tonight for a steak dinner."

We sat around our camp with the wagon train, down at the fairgrounds. The smell of steaks on the big barbecue filled the air and I could feel a pit of hunger in my stomach.

"Where's your back up vehicle?" the wagonmaster, Red, asked me, as we settled down to our thick steaks and green salads. He had a plate heaped high with beans and steak and he balanced it on his knee as he ate.

"It's just us. The three of us, these horses and the mule," I told him. The steak was so good. I savored every bite.

"We have already been on the road for six weeks," he told us. "Hopefully we will reach Sacramento by the end of August."

I could see why they called him Red. Big red curls hung down over the collar of his cowboy shirt. He had on a big six gallon hat, made of the finest felts. I wondered to myself if it ever made him lose his balance, it was so huge on his head. His wife, Irma, had a cowboy hat on her head that was almost as huge as Red's. She was having a grand time, leading the way to Sacramento, slowly, in the motor home.

"So you are just out here with your horses and the mule and your saddle packs. How many miles to Spokane from here?" he asked us. We were eating like a pack of half starved coyotes. It wasn't that we didn't like the food we had with us, but it sure wasn't steak and salad. I could tell already, the mixed grains for breakfast and dinner would sure wear thin by the time we reached our destination.

Debbie stopped eating and said, "Oh, close to a thousand miles or so, the way we plan to go." She wiped her face with the back of her sleeve. Red's mouth fell open. He still couldn't believe we didn't have a motor home following us with extra supplies.

I rode Cowboy uptown, to pick up our mail in General Delivery at the Post Office. For a young horse he wasn't afraid of much, even though his Appy eye made him look a little wild.

"Where you headed?" I heard a quiet voice behind me, as I slid out of the saddle in front of the Post Office. I turned to face an ancient face under a cowboy hat that was at least half as old. He peered at me with squinted eyes like he was still in one heck of a serious dust storm, but he had a kind look in his eyes, what I could see of them. He smiled and stuck out a hand. I reached my hand out and grabbed his. Sagebrush and barbed wire. He shook my hand slowly and for a long time, until it started to feel like a saddlehorn.

"Where you headed?" he asked me again.

"Up to Spokane," I told him matter of factly.

"Been there," he said. He dropped my hand and I wrapped my fingers around Cowboy's reins. "Cowboyed all up and down the State of Wyoming. Been in Montana and Idaho too. I know Spokane, way up North, beyond most of Idaho, not really as many cowboys up that way as there are down here. That's mostly lumber up that way."

"How many mules you packing?" he continued.

"We only have one, and her name is Sarah Jane. She's out of a white Appy mare. She's the best animal we've got."

"And all the rest are horses. How come?" he asked me with a smile on his face. "How come no more mules in this outfit?"

I stopped and thought about it and really couldn't answer that question. This old-timer knew what we were rapidly finding out. Mules were made for this.

I looked through the letters. Debbie had three cards from Johnny. I had one from Jill Tipton and another from Mom and Dad. Mom had popped a five dollar bill in the envelope before mailing it. I immediately stuck the bill in the front pocket of my jeans. Five dollars seemed like a lot of money on the trail, with all those days in between places to spend it. Most days there was nothing to spend money on, because we were beyond the last electric pole and up the trail. The five dollars would buy a few dinner salads, heavy on the saltines.

Dave the horseshoer had driven three times up and down Highway 150 South, and camped out there in the sagebrush. I found him out in front of the Post Office, sitting on the stairs with Trampas, waiting for me. My heart raced when I first saw him. He looked so beautiful sitting there. I had forgotten what a wide open smile he had. He had three nectarines for me, in a worn brown paper sack. We walked down the Main Street of Evanston with Cowboy and the dogs. No one was ever so happy to be in Evanston, Wyoming as we were that day. It had taken us fourteen days from Park City.

Dave and Sherry Thompson showed up with John's horse,

Red. He's a big brick of a Quarterhorse with kind eyes and a beautiful long red mane. If we didn't have so much stuff with us, Debbie could use him, but he belongs to John, so from now on we'll probably pack Chief, and John will ride Red.

"How long will you stay?" I asked David as we rode Cowboy and Sarah Jane bareback in the fields behind the fairgrounds.

"I have to get back down to Park City tomorrow. I have a lot of people waiting for me to shoe."

We galloped the horse and mule in circles, and it started to rain. The rain in these clouds comes down in sheets, with lightning and thunder. Cowboy bolted forward, and I almost fell off. We got sopped in the rain, a warm rain that soaked us to the bone, but we weren't cold.

Deb and John, meanwhile, were hanging out under the shelter we put together with the tarps. Everybody walked downtown to dinner. Dave and I let Cowboy and Sarah Jane go with the other animals. They were really wet too, and immediately rolled in the soft mud in the pen.

David and I hid under the bleachers for two hours, talking and staying out of the rain. The last two weeks have seemed more like two years. It is incredible to think it only took our friends a few hours in a car. We covered the same distance in two weeks! I find myself looking towards the North. Two days and I am already anxious to get back on the trail. I can see from the saddle, a long way, and I like the view from there.

"Go and see Russ and Barbie Doll down at Nick's Bar, if you like good country." She never turned away from the bar mirror as she said this, looking at Dave and me in the mirror. We drank a draft, and listened to Willie Nelson on the jukebox, singing my favorite song, "I'd Have to Be Crazy". We walked down the Main Street, holding hands and singing old cowboy songs.

We veered into Nick's Bar and grill. We could hear a woman wailing Patsy Cline songs from inside the smoky tavern. Russ and Barbie Doll were in the middle of their second set; they had been playing since seven.

"Welcome," Russ said to us, as we scooted into the black upholstered chairs in the front row, right up next to the dance floor. Russ had no teeth. He had a royal blue cowboy hat on, and a western

shirt that was made especially for the Bicentennial. It was red, white and blue with a big American flag on the back. He had a royal blue silk scarf around his neck.

His outfit matched Barbie Doll's. She was the Trucker's Sweetheart. She had the tallest blonde hair I have ever seen, and heavy makeup; dark blue eyeliner with lots of mascara, enough to make any lashes droop, and hers did not. Together, they sang and played the most beautiful slide guitar and pedal steel. Old Mike behind the bar gave us a free beer, when he found out I'd ridden my horse all the way from Park City.

Barbie's eyes twinkled as we danced the Western swing and smiled back at her. As they played and sang love songs to each other, the same love songs they'd been playing for years, David and I twirled the night away on the tiny linoleum dance floor.

"You're riding to Spokane? I grew up there, Sweetie," Russ told me. "Me and Barbie, we've played all over the West. From Spokane to Bakersfield, and as far east as South Dakota. Ever since we were nineteen, we've been playing music together. Never had an argument to speak of, aside from little ones, like what key to play a song in. We have lived in harmony, you might say!" He laughed.

"Russ was everything I ever wanted in a man," Barbie Doll said in her raspy, smoky voice. Even though she sounded hoarse when she talked, when she sang, her voice sounded smooth and sweet. "He showed up one day and stole me away, right from under my papa's nose."

"Playin' the bars ain't easy," Russ said seriously. "Sometimes booze makes people real noisy, and they don't listen. It gets hard to play then. But when they listen, and they're dancin', well, there's just nothing like it. Ever since I first started playing the guitar, I have loved to play for people."

"Back in Spokane, when I was a young sprite, I used to play at the grange halls and the churches, every chance I got. Back then, the only thing some folks had to look forward to was the dance at the hall. I played along with the band when I was only ten or so," he continued, "but I always hid outside where they couldn't see me or hear me, until I could keep up with the best of 'em. Then I came inside and got up on the stage, and they haven't been able to drag me off yet."

"You know," Barbie Doll said proudly, "Russ is one of the best pedal steel guitarists in the whole country." She put her hand on his shoulder and said, "Honey, we'd better get back up there. The crowd's starting to get a little restless."

We wandered back to the fairgrounds and slept under one blanket in Stock Pen #9.

B. Shields '94

## The Long Road to Cokeville

Wyoming breeds mosquitoes at an alarming rate along the irrigation ditches. The road to Cokeville was paved with mosquitoes; I had shorts on most of the way, and the annoying little insects fed on my legs. They are hard on me especially, since I have a bet going with Dave the horseshoer, and cannot wear any repellant.

"I promise you, Jod," he said to me right before he headed back to Park City, "if you don't wear repellant, pretty soon you will be immune to them. You won't taste good to them any more."

"How long will it take?" I asked him. "Three months?"

He laughed. So far I wish I never would have made this bet with him. I don't think he realized how many mosquitoes there really are out here. Debbie has some of that Army surplus bug stuff from Vietnam, and uses it like perfume. They seem to leave her alone.

I got off to open a gate and they zeroed in on the tender pinkness of my calves, particularly enjoying the back of the knee. My legs were covered with mosquitoes.

"I wish my jeans weren't packed away on the mule," I whined to Debbie.

It was torture today; long, hot, and miserable. My legs were welted solidly from the top of my grey wool socks to the bottom of my green shorts, and a little beyond.

We were fifteen miles south of Cokeville, heading up the irrigation ditch on a perfectly graded dirt road.

"Just a second, Cowboy," I said to my horse. "I need to tighten your cinch. This saddle is about to fall off." It was very loose, so I lowered myself carefully to the ground. I could instantly hear the buzz of the mosquitoes rise to a crescendo, in a feeding frenzy, as they headed for prime positions; the best my thighs and calves had to offer. Their favorite place to dine was the tender inside of my thigh, right below the line of my shorts. I tried to stay calm, but I was about ready to blow.

To make things worse, Deb and John had ridden ahead of me, and were by this time almost out of sight, on top of a little rise on the road about a quarter mile ahead. There's nothing a horse hates more than to lag behind the herd. To say the least, Cowboy was more than a little excited about it. Robin circled us nervously; she also was not interested in losing the mule who carried her dinner.

"Easy, Boy," I said to him, as I loosened his cinch before retightening it. He watched the top of the bluff carefully, his big brown ears pointing earnestly towards the horizon, intent on his herd, as Comanche and the other animals disappeared from his view. This was not something he liked; in fact it was the one thing, besides the rustling of raincoats and tarps, that made the spotted horse very anxious.

Unfortunately, in that same moment, a yellowjacket landed on Cowboy's belly. I saw the insect land, half a second before my horse exploded, leaping straight up in the air, about four feet off the ground; straight up, like the Roadrunner, his legs a blur of movement as they formed a wheel under him. I blinked and he was gone, bucking insanely down the road through the sage; legs flying back behind him, kicking, jumping, trying to lose the yellowjacket and the saddle. I watched as my meager household shot off his sides, as he kicked out his legs with such force he truly looked like a cartoon horse. His only concern was to catch up with Comanche, Sarah Jane and the others.

I fell backward into the sandy soil between two sage bushes and watched as Cowboy became a tiny dot on the horizon, then disappeared out of sight. I sat there laughing silently, then got up, dusted myself off, and walked stiffly down the road. Robin was laughing at me as only a dog can laugh, with her big pink tongue reaching out for the canteen. Just as she realized that the canteen had disappeared over the ridge, along with everything else, she looked at me with sincere Labrador concern, urging me along through the sage, in the direction of my itinerant band. I knew that Cowboy had caught up with Deb and John and the pack train. I hoped they had caught him and were up ahead waiting for me.

I found my saddlebags first; thrown off the side of the road into the middle of a sage brush. They were empty. My saddle had come off around his tail and back legs, because the cinch was still fastened together. I smiled, picturing him wriggling out of the saddle.

"There's my address book, Rob," I said to my dog, who was

nosing her way from page to page of the book, finding the A's and then the B's, and so on, up the dirt road to Cokeville. I found my canteen and sat down in the sage.

"Here, girl, here Rob, have a little drink, your tongue's getting pretty long!" I said to her. She gracefully trotted towards me, dropping the M page of the address book at my feet. "Thanks, girl." I cupped my hands and she licked at the water in my hand very slowly and carefully, so she didn't lose any. There was my toothbrush and toothpaste, in a plastic bag, in the barrow ditch. Then I came across my hairbrush, my tape recorder, seemingly unharmed, and my notebook, all in the same big bush, flung there, then suspended, hanging on the stiff branches of the aromatic sage.

I picked up the rest of my belongings: the lucky horseshoe I had carried in my saddle bag since the High Uintas, a red bandanna, some Band Aids, a Chap Stick, skin cream, three pens, some hydrogen peroxide, some gauze, sunglasses, letters I had received in Evanston, and a little bag of rubber bands and leather ties that almost escaped my eye, pitched under a sage brush. I walked along, fairly confident that I had everything, and walked the rest of the way at a good clip with my saddle over one shoulder and my saddlebags over the other.

"How does Cowboy carry this thing?" I said to Robin. We caught up with Deb and John a mile later, just enough time to work the crink out of my legs. They were eating peanut butter sandwiches and dried fruit by the time I caught up with them. Sarah Jane and the horses, including my spirited Cowboy, were tied to fenceposts.

"Boy, Jod, I'll tell you what," Deb said to me through a mouth stuffed full of fluffy wheat bread and peanut butter. I could barely understand her muffled words. "That horse was flying when he caught up to us! He didn't slow down until he was head to head with Sarah Jane. I swear, the boy's in love!"

I put out my hand and pouted, begging for a sandwich, then dropped to my knees and really begged until John threw me a dried pear. It tasted better than anything I had tasted in a long time. I savored the sweet chewy fruit and looked at Deb, not saying a word. It would take awhile to live this one down. After a half hour or so I packed up Cowboy, tightened the cinch, and we headed towards Cokeville.

This land is a place where the golden grasses dance in the wind and the sky is immense and very blue. To our east is Commissary Ridge, and beyond, way off in the distance to the northeast, I can see the Wind River Range, the slopes of the Rockies and the Continental Divide. I heard there's a trail up there that runs all the way from Waterton Glacier in Canada to the Mexican border in New Mexico. I would like to take that ride sometime.

Directly north, the Salt River Range stands, with the Teton Range beyond, the jewel of the West. It will take us two weeks to get there from here.

Orson Nates was waiting for us by the gate, as the Wyoming sun disappeared into Idaho and a purple light covered the land.

"You can stay down behind the barn," he said to us, pointing towards a huge wooden barn the size of a city block. He wore a red shirt, overalls and Cowboy boots, crossing his arms over his hay bucking chest, undoing them only to reach in his back pocket for the Copenhagen tin he kept there.

"The critters will like that good feed in the big corral. You can keep them in there overnight." He spoke softly and directly at my sister, taking in her long brown braids and open smile. Cokeville is seven miles from this gate," he added, in an official tone.

We spent the evening  counting all the bites on our legs. As the moon came silently up over the ridge, it turned the Bear River, wide and slow, into a shining silver ribbon. Robin swam across it, and back again. She shook the water off right next to me, almost losing her balance.

"Thanks, Girl, but I'm not thirsty anymore," I said to her as I watched the water fly off, sizzling on the hot rocks surrounding our fire.

I'm not sure how much time passed there by that fire, or by many others. The time just passes, looking into the fiery orange depths of the wood fire, until it disappears into smoke, and it's time to sleep.

"Cokeville, tomorrow," I said aloud to the fire. Deb and John were already asleep; neither one answered. I stayed up until the fire died down and listened to the frogs' voices, harmonizing baritones, echoing off the river's steep sandy edge.

As usual, Debbie was the first to rise and stir the coals. We would still be back in the Uintahs if I was in charge of getting us going in the morning. Sometimes the amount of stuff we have with us overwhelms me, and I can't fathom packing it all up again. As time goes on, we are starting to get a routine going. Deb stirs first and shakes John, gets the coals going again and starts the water boiling for coffee. I am still asleep; if I'm not then I pretend to be, and so does Robin. I'm not sure why she does it, but I wait until I can smell the coffee bubbling away in the old black coffee pot.

"Jod, the coffee is hot, dear," she says to me wryly and throws a pine cone at my head.

"Cream and sugar," I say to her, and roll over. John gets up and pulls on his down vest; it's already looking like he has had it on for several years. He heads out to check on the horses, to make sure everyone is okay. Whether they are in a corral or picketed out, they are always ready for something new to happen by the time we get going, which is usually, thanks to Deb, around seven or so. I have been naturally slower to awaken than my lovely sister for my entire life. The chipper stuff, first thing in the morning, annoys me greatly.

I pull on my jeans and put on a less dirty pair of socks. I pull my hat on and go out to see my horse in the lower corral down behind the barn. The morning sun is bright and ricochets off the river in bright bolts of light. He whinnys to me, his big innocent eyes looking at me, his soft ears facing me, directly.

"Morning, Boy," I say to him, handing him a granola bar, or a good half of one, I found in my pocket. It was perfectly fine with him, once I unraveled the thread from the sticky oat bar. I could feel the warmth of his breath on my hand. He chews, and his giant jaw grinds away, putting every part of his face in motion. His nose is the color of wheat right before harvest, and is very soft to touch. I warm up my hands on his warm hide, and watch the morning mists rising off the river. I can smell the coffee brewing up there at the campfire; it mixes with the smell of the alder we are using for fire wood.

After the usual gruel, some cowboy coffee and some dried fruit Debbie had stashed away in her own bag, we saddle up the animals, one by one, until everything that is on the ground, scattered around in our camp, somehow ends up back on the animals. Then we take one quick look around camp, looking for wayward forks, socks, bits of trash we had missed. What had only moments before been a disaster area is once again a natural place, with its grasses only slightly bent out of shape.

Cokeville.

This particular morning quickly became the afternoon, and we limped into the little two streeter, Cokeville, at around one or so. Debbie was leading Sarah and Comanche. I was walking next to her, leading Cowboy. John was riding Red, leading Chief. We were all a little sad, because we saw what was happening to Chief. He needs time off to heal.

We all knew we would probably end up trading him for another pack horse, to someone who could let him sit and heal in a pasture for the summer. We were thinking about this when we pulled into Cokeville. Debbie and I walked, side by side, followed by our animal friends, down the Main Street, passed the three cafes, the church, the store, kicking up dirt, and turning the heads of every local who set eyes on us; part curiosity, part "Welcome to our town" and part "When are you leaving?"

We found the rodeo grounds in Cokeville by just following the Main Street to the end. There are only a few streets in Cokeville; it's a really easy town to find your way around. We let Red, Chief, Cowboy, Sarah and Comanche go in the little corral back behind the arena. Unfortunately, Chief's withers look really bad.

It was the really hot day, south of Sage, when we went without unpacking the animals at lunch. That mistake is going to get us after all, I'm afraid. The packsaddle is too narrow for him, now that he is losing weight, and rubbed on his withers until he was sore.

"Never pack a high withered horse." This little piece of advice came too late for us. I hate to think we did this to the poor old boy.

We would never forget Cokeville, Wyoming, with its one main street with three cafes, the Midway, the Red Dog and the Coke Villa. Every cafe  has a great jukebox. The whole town smells like coffee and bacon from about six o'clock on, just as the sun gets the birds singing, until about eleven, and then it smells like hamburgers. The three greasy spoons have been suspended in time, and their decors have never been changed very much. Some of the waitresses have been there for twenty years or more, and the seasons change while the cafes change only the grease and the calendar, a free one the Hardware Store gives to everybody. The three of us stood out like sore thumbs.

They stared at us as we walked into the Midway — John in his red vest and maroon cords, Deb in her red and white gingham blouse and dirty blue jeans, and me, the one in the dirty everything. I had managed to get about three times as dirty as anyone else and all my clothes rivaled John's vest.

We ordered dinner. I stuck to my usual dinner salad with saltines, and Debbie ordered a baked potato. John had his usual, spaghetti with extra meat balls. John always ordered spaghetti and garlic bread.

We sat in the tiny, sticky plastic booth and listened to the songs I had chosen on the juke box. The rest of the people in the Midway, all locals, asked us a steady stream of questions about how far we had come, what it was like, if we'd been lost, how we were enjoying Wyoming, and wasn't Spokane a long way from Cokeville! They were right, Spokane was still a long way from there. And we had two animals who were not going to be able to continue on. Comanche, Debbie's gelding, is still in trouble with the swelling in his ankle. He is going back to Utah in a horse trailer; this is definitely the end of the trail for him. And Chief will not see a pack saddle again until his infected withers are healed.

We organized our gear right there by the rodeo ring, until we could no longer see, listened to the trains as they passed on tracks a stone's throw from our camp, and watched the Milky Way pour across the sky above Cokeville like you wouldn't believe unless you saw it for yourself; a solid white band of stars across the black sky. We had finally reached Cokeville, the irrigated oasis at the end of two hundred and fifty miles of sagebrush and cow skulls. We even saw a horse skeleton stretched out across a cattle guard. It had been there a long time, and every bit of hide was gone, except for a long black tail.

The mosquitoes left about a thousand red calling cards on my arms and legs. The mule needs a bath, and is not nearly as white as she used to be, since she has been rolling in some of the reddest of clays and the blackest of muds. Red needs the usual, more oats than the rest, but he's a good horse, big and kind, steady as he goes.

John's and Red's hair are the same color.

The next morning, we met Ray. He walked slowly towards our camp behind the arena, leaning heavily on his cane. He walked with a limp, with his little fox terrier at his heels, who trotted in place, and was no more than fifteen inches tall.

"I never go anywhere without this cane and this little dog," he said to us, pointing the cane at the little yellow tap dancing dog with the bulging eyes and the tiny claws.

Ray was no beauty himself. He squinted out of red eyes behind a big red nose; he had the face of a beat up but not beat down cowboy. Under all the cragginess of his old, beat up face, he looked like a young man, at least when he set eyes on Debbie. It was love at first sight, we could all see that.

"You are comin' home with me." He poked at the dog and it dodged the cane with agility, having been dodging since puppyhood.

This bent up old cowboy wore a white cowboy hat with a brim stained black from years and years of sweat. His bushy grey eyebrows stood out like dark thunderclouds on his face, shielding his puffy eyes from the relentless Wyoming summer sun. His teeth were not all there, and still, when a smile broke across his face, the sun came out. We knew right away that he was serious, we were going home with him. He wasn't there to argue.

"Got to get you all out of this Rodeo Arena. So pack your bags."

We packed up and walked our herd back through town, past the cafes, to Ray's house. His place was old, old as the hills. His back yard had a couple of old corrals in it, a perfect place for the animals. There was lots of untouched grass back there, just waiting for them.

Ray walked slowly up to Chief and squinted at his withers.

"They look bad," he said to us. "He doesn't need to pack anymore until that heals, that's for sure. He'll just have to travel bare naked with you the rest of the way, or you'll have to trade the bugger off." He made the terrier jump over his walking cane again. The dog was always waiting for him to do that.

"I'm one of the last of the old-timers," he told us after we unloaded the animals in his backyard. "They're all dead, most of 'em. For some reason, the Good Lord makes me live! All crippled up with this dancin' dog! And now I know why!"

He invited us into his little house, warm with the coal fire. We sat there by the wood stove on chairs Ray provided for us, all of them different and very old. I found myself hoping mine didn't split into a thousand pieces underneath me. Ray stoked the fire, grabbing chunks of coal from a box next to the stove. I looked around the house. It was very small and it was painted green with yellow trim. The ceilings were low and junk mail and magazines had not been tossed, ever, by the looks of things. Ray's mantle had a trophy on it and a clock. His couch was big and soft, light green with a huge, puffy cushion in the middle of it, covered with little dog hairs. The coffee pot was always hot at Ray's house. He liked company. But in Cokeville, everyone had already heard this old man's stories.

"I was born lonely," he told us. He pulled out his harmonica and played a sorrowful tune. "Been lonely since I was born, until now," he sang to us.

"I've been a trapper, I've been a horse trader, I've been a rodeo cowboy, and even a rodeo clown, do you believe that? Well, it's true. I rode in some of the rankest rodeos in the history of the West, all the way over to Laramie. I made my money that way for awhile! But then, you know what happened to me? I got bucked off one too many times and had to quit." He looked sad when he thought about the rodeo. He had ridden the range for many years, cowboying across Wyoming and Idaho. We listened to his stories with interest.

Every morning, we were invited for bacon and eggs. We all sat around the old green formica table while he fed us his potatoes, eggs, pancakes, and cowboy coffee.

He gave me his old felt Alamo hat that has patches on it, in places where he creased it over and over again. He also gave me an old cowboy shirt, this incredible blue one with silver snaps.

Deb and I cleaned six months of dirt out of his corners, beat his rugs, washed his floors, did the dishes from a pile that almost reached to the ceiling, baked pies and cooked meals. We picked some daisies and put them in a glass jar on the kitchen table. Ray told us, "I ain't seen flowers in here since my Mother's funeral."

We went to church on Sunday morning with Ray at the Mormon Church, and he paraded Debbie and me with pride, then took us to a big old time B-B-Q feed after church.

"Endless macaroni salad, John," I said on our way down to the picnic. John was practically drooling. He was really looking forward to the potluck.

We sat on the grass with Ray and his son and daughter-in-law, Barney Ray and Bonnie Jean. There was ample macaroni salad, and that wasn't all. There was chocolate cake, ribs and chicken, baked beans, garlic bread, coffee with milk, and cookies to take with us in our saddlebags.

Then we headed out to the rodeo, as Ray's guests.

"I'm too old and broke up to ride, but you better believe there was a day..." Ray said to us as the rodeo began.

It was a real local rodeo with steer riding, bronc busting, barrel racing, and single and team steer roping. The Rodeo Queens from Afton did a special for the Bicentennial, about the American flag. All of the horses were draped in the stars and stripes. The Rodeo Queen read a monologue piece about the flag, over a crackling speaker. Ray was beaming. He sat next to my sister the entire rodeo, explaining every event to her.

After the rodeo, I did not go straight back to Ray's place. I stayed in the rodeo grounds parking lot and talked to a man with long hair and a van! When I walked back to Ray's, there he was, sitting on the back bumper of his Scout with his rifle on his lap, "ready to put some holes in those hippies."

Later on, we all sat around his kitchen table and he told us stories. His coffee was strong, and he served it with canned milk.

Ray recited this poem to us after a pork chop dinner. He stood up, put on his hat and walked around the small stuffy room. I could hear the linoleum crack under his feet as he walked. The little dog jumped out of the old chair and followed Ray around the room, in double time. All of a sudden he remembered the poem and started in, as we three sat there in silence.

*"I rode into old Cokeville the morning of the fair.*
*Entered in a bucking horse a funnin' in the square.*
*Knocked around town, had nothing else to do*
*I could feel that nerve was slippin' and went and hoist a few.*
*Then I heard the band a playin' and headed for the track.*
*Went and slapped my saddle on my old nag's back.*
*We were a happy bunch of boys*
*Seen a couple races, heard a lot of noise.*

*The judge hollered,*
*"Come on up here you punchers get ready for the draw.*
*I got an old bay mare just as handsome as a squaw".*
*When I stepped upon her the crowd was mighty still.*
*Seen those punchers grinning 'cause they knew I was gonna*
*spill.*
*Grabbed my hat and hollered and hooked her in the flank*
*hooked her in the shoulder with the silver mounted shank.*
*She left this earth and made a ball*
*And made one leap towards the Grand.*
*I reached down to safety and lit down on the sand.*
*The crowd hollered, "Rotten, your riding's pretty cheap!"*
*So I beat it into Utah, and went to herding sheep!"*

John was sitting on the old couch, Deb was at the table. After the poem Ray looked right at my sister and said, "You know honey, I wish you were gonna stay right here with me, forever."

He wiped his eyes with the sleeve of his threadbare cowboy shirt.

Two days passed and we knew we had to get going. We'd lead Chief to Jackson bareback. He watched us pack up in his backyard while the dog danced around him, always ready to jump over the cane.

He stood in the driveway and watched us leave, and tapped his cane on the dusty road.

"If I was a little younger, honey," he said to my sister, "I'd ride on up to Spokane with you. There was a day, you know..." His words cracked in his throat.

It was not easy to leave this old man there by the railroad tracks. Somehow, I just knew I would never see Ray again. We rode north in silence, the only sound was the animals' hooves on the dirt. I looked back and saw him standing there, with that little terrier poised by the cane, the two of them watching as we rode on up the road towards Jackson.

"I hope I didn't break his heart," Debbie yelled back at me. She was leading Sarah. Horseless, she walked with such determined vigor towards Spokane we could hardly keep up with her.

"Well, if you did, it was probably for the last time," I said to Debbie, reaching down and adjusting my saddlebags so they were

even on my saddle.

We were all glad to be back on the road again. Debbie and I didn't talk about it but we were both really glad to be out of Ray's kitchen, though we both had, four days ago, craved the warmth of the wood stove and coffee he made us, thick with sweetened milk.

## Rattlesnake For Breakfast

Three candles light up this tent. It is about ten-thirty at night, and we are camped two days from Jackson Hole. We rode up the Salt River Range to the Gros Ventre Range. Now we are straight across from the Grand Tetons.

At thirteen thousand seven hundred feet, Grand Teton is the highest mountain around here. They told us down in Cokeville that there are eight summits in the National Park over twelve thousand feet.

The Wind Rivers, to our East, are inviting mountains, rounded with age. It is sometimes difficult to pass these mountains without disappearing up the draw and into the back country.

This is where the Continental Divide separates the waters. The Yellowstone flows into the Missouri and the Mississippi River and on to the Gulf of Mexico. The Snake works its way to the Pacific Ocean through the mighty Columbia. The Divide follows the Wind River Range, the Absarokas through the heart of the Yellowstone, and on up into Canada.

The aspens, cottonwoods along the river, the light off the Snake, with the Tetons rising up to the sky — this is definitely God's country. I just hope God likes motor homes, because there are lots of them on the road to Jackson. The old wagon trails run up the valley too, so we are able to stay off the road. Still, we can hear the sounds of the highway echoing off the mountains, rising high to the West, as we head towards Jackson, where the trails of the mountain men once converged.

Everyone else is already asleep. I can hear Debbie and John's slow and even breathing. I wonder what they are dreaming about. I know Robin is dreaming. Her legs are moving and her eyes are twitching. She is probably chasing a bear or getting chased by one. I bet John is dreaming about his next spaghetti dinner.

I like being the only one awake. I can hear Cowboy and Sarah, picketed close by in the greenest clover we've seen for awhile. I can hear their breathing as they move around on the end of their picket ropes.

It's been awhile since we all slept in this tent, but the clouds that cap the Grand Tetons threaten rain. They are a dark charcoal color, with highlights of lighter greys, like the smoke of a hot, uncontrollable fire.

I can't take my eyes off these grand peaks and this mighty, shimmering river. The moon is half full now, and the small stream by camp is glistening, covered with stars of light, reflecting like a ribbon of silver. Chief is grazing very close to the door of the tent.

I just went out and said goodnight to Cowboy and Sarah. Standing there in the moonlight, leaning up against my horse, I could feel the warmth of his coat, and could hear him breathing, slowly and quietly. He has put in some long days lately. I can tell he is getting used to the pace of the trip, and feels the excitement of the day to come just as we do, at night dreaming about whatever it is that horses dream. I know he is satisfied with the beautiful clover at his feet and has had his fill.

The moon shines in his eyes and he looks at me, softly nudging me with his head. Sarah and the river are both glowing in the moonlight. There is no way I will ever forget this camp on the edge of the river. The night air is so still and cold. The animals are sleeping or eating quietly. The mountains rise up to guard us against too big of a sky, bright with stars.

I could stay here and watch this river flow for the rest of my life. I know I would never get tired of this view. I guess it gets down in the minus degrees in the wintertime. Relentless snowstorms blanket the area and the motor homes are gone, long gone to Arizona.

I couldn't have asked for a better horse unless he was a mule! He has such a nice gait, fast and smooth. Cowboy can really move, and covers the miles with ease. Long after the other horses have slowed down, he is still walking with his ears forward on the trail ahead. He is made of Nez Perce mountain mare and stallion, sure footed, graceful and smart.

As time goes on we become more used to this life on the road, and it's easier and easier as the days go by. The saddle makes it up on Cowboy's back in the morning without effort, and he stands still while I adjust his bridle and even out my saddle bags, tying on my coat with the latigo straps.

We prepare for the day, never knowing what it will bring. All we have is a map showing the road up the valley and over the hills into Yellowstone. The river is directing us up this most fertile high mountain basin, carpeted in spots with granddaddy cottonwoods, their leaves glittering golden yellow in the morning sun.

We rode to Moose from our camp at the White Grass Ranch. We crossed the sagebrush for hours, surrounded on both sides by the mountains. I am amazed at the beauty of this place. It feels so much kinder than the country between here and Evanston. I love sagebrush, and like to keep it in my front pocket. I take a little bit and smash it behind my ear for perfume.

I met an old woman, with white hair and a big cowboy hat, sitting on the porch of her log cabin, and she took me in, fed me, and filled up my water jugs. If I hadn't ridden down her driveway I never would have met her. I needed water and as it turned out she was ready for company.

"Deb, you and John wait for me at the junction, O.K.?" I jumped up on Cowboy after lunch and left them by the side of the road where we had unpacked and let the animals graze.

"We'll probably still be here when you get back. I want to take a nap," Deb told me as she lay on her back in a grove of big cottonwoods. The branches were playing a soft melody and it was putting them both to sleep.

"I'll fill all our water containers," I said, as I started to trot off on Cowboy in the direction of the log cabin, with four jugs tied to my saddle horn. I rode down the dirt driveway lined with wildflowers.

She watched me approach, signaling me to come on up on the porch.

The cabin was made of big pine logs, ancient, well oiled from the hands of generations. Chairs were backed up under the windows, and a grey cat lay in the biggest of the chairs on an old horse blanket. Old spurs, saddles, branding irons and wagon wheels were covering the far end of the porch. There was an ancient saddle that looked well over a hundred years old. Around the horn there was an old rope. Antlers leaned up against the wall.

"It was built in 1918," she told me. "All hand made. The

same folks lived here until I bought the place in '45. I never married; lived here all this time with a bunch of dogs, cats, raccoons, deer, bear, elk, and skunks. I never meant to stay single like this, but nobody ever came and found me out here, at least not the right one." She laughed.

"Can I tie up my horse and sit on the porch with you for a minute?" I asked her.

"Sure." She looked at me with bright blue eyes. She had deep wrinkles around them and I could tell she had laughed a lot. She had a red bandanna tied around her neck, and little black cowboy boots peaking out from under her well worn Levis. A big turquoise bolo tie graced the front of her cowgirl shirt. She saw me admiring it.

"An old mountain man friend of mine, we called him Piercy, gave that to me when he come down one year after the first snowstorm. He lived in the Wind Rivers all year 'round and only came back down here for supplies and to wait out the snows. Sometimes he would stay in the little meat house out back. See the log building back there?" She pointed around the corner of the cabin, rising halfway out of her chair.

"What a beautiful cabin," I said to her. I ran over to Cowboy who was already loose. Somehow he had undone the knot I had tied.

"Anyway, Piercy would come down out of the mountains once in awhile and this is where he stayed. He was always welcome here. In town, people always understood that he was born a century too late! He smelled pretty strong when he first rode in on old Sally, his piebald roan mare. I'd say to him, I'd say, "Piercy! You gotta get cleaned up! Or I won't have you!" And he'd laugh, set his horse up in the corral, and take off that stinky deer hide coat he wore that he said was a gift from a Nez Perce medicine man. I'd draw a tub for him and he'd sit in there, just sit in there for hours and hours until the water was almost cold. I'd stoked the fire up real high, and get the cabin real warm inside, and slice him off a piece of huckleberry pie, or whatever dessert I had made for him. He'd sit at my kitchen table for hours, trying to remember how to talk to humans again. That feller was more used to the company of his horse than anyone else. He'd sit there, kinda mesmerized by the heat of the wood stove, and finally he'd start talking, telling me about his summer in the high country; the bears he saw, the deer that grazed in the meadow where he stayed for months at a time, and the elk in the fertile meadowlands up there.

She stopped and said, "How about you? Do you want some coffee?"

"Sure, I'd love some," I said. "I just came up to see if I could fill up our bottles here. My sister and another friend are under the cottonwoods up by the road. They are probably sleeping by now. It's been a long day for us already! My sister Deb wakes us up early so we can get some miles in before we unpack again and take a lunch break. It is definitely slow going," I said to her, "at three and a half miles per hour."

"Where are you going?" she asked.

"Up through Jackson and Yellowstone, through the great state of Montana and across the Panhandle of Idaho to Spokane," I said, all in one breath.

"That's a heck of a long way from here," she answered, "even in a car. You came from where?"

"From Park City, Utah."

She looked at me in disbelief but could tell I was telling the truth. She grabbed my arm and led me into the yellow log home. On the mantle was a moose horn, she told me she had found it in the road on the way to town. The wood floors were covered with the most beautiful Navajo blankets. The fireplace was made of river stones, and I could smell the fire from last night. The water was boiling in the kitchen and she was making us coffee. Old cowboy prints in ornate gold frames hung from the logs all over the cabin. She had an old record player; it looked like the first one ever made.

"You know, you are more than welcome to stay here, all of you," she told me. "It's been lonely since Piercy's been gone." She walked to the window and looked up at the mountains for a second, looking way back up the Divide. "Haven't had a horse in the old corral since then. You know, one winter he just never showed up," she said.

"When was that?" I asked her.

"Ten years ago now," she said sadly and smiled. Her face lit up and she continued.

"I waited a long time, about ten days or so, waiting for old Piercy to show up. I had the old meat house fixed up for him, extra pies and all sorts of newspaper articles I'd cut out to show him when he got here." She stopped and stood there for about a minute or so before she continued on with her story. "Finally, the Forest Service sent a guy out to tell me that they found Piercy and the horse. They figured a lion got 'em both. It was real hard for me that first winter. It seemed like it would never stop snowing. Piercy had no living family that anybody knew anything about, and they buried him below Gannett Peak. It's been ten years since he's been gone, and I can still picture his face like it was yesterday."

We sat on the porch for an hour or so, drinking coffee with milk and brown sugar. After filling up my water bottles, I got back up on Cowboy and started up the driveway.

The purple lupine made the air smell with its musky perfume and literally blanketed the ground in some places. There were about seven tipis, out there in the sagebrush. We rode along in silence; John Pierre on Red, leading Chief, me on Cowboy and Deb leading Sarah. It is going to be along walk for her, all the way to Spokane. I bet she misses her horse Comanche.

The clouds are always there, all summer long, hovered up over the mountains. Each night it rains on the massive peaks, jagged and dark. Every morning the earth is washed clean. The sagebrush is cleaned of the day's dust, filling the air with the perfume of the high desert.

Jackson, Wyoming

The tourists in Jackson cover the town in the summers. Small faces show through mesh screens of the motor homes, smiling and waving when they see our pack train, riding down the barrow ditch. Their smiles and waves give me butterflies in my stomach.

We rode into town, under the Antler Arch, across from the Million Dollar Cowboy Bar. John stayed with the horses and the mule, and Deb and I headed up the road towards the Chamber of Commerce building. Once off Cowboy and on the ground walking, I realized the perspective was much different from the back of my horse, moving along at a swift pace, the ground moving beneath his sturdy hooves.

"Hi!" I said to the woman behind the desk, "my name is Jody Foss. My sister Debbie here, and our friend John Najar, are travelling from Park City, Utah, to Spokane, Washington." I could see her apparent lack of enthusiasm. She didn't want to know my name, just to get on with it.

"We are riding the whole way on horses and mules."

She looked me up and down as if to say, "That doesn't surprise me."

I looked down at my shirt. There was a huge stain, bright red, from the Betadine solution we'd been using on Chief's back. My jeans were very dirty. My hair was pulled back with an old faded red bandanna. I looked as if I had just spent a few too many nights in the sagebrush. We definitely had not spent the night at Teton Holiday Inn.

"What can I do for you?" she asked.

"We need to find out where we can camp," I answered.

"There are no horses allowed in the campgrounds."

"Oh. Any other places close by?"

"Not that I know of," she answered.

Deb was methodically chewing her fruit leather. The sun glistened off her long brown braids, hanging over her checkered shirt. John and the horses could be seen from a great distance. We walked back down the road towards him and the rugged looking pack train, framed by hundreds of antlers, arching towards the peaks of the Grand Tetons. They are formidable castles, and Jackson looks like a toy town in comparison. Such beautiful log buildings! They are shiny and well worn.

Jackson would have been more fun if we had padded wallets. I didn't even have a wallet, and kept my dwindling cash in the front pocket of my pants.

"I wish I could figure out how to get it reproducing in my pocket," I said to Deb.

"Who doesn't?" she said to me, smirking with her eyebrows raised. She had the smile of an angel. Mine goes down on the ends.

We looked like saddle tramps, and there was no way to get the dirt out anymore. We looked especially dirty down here in town, next to these spanking clean tourists, straight from a morning shower out at the dude ranch. The streets are busy, with people in polyester pants, swinging bags full of fuzzy bear banks and cedar boxes with pictures of the Tetons or Jesus glued to the top. Even after a trip to the laundromat, our clothes remained stained from the soot of the fire, the sap of the pines, faded from the sun.

"We should have packed dresses," Deb said to me.

"Yeah," I answered.

We walked together into the famous Cowboy Bar and looked around. The bar stools were real saddles, polished to a fine sheen by millions of Levis. The bar itself was covered with real silver dollars.

"What can I get you two cowgirls?" The bartender looked at us and smiled.

"Oh, we'll just have water for now," we told him.

"Big spenders," he said, laughing.

"Really, we've been in the saddle all day already," I told him.

After a few minutes we had decided to put the animals out of town, then we would come back in and shower at the campground, and go out to eat. The horses and Sarah were happy to graze on the rich meadow grass.

"Food, food, food!" John chanted. Debbie and I marched behind him, trying to stay off the road. Motor homes flew by us, passing each other with three inches to spare. We walked downtown and into the first restaurant we saw. We were all hungry and ready to eat. It had been a long time since breakfast.

"What would you like to order, sir?" The waiter was dressed in a black and white suit coat. He even had a little towel over his arm.

"Where are we?" I said to Deb under my breath.

"We're not sure yet," John looked up at the waiter, standing above him. "We still need more time to decide."

I had already dug into the basket of saltines that sat on the table, invitingly, when we sat down. I just smiled and kept my mouth closed, so the crackers didn't fall out. The waiter made a funny "humpf" sound and walked away, but not until he had glanced up at the crowd of hungry tourists waiting at the door to be seated.

"Four dollars for an order of fries. This is outrageous!" my sister said in an loud voice. We had been out on the trail too long.

"I'll just get a dinner salad and crackers," I said, "my usual fare."

"I want spaghetti," John added hungrily, "but I won't spend seven dollars. Maybe we should try another place. This has got to be

the most expensive place in town."

Debbie and I both knew that John was overly hungry, and he was ready to eat. His body was like an engine on a motorboat; when he ran out of gas, it didn't matter where he was, he would be out of gas, period, even if he was still a quarter-mile from shore.

The waiter returned to our table with the owner of the hotel, and said, "Excuse me, sir, but perhaps you and your friends would like to dine somewhere else."

I looked at John. His shaggy red beard would never be a real good looking one, with its thin places. His hair was sticking straight out, all puffed up like a chestnut Afro. His shirt told the tale of many a campfire.

Debbie was the first to speak up. "You are actually kicking us out of here? Really?"

The waiter looked down at his feet. "If you are going to be complaining about the prices, yes."

"O.K. Let's go everybody. We don't want to eat here anyway," Deb said loudly. She would really surprise me sometimes, striking back like a rooster, cornered in the barn.

We walked out of the hotel restaurant, one by one. I wonder, now that I look back on it, if we didn't smell like saddle leather and wood smoke from the campfire. The longer we spent on the trail, out in the sagebrush, the more comfortable we became there. It became evident that slipping right back into town wasn't easy, when we were always in those same old clothes.

We are now camped fifteen miles south of Colter Bay, near Jackson Lake. We are staying on Senator Hansen's leased ranch, home of a thousand head of Angus overlooking the Tetons. It is raining again.

"I can't believe we are actually going to trade him off," Debbie said to me as she tried to wash the dried up oatmeal out of our skillet. The scrub pad had long since lost its ability to scrub. Deb spent five minutes trying to scrape out the pan, finally throwing the scrub pad in the trash bag and the skillet back on the fire. "I'll burn it off," she said as she stood up and walked over to Chief.

She took her hands and spread them out, rubbing the big brown and white Paint horse down his sides. The infection from his withers had spread little bubbles under his coat from the swelling.

"We did our best, Deb," I said to her.

"I just can't believe we're going to go on without him. I wish he could just follow us, without a thing on his back. I know he's going to miss Sarah. Besides, we'll miss him too," she said quietly.

I looked at Deb and Chief together, and thought about the long road we had travelled with him. We both felt sick that we had caused this injury to his back because we failed to check his pack that long, hot mosquito day down near Cokeville. His withers, high and large, weren't protected enough from the sawbuck saddle. All it took was one hot day and a crooked sawbuck to cause this awful sore on his back.

"He'll be better off staying here at Tarpin Meadows. They'll give him the rest of the season off, and after he gets better, he'll work as a dude horse for the rest of his life," I added. Tears welled up in my eyes and I tried not to cry.

We traded Chief to these two wranglers from Tarpin Meadows for a mule named Cadillac Annie.

"We'll take good care of Chief," the bow-legged old-timer of the outfit assure us.

"He's a good horse," Debbie told him.

"I think you will like Cadillac Annie. She is a serious little critter, and not a real friendly mule, but she won't kick, I know that for sure. She's sure footed on the trail, and always uses her head, as most mules do. She's not older than twelve, I'm fairly sure, by looking at her teeth. She's been here for as long as I can remember. We'll heal up the horse and work him into our string. But the little mule's gonna cost you an extra hundred dollars. She's a strong little mule with a good head on her shoulders, I promise," the old-timer said.

When the truck drove off with Chief in the trailer, Sarah was bucking and braying in frustration. She ran back and forth on her picket rope, crying out for her friend Chief, desperate to get free and go find him. Each time she cried out, tears welled up and my throat hurt. It's hard not to regret what happened. A Canada goose is flying south and honking overhead.

We got rained on heavily, and slept next to the old National Park Service corral in an abandoned log shelter. In the morning, we left out our shoes, down gear and the tent to dry out before we packed up and headed on.

The road to Flagg Ranch was narrow, and we had to travel along the highway. There was not much of a shoulder. The smiling faces of Louisiana, Texas, Michigan, California and Montana greeted us with surprised looks and waves as they passed us, on their way into Yellowstone. We must've been a sight to see, the three of us popping out from the ponchos, yellow plastic arms waving to the passing cars.

Ever since I did that double flip off the back of Cowboy, I'd been limping a lot on my right leg. Sarah Jane's rope got stuck under the boy's tail, and he shot forward, out from under me with a calculated buck. I landed on my right leg and a sharp tree stump. Cowboy raced off after Sarah Jane, who was trying to catch up to Red and John.

An old man who ran the gas station gave me some meaty bones for Robin to chew on. She was ready for that!

Together, after dinner, Robin and I walked up the trail last, after Debbie and John. I felt the glow of the moon on my skin. It will be full in two days.

"Deb, you take care of my horse, and watch out if he starts to dance."

"Don't worry, Jod," she said to me, smiling, "I won't let him get away from me."

"You take care in the Park with the dog, Jody. And don't take rides from anybody weird, okay? We don't want to have to come looking for you," Debbie said as she packed her saddlebags on Cowboy.

"On horseback, it could take awhile to find you, Jod," John added. "I hope you have a good walk. Think of us in Bear Country."

"As they say, rules is rules," I said. "Otherwise I'd be walking with you. No dogs allowed on the backcountry trails. I'll see you in West Yellowstone." It took a lot of courage to say goodbye to my whole outfit, there by the wilderness sign. I put Robin on a leash, grabbed my small back pack and stuck my thumb out.

"See you in three days," I reminded them as they rode up the trail. Deb was in the lead, on Cowboy, leading Sarah Jane.

"Feel good to be riding again, Deb?" I yelled to her, as she disappeared out of sight. John was on Red, leading the new pack mule, Cadillac Annie.

I stood there with Robin on a leash and my thumb out for over an hour. I was missing my horse already. The motor homes rumbled by on their way into the Park.

"I hope they'll be alright back there," I said to Robin. She had stopped looking up the trail. It was just she and I now. Finally, an old Chevrolet pick-up slowed down and pulled over in a turn out. I got in the back, jumping over the tailgate with Robin close behind. "Thanks," I smiled and waved to the driver, an old man. He looked like a local.

"Just heading into the Geyser," he told me, "to pick up my daughter at work." He had white bushy eyebrows that stuck out from his face about three inches, and under them, bright green eyes.

"Perfect," I told him.

He dropped me off in front of the Old Faithful Lodge, the world's largest log hotel. I walked into the lobby, and wandered around. Now I was all alone in the Old Faithful Lodge cafeteria, sitting at a long linoleum table, covered with the scratch marks from many a meal. Robin waited patiently out by the front door. I could see her shadow plainly, but could barely see her, leaning up against the exit door. This was an adventure in itself. I was without my horse — a horseless girl with a sleeping bag and a big brown dog.

I hoped Deb does okay with Cowboy. She had only ridden him a few times, and he can be tricky. I wondered if those guys would have a major bear experience. Meanwhile, I was going to enjoy this warm building and the warm shower.

The basic tourist in the park does not want to stop for a hitchhiker with a dog. I wondered, how is Cowboy? Then I thought I should be more concerned about Deb and John. They might look pretty tasty to a bear! I wished I was with them, still it felt good to be out on the loose with just the dog. It was tough out here without my horse.

I had never seen such a huge log building in my life. The lobby has a ceiling ninety feet high. There are four stories with log balconies overlooking the lobby. I was standing on the second floor looking at all the tourists and guests milling around downstairs.

"Ever been here before?" A cowboy, about sixty or so, was

standing next to me, reading a Western Horseman magazine. He looked up from his magazine and smiled.

"I came here with my dad and mom years ago, when I was six or seven. It's been a long time," I answered. "I'm on my way to meet my sister and a friend over in West Yellowstone. They are taking the wilderness trail, through the back country."

He looked at me and squinted. "On foot?"

"No, they are riding horses and packing two mules. We rode all the way up from Utah, and we've still got a long way to go, all the way to Spokane." I could see Robin downstairs, sleeping very politely out of the way of the heavy door. People hardly saw her; she had a way of being invisible when she was sleeping under a "No Dogs" sign.

"Mules?" he asked. "They're packing mules?" he said again.

"Yep. Two of them."

"I grew up behind a team of mules. Daddy started me farming when I was three. That big old team he had, Sassy and Franny, they were a powerful pair, and they worked my daddy's ground for him until he died." He stopped and looked down at the lobby, thinking.

"Yep, by golly, those mules outlived my dad." He laughed a little. "Mules can live to be forty, forty-five sometimes. Some of the old mule teams on the farms where I grew up, back in Oklahoma, stayed with the families through three generations. I remember getting up at three a.m. to wake up those mules and get 'em fed. That was my job. I was too short to harness 'em, so my big brother had that job. I could walk up and down those rows with those two mules for days on end, working up and down the rows, acre by acre until it was all plowed. Then we'd seed. We couldn't have done it all without those two mules!"

He had put his Western Horseman under his arm. "Mules are some of the most intelligent animals. Those mules of mine always knew when it was quittin' time. They always knew when it was time for their grain. They had little clocks in their heads, I guess. They would never overeat, either. Can't say that for the rest of us!" He patted his belly. "Speaking of eating, have you had lunch?" he asked me.

"No, I haven't," I said. "But I was thinking of going down to the lodge and eating a salad with some saltines."

"Let's go!" he said.

Downstairs, we ordered sandwiches and coffee, his treat.

"I came out here from Oklahoma back in the Forties. I always wanted to be a cowboy. There weren't much cowboyin' going on then, but I managed to talk myself into a job on a ranch outside of Red Lodge, Montana. I got on because I told the guy I knew all about mules. He said, 'If you know mules, cows and horses are a snap.' I always said that the mules got me my cowboyin' job."

"I used to ride a little Quarterhorse, a mare named Sweetheart. Everybody on the outfit had a nice little Quarterhorse. I used to ride Sweetheart thirty miles a day, and sometimes I'd stay out for three or four days, just riding around in the Absarokas. My favorite place is the Stillwater River and the Gallatin Range. I could tell you some places to go that you wouldn't believe!"

"Worked from Red Lodge up to Great Falls and as far West as Kalispell. Never went back to Oklahoma, though," he said, as he finished off the rest of his sandwich. He looked at his watch and realized he was late. He'd forgotten that he had promised the grandkids a trip to Fountain Paint Pot.

"Thanks for the sandwich," I told him.

"Here." He stuffed a twenty dollar bill in my hand. "Keep it. Buy yourself some dinner tonight."

I sat in the dining room until it closed at midnight. Somehow, I managed to find a bed in the men's dorm, after everyone else was asleep. Robin slid in under the wire webbing of the cot and fell asleep instantly. I thanked the cook from the dining room for sneaking us in. I fell asleep after a little while, thinking about Cowboy, Annie, Red and Sarah Jane, and about Debbie and John, out there in the back country of Yellowstone.

"It's chock full o' bears," the cook had told me as we walked silently into the men's dorm. "I can see why they don't allow dogs back there. Many would never make it home."

I rolled over on my cot and looked straight into the face of a man in a green uniform — not usually a good sign. He was standing next to the cot, looking at me, then at Robin, who was cowering under the bed, then back at me.

"Who told you this was okay?" He glowered at me, and actually looked pretty upset. I could see his face reddening by the second.

"Um, well, I don't know his name, but it was late, and I can go now." I was trying to simplify everything by having the conversation be over. We would just get up and disappear.

"Well, for one, there are no dogs allowed in here," he said in a loud tone, "and secondly, there are no girls allowed either."

"What's worse?" I said to him quietly and smiled. He started to smile, and stopped himself. "You'd better get your stuff and go. Next time, ask me."

"But you would've said no," I said to his back as he walked away. I gathered up my stuff and headed back outside into the warm morning sun. Getting the rest of the way to West Yellowstone was no problem. I just walked, and Rob lead the way. We stopped and looked into the Sapphire Pool. We walked by the Great Fountain Geyser and the Fountain Paint Pot, and a marker in honor of the Nez Perce Indians. They tried to escape the U.S. Army troops under a relentless General Howard in 1877, heading north on their way towards Canada.

Finally, we reached the mighty Madison River, as it flows west, and made it into West Yellowstone on the third day, in time to meet Deb and John. I looked forward to seeing all of them again. Stopping at a little cafe on the way into town, I sat down at a little booth next to the window.

"Coffee?" the waitress asked me. She was at least seventy years old.

"Yes please. I'd love some. And a salad with some saltines."

"Where you headed?" she asked me, pouring coffee into my cup and tossing a salad at the same time. She took the dressing and squirted it onto the salad and put it on a plate in front of me, next to a basket of saltines.

"Heading to Spokane. It's still a long way from here," I answered.

"Where's your car? I didn't see you pull up," she said, as she wiped the counter and straightened the napkin holders.

"No car. We're walking. I was riding, but my sister took my horse and they are coming through the back country. I'm supposed to meet them in town this afternoon sometime," I explained, as I tried to talk with a mouth full of lettuce and saltines.

"Back country? It's full of bears, and bad bears, too. They put all the grumpy ones back there, the ones that get too greedy with the tourists' food. They are the ones to watch out for. Just get between a mama and her cub, and well, you know the rest of that story!" She laughed.

Her face lit up and she adjusted her hair net. It had slid to the side and was almost hanging over her eye.

"I've been here my whole life," she told me, lighting a cigarette and brushing the smoke out of our faces with her bony old hand. "Worked here thirty years. My husband had always been a logger, from here to Bozeman and up to Butte. He worked in the mines, too. Always been a hard working man until a year and a half ago, when the logging truck rolled over on him. I can hardly stand to see him sit around the cabin. It drives me nuts! He hates to think this world can go on, with him just sitting there, listening to the squeaky screen door and the radio."

"I'm sorry," I said to her.

She noticed Robin, waiting patiently by the front door of the cafe. She went in the back and brought out a big meaty bone for the dog, opening the door and dropping it at Robin's feet.

I waited two more days before Deb and John and the pack train showed up in West Yellowstone. I got cleaned up, ate salads at various restaurants, and tried not to worry.

"They are just confused," I would try to remind myself. "Not a bear in the world would take on that garlic eating crew." As the days passed, and they never showed up, I really started to worry, and was ready to go looking. That's when they showed up, riding down the Main Street of West Yellowstone and down to my camp by the river.

"We woke up one morning to a steaming pile of bear droppings," Deb told me seriously. "Right outside the door of our tent. We could hear them, checking out our camp all night long, but they never did get a thing," she continued. "John and I got a little confused, not lost, and took the wrong trail off the pass. It was only twenty or thirty miles longer the way we came."

"I was just starting to really worry," I told her.

Dave Thompson showed up with his nephew Gary from Ohio.

Dave had figured Gary could walk the rest of the way with us, since he was in Salt Lake without anything real exciting to do. We all agreed it would be no problem. It was a wide open road and there was plenty of room.

"When Dave told me what you all were up to, I had to come up and join you," he told us that first night at the campfire. "That is my dream, always has been. I grew up in the hills, living like a mountain boy. Ever since I left home I haven't been in the mountains, living over a campfire. It's good to be walkin' with y'all," he smiled. "And besides that, I can get us some rattlesnake for breakfast," he continued. "I promise."

Deb and I couldn't believe he had said that. And he was dead serious.

We got the horses and the mules shod; Dave Goble and his friend Ben came up to do the job, all the way from Park City. We were ready to go, heading West towards Henry's Lake.

We found ourselves in Alice's restaurant at Lionhead Ranch, eight miles out of West Yellowstone. People from all over the country come here to dance in ruffles and cowboy shirts, and stay out in the campground in their trailers. It is five p.m. and we are taking our noon rest. We never seem to be on the road early enough to really stop and rest at noon. I just looked up at the sign and read that the coffee is ten cents a refill. I just had ten cups.

The horses and the mule are tied up around the back, enjoying the grain we fed them. They needed a break. Now we'll head up the road to Henry's Lake. I am going to ride the lower route to Dillon and the others will take the high road. I want to see what it is like to travel alone with my horse and the dog. It will be just the three of us for almost a week.

We rode through this southeastern Montana country to a small log coop, where we built our fire. We had soup, tea, and grilled cheese sandwiches. Everyone was asleep in the log coop. Robin had taken over my sleeping bag, and I sat out here under the heavens, and all the stars were so bright. Sitting in front of the fire, I could look back and remember a lifetime of campfires. I always felt safe with the embers glowing.

The man at the laundromat in West Yellowstone, Montana,

said, "Here, kid. If they fit you, take them. Those shoes have been here for awhile. Try them on." And then he said, with a funny smile, "They look like they've already seen some mountain miles." They were now on my feet: red tennis shoes with white stripes and funny toes, covered with white rubber. They were two inches too long and they made Debbie laugh. They make me feel like I am getting there a little bit faster. Size nine, and three and a half miles per hour.

At the summit of Red Rock Pass, we met a man by the name of Robert Wuthrich. He rode up on a tiny motorcycle. He was in his seventies, and was healthy and full of life.

"Where are you guys going?" he said to us after he turned the bike off and walked over to Sarah Jane. He was petting her, scratching her ears.

"Over the Gravellys to the Bitterroots and over the Divide to Salmon, and then up the Bitterroot Valley, and eventually to Spokane," Deb said, as she took a bite of the apple cake he offered her.

"Long ride. Mind if I come along on my motorcycle?" He laughed. I loved this man's face. I could tell he had spent his life in the mountains. He was from Switzerland, and he and his brother had been in the Yellowstone since 1910.

"I live by this lake, and it reminds me so much of the old country," he told us. "I love the winters here, when the snow is deep and the animals all come in close. I love to watch the moose move through the valleys and the elk herd, the deer and even the skunks and bears, all of the animals. I take pictures of everything, just live in a little cabin down here, not too far. I wish you were coming to stay down at my place," he added.

Later he and a younger friend of his came and found us at our little camp next to the old cabin. None of us wanted to sleep inside — it was too dirty. We built a campfire in the shelter of this old cabin. They stayed and talked to us, and we made them some campfire coffee.

We sat around the campfire until the last rays of the setting sun disappeared to the west, and the fire died down. Robert and his friend said goodbye and we all fell asleep, in front of that old abandoned cabin. In the morning, I was just waking up when I heard one gun shot, followed by silence. Gary walked towards the campfire with his shotgun in one hand and a three-foot-long rattlesnake in the other.

"I promised," he said, as he got the morning fire going for our coffee and rattlesnake breakfast.

I told Deb and John and Gary that I planned to go alone on the Blacktail Deer road, and I would meet them in Dillon. It seemed like a perfect time to try, since the road to Dillon split, and both ways were clear and direct. They'd take the high road, I'd take the low road, and we'd make it into Dillon around the same day. "It's some pretty quiet country," Robert had told us. "Nothing much but a bunch of cows and rattlesnakes between here and Dillon."

B. Shields ©1994

## *Travelling Light*

They hauled my gear down to Price Ranch Junction in the truck. It felt good to be riding Cowboy, free and easy, galloping down the road, light hearted. He was free of his saddle bags, the sleeping bag and blanket. All he had to carry was me. As we slowed to a walk, I was surprised by the wide silence this land has. Only the sound of hoof following hoof broke the quiet.

I realized then, as I rode my horse in the dark towards the ranch, that, being alone with the animals, I was able to hear much more. Debbie and John weren't there to talk to about what we would eat when we got into town, if we were lost or just confused, or where to camp. I had to ask myself these questions now. Conversations with the horse were much shorter.

"Cowboy, are you getting tired? Are you ready to find a watering hole, Boy?" And, of course, Robin is always a good conversationalist. The rest of the time I was the listener. I was absorbed in the absolute silence of the country.

I slept at this abandoned ranch, out in the sage in front of a little cabin. It was not the kind of cabin I could see spending the night in. Old cans, old clothes, strewn about on the floor and rat scat everywhere. I figured I would sleep outside. I felt safer out there, using the building as a shield, as a wall to build my evening's shelter around. There was a big pile of deer skulls and antlers on the ground behind the cabin. I camped as far away from them as I could.

There were more stars last night than I have ever seen anywhere else in my life. I felt a deep sense of peace; my dog sleeping by me, my horse lying in the pasture below me. I like being away from all the stuff we brought with us. This is so different, being on the low road without them. I find myself trying to picture their camps and where Sarah Jane was picketed for the night. I can tell Cowboy is missing the other animals too.

A cowboy came by, slowing down to keep pace with us.

"Where you heading?" he asked me, his arms bunched up around the steering wheel. A coffee cup on the dash steamed up the window.

"Dillon right now, Spokane by October," I answered. He didn't look surprised. He looked like he had ridden many miles himself. His dog, a black and white Australian Shepherd, looked down at Robin from the bed of his truck. Robin was cautious, but the dog stayed in the truck. Those cowboy dogs are really smart.

"Well tonight, up the draw, watch out for the grizzly. They bring 'em out here from the Park. Keep your gun loaded!"

I didn't get a chance to tell him there was no gun. He waved and kept driving. I wonder what he would've said if I told him my only weapon was garlic and a Swiss Army knife. I climbed up the dirt road into the hills above the lake. I ended up on the other side of this small divide, and rode down Blacktail Deer Road, heading northwest towards Dillon, between the Pioneer Mountains and the Gravelly Range.

Another cowboy drove by in a blue Chevy pickup. He slowed down and came to a stop by a cattle guard. He got out, checked the fence and said, "Hey, if you find my mule out here, you can have him!"

"Are you serious?" I couldn't believe what he had said.

"Yeah, he always jumps real high, right out of the truck, and takes off with his saddle on. He hates to pack salt, and that's the only reason we have him. He's useless. I've had it with him!" He laughed and drove off, heading back towards the main ranch. I thought no more about the mule that day.

I was once again in awe of the beauty surrounding me. It is not like the mountains, but vast and wide and lonely, and to a stranger, it looked deserted. I guess the Matador Ranch in Texas owns it all, and these cowboys are stewards to the huge herds. They are used to being alone in the middle of nowhere. It seemed every house I saw was boarded up, deserted — as if everyone just packed up and left this stretch of Montana.

Thoughts of the bear were paramount. He had said to keep my gun loaded. What would Robin do, would she back down from the grizzly, or would he just grab her and eat her for hors d'oeuvres? I wasn't sure.

I decided to solve the problem of the grizzly. I would not sleep in his area. I'd pull down my hat and put on all my warm clothes, and forget about the fried potatoes and onions I had planned on cooking up. I would eat raisins in the saddle, and keep going.

I was a night rider. Only the shadow of my horse could be seen, and I hoped nobody was watching. I felt a cold chill when I thought about the bear following me in the dark. How would I know? Would Cowboy smell him and take off? Would Robin bark? As we rode into the night, on the long, flat road up over the Divide, everything was cloaked in darkness and I could barely see my hands on the reins. The sound of the hooves on the dirt comforted me and I rode on for two or three hours.

I kept hearing that sound but no sound, that twig breaking behind me. Then sounds of something running, then nothing again. I turned around and stopped Cowboy, staring back into the dark.

I could barely see, in the shadows beyond the dark, the shape of something, something standing very still, as still as I was. Cowboy turned to stone, all his senses stretching towards this unknown form, trying to see, smelling the air. He was frozen, eyes bugged wide open, staring at something. Then he snorted.

It was the mule! I could make him out now. His long brown ears, his thick neck, straps from the sawbuck hanging down to the ground. He was so curious about us. He came closer. Seconds passed, and then he turned and ran off into the blackness. I could hear him galloping through the sage, heading back up the Divide. Then nothing.

We stopped, later on, down the road and slept next to the barbed wire fence, at the side of the dirt road. I picketed Cowboy to the bottom of a fence post and he grazed nervously, one eye on the road behind us.

The mule had made me less afraid of the ever-looming grizzly bear, and, anyway, we got too tired to ride any further. I knew the penalty for horse rustling in the state of Montana was the hanging tree, and I wasn't sure if the cowboy who said "keep the mule" actually was kidding, and the mule probably belonged to the Matador Ranch. Still, the next morning, while cooking up my coffee on a small sage fire, I hoped to see the mule again. Searching the hills slowly through my binoculars, I saw him. It was the same mule, a big light sorrel mule with a black cross on his back.

A lone eagle soared above him, maybe they were keeping each other company out there; it was too sparsely populated by man or beast to be too choosy about company. He was walking down the mountain, on Blacktail Deer. I smiled to myself.

He spotted Cowboy as we rode up behind him. He stopped and let us pass, his large, gentle eyes watching our every movement. He followed us, very curious about the horse. Robin kept far away from this mule, and was wary of its back feet. She didn't know him, so she didn't trust him. She had learned a lot about living around the feet of horses and mules the last few months.

I stopped, and since it was raining, I built a small fire in the shelter of some willows next to a creek that found its way through the marsh grass across the Divide. I cooked up some soup and waited.

After an hour, Cowboy and the mule had inched closer and closer to each other, and were now only a few feet apart. The mule was more than willing to make friends with the Appaloosa, but was wary of me. I inched closer myself. I gently slipped my lead rope onto his halter. I smiled at him, triumphantly. He was my captive now.

I made myself a cup of java and thought about this. We could sure use another good animal to pack our gear, and then Deb could ride Sarah. I looked back at the MX branded on his hip. His big eyes looked at me; he didn't mind being tied up. I figured I could take him on in to Dillon, call the ranch and see if they wanted to sell him. But I didn't have money to buy him. What if they thought I was stealing him? Dillon was still close to fifty miles away.

I knew, in my heart, the mule belonged to the ranch, and the cowboy didn't really own him. They were both hired hands. On the other hand, I thought maybe the heavens had rained a mule upon me, and I should just take it and be thankful. That is what I call wishful thinking.

I decided the mule would stay behind so the cowboy could pick him up. He would be looking for him again, probably calmed down from a good night's sleep. Walking away from the mule was a really difficult decision, one I made and wasn't sure about. But the salt mule stayed behind, for right or wrong. We packed up, shooed him back up the road, and headed out towards Dillon. We watched him watch us as we disappeared out of sight, and rode down into the lowlands.

I was used to travelling alone. Cowboy was my swift walking vehicle, Robin my closest companion. The Montana sun was hot, up to eighty during the day. We rode long days, sometimes twenty miles. The dirt road was an expressway, compared to the narrow trails of the Uintahs. The low hills of the Blacktail Deer were wide open. Every fifteen miles or so, another abandoned ranch would appear on the horizon. The old posts of the corral looked like petrified wood; very shiny and hard, having survived many heavy winter snows.

"It gets down in the minus thirties out here sometimes," a cowboy had told me back at the Lionhead Ranch. It's one cold you-know-what in the winter out here."

After six days of riding, I could see Dillon off on the horizon. I had been out on the lonely roads of abandoned ranches and was once again on the edge of civilization. I looked forward to putting a quarter in the juke box to play my favorite songs, having a shower, and eating a dinner salad in the local cafe. Ordering coffee in the greasy spoon and having it served to me was one of life's greatest pleasures.

We had listed Dillon on our itinerary, so hopefully the General Delivery would have letters for us, maybe even a package. Mom was always sending us little packages for the road; usually dried pears, apricots, a pair of socks, a five dollar bill, and some Vitamin C. Cowboy would get to spend a few days on pasture behind the rodeo arena, and have some grain. We had run out a few days earlier.

About seven miles from town, a Toyota passed me and stopped. I signaled Cowboy to a stop. These guys, Jim and Kelly, worked for the Bureau of Reclamation and were out gathering samples from the rivers.

"When you get to town, give us a call. We'd love to talk to you more about your trip."

"Okay, and thanks for the water." It was icy cold. I got down out of the saddle, pulled Robin's bowl out of my saddle bag, and poured her some.

For almost a week, I had only spoken to only a few people. The silence had cloaked me, the hills made me feel safe.

We had a feeling of complete harmony, at one with this

blessed road. For hours, before I fell asleep, I would stare into the blackest of skies, deep in layers of stars. My fire slowly turned to a smoking pile of ashes, and I would fall asleep, with warm Robin to lean against.

People driving in cars and walking on the streets of Dillon looked at me and smiled. I watched our reflection in the windows of Main Street, riding Cowboy to the ring behind the rodeo grounds. It was close to downtown, ideal for us.

Cowboy rolled the minute I got his saddle off. Robin was excited too. She raced around the field. I tethered Cowboy and hid my saddle, tack and bags underneath the bleachers, and immediately headed for downtown.

Dillon is built around the train track; switching rails, loading docks, and the old Dillon Hotel. Of course, I wouldn't be staying there. I was down to fifteen dollars.

I headed into Skeet's, home of Famous Pies, next to the Casino Bar. I had heard stories about the homemade pie at Skeet's all the way from Wyoming. "It's the best pie in the West," people would say wistfully. I was going to try it for myself, even though I didn't usually care too much for pie.

There were two men leaning up against the royal blue tile wall in front of the dusty window of the bar. There was a poster advertising Miss Riley. She wore a sequin gown and had a microphone in her hand. They watched me, through red, squinty eyes of a two day drunk, as I headed into Skeet's. I knew if Debbie and John and Gary had made it to Dillon, the waitress at Skeet's would be the first to know.

The magic of the quiet trail disappeared as I entered Skeet's. All the waitresses and the people at the counter looked up. I smiled, paused there for a moment and then sat down at the counter.

A grey haired, middle-aged man smiled at me, and asked, "Are you the one who just rode in from Utah?"

"Yep, that's me. I just got to Dillon an hour or so ago." I found the words sounded awkward to me. I had probably talked less in the last week than I ever had in twenty two years of life.

What was clean to me on the trail was definitely not clean in town, under the bright lights in Skeet's. I don't know what I must've smelled like. A horse? Sagebrush and wood smoke from the fires? I caught myself thinking how very much I would like to get cleaned up. Get the dirt out from under my fingernails, wash my hair, and take a nice long shower. It had been a showerless trail since West Yellowstone.

I sipped the coffee. I took the half and half in the silver container, and dumped a lot of it into my cup. As the white and brown converged, I searched for words.

"Yeah, I just rode over from Henry's Lake. I expect my sister and the boys will show up today! They're coming in on the other road, the upper road around Red Rock Lakes." He turned on his stool and looked at Robin. She was asleep on her side, taking up a good part of the sidewalk. He smiled.

"So where are you headed?" He asked me, as he cut through a piece of berry pie with his fork.

"Spokane, Washington. It seems like a long way from here."

He shook his head and laughed. "Hope you don't mind me saying this, but you have guts. I wouldn't sleep out overnight in the mountains if you paid me."

I ordered my dinner salad. I cherished every bite. The Thousand Island dressing slopped down the outside of the bowl, dripping down onto the Formica counter. I had to hold onto the bowl with each bite, to keep it from flying onto the floor. I crushed saltines, several packages of the white wonders, onto the salad, mixing them in with the brown lettuce. Oh! There was a little piece of a beet. We both sat there in silence for a few minutes.

"If you would like, you can come over and shower in my motel room at the Royal Inn. Check out time isn't until one. I am getting ready to leave now." He bought me a coffee to go and drove me to the Royal Inn.

Riding in the car was very strange. Although we never got going faster than thirty or so driving across town, it was much faster than the slow pace I had grown accustomed to. I found myself pushing down on the floor mat in the car to slow it down. I looked out the window as the blocks disappeared in a flurry and in minutes we pulled into the parking lot at the Royal Inn. It would've taken me ten minutes to get there on Cowboy. I said goodbye to Mr. Farmer, and thanked him. I had been in Dillon only an hour or two, and my shower wish had come true.

I padded across the clean soft carpet in the room and headed straight into the bathroom. I had not looked in a mirror for two weeks. I was very dark skinned, my blue eyes shining. Smiling at the face I saw in the mirror, I stood there in my dusty cowboy shirt, dusty bandanna over dirty hair and, my dusty, dirty jeans over dusty shoes. I set the shower, keeping my hand under the spray. When it reached that perfect temperature, I undressed, the red dirt sifting out of the cuffs of my jeans onto the white tile floor. I walked into the white shower stall and closed the curtain, and watched a week's worth of red Montana dirt disappear down the drain. I stayed in there until the water ran clear.

I think people are used to seeing horses on the street around here. I rode Cowboy all over Dillon, and nobody seemed to mind. Cowboy liked to look at his reflection in the store windows on Main Street, especially since he misses Sarah Jane. He stopped and looked at himself in the glass, and then bellowed at the top of his lungs. His whinny echoed up and down the streets of Dillon. Robin seemed glad to be in town. Her feet were sore and she was tired.

I was cruising the aisles of Safeway, looking to buy something I had been missing, but I wasn't sure what it was.

I heard a voice over the intercom. "Would the young lady with the Appaloosa tied to the post in front please come to the cashier." I jogged to the front of the store and there he stood, the store manager, with a shovel in one hand and a broom in the other.

"I don't assume you have your own shovel," he said with a smile. He handed them to me. I got the message. I went outside and cleaned up after Cowboy, donating the manure to a flower bed of desperate looking marigolds. After the incident at the store, I jumped up on Cowboy and rode back to the rodeo grounds. On the way back to the grounds, Cowboy stopped in his tracks and stood very still for at least two minutes.

"What is it, Boy?" I asked him. He was shifting his ears back and forth against the wind. He put his nose up into the wind to get a better whiff of the air. A big horse fly landed on the inside of his leg, and he stamped his hoof on the ground, but never took his mind off the wind and the scent it was bringing his way. "Come on, Boy. Step up," I said to him, giving him a little tap with my heel. He wouldn't move. Still as a statue in the square, he listened, and then

131 — Travelling Light

he whinnied again at the top of his big lungs.

Off in the distance, Sarah brayed. The familiar sound came resonating up Main Street and then echoed long enough for Cowboy to be sure it was her. He whinnied again, and walked down the street in the direction of the bray, at a fast walk. There was no stopping him.

From a distance, way down the road, I saw them walking towards me. Debbie was in front. John and Gary were behind her. The road widened and then they all walked side by side. John was riding Red and leading Annie. Deb was leading Sarah Jane.

Gary, leading his puppy, Beauty, on a rope, had a hillbilly walk. Our worlds were very different. Gary grew up skinning rabbits for the stew pot while I was shopping for groceries with my mother. I liked to listen to him talk, the way he said things like "talk at ya" and "y'all".

His little black Labrador, Beauty, stayed on her rope and was very well behaved. I was glad Gary was with us. We were in the middle of the trip now, and the road stretched out beneath us in beauty.

"We're camped out on the Sweetwater Road. We just brought the animals in to see if we could find you. Do you want to come out and stay at our camp tonight?" Deb asked me. "We met a real nice man on the way in, who offered us his pasture for a few days."

"I think I'll keep Cowboy down at the rodeo grounds again, and catch up with you guys tomorrow," I decided without thinking. It just seemed like less trouble, and it was almost dark. After we told each other a little about the trip to Dillon on different roads, I rode back down to the rodeo grounds.

That last night at the fairgrounds, in the pouring rain, I was getting soaked and decided to leave my stuff under the bleachers and go up to Skeet's for some coffee. I checked on Cowboy and headed up the grassy hill and over the tracks to Skeet's. Once I saw Deb, John and Gary and the other animals, I had lost all desire to be alone and felt sorry I hadn't just packed up and followed them back to their camp on Sweetwater Road.

The Casino Bar was hopping. I could hear the pure country voice of the sequined Miss Riley. The blue tile front reflected red and blue neon. I walked into Skeet's. Robin got as far under the canopy outside as she could, to keep from getting soaked to the bone.

The rain was falling in sheets off the canopy. I picked an empty booth and slid into it. I looked at the plastic menu, and wiped the rain from my face with a paper napkin, watching as the coffee filled my cup, swirling in comforting warmth. I realized I was really pretty wet, and found myself wishing again I had moved up to Debbie's camp.

I was sitting alone there, and this bearded troll showed up.

"Hi. I'm Yukon Jack," he said loudly. "Mind if I sit down?" He was already sitting down across from me in my booth. He took the creamer container in his hand, raised it to his lips and sloshed it down, drinking it all until it was gone.

"Waitress, please get some more cream for her coffee," he ordered. The waitress returned with another cold cream container, the stainless steel kind. He instantly  gulped it down again.

Yukon Jack was one rude fellow. He was really broke and was passing through on his way back from the Yukon. I pampered this Yukon Jack way too much, by not telling him what a jerk he was being, drinking the cream every time the waitress brought a new container, four of them before he stopped.

He jumped up and sauntered out the front door. I think this character lived on creamers. The worst thing about it, he knew I was staying down at the fairgrounds. I ran back in my poncho to the rodeo park. The wind was howling through town and it was pouring rain.

I felt like a sitting duck. I pulled out the tarps and laid them out next to the bleachers. I pulled my sleeping bag out of the garbage bag I kept it in, and rolled it onto the plastic. I pulled another tarp up over my head, making sure it was tucked in on the edges. Robin went over and crawled under the bleachers. With the wind and the rain, and listening to any sound that might be behind the other sounds, I could not fall asleep for the life of me.

I heard splashing footsteps in the mud on the racetrack. They were heading my way. Robin growled and jumped up, and I whispered, "Here, Robin, here girl." I could tell it was Yukon Jack.

"Hey, you awake?" I stayed quiet, trying to fake it. I was scared. I didn't want to start anything. I was thinking about what to say when he grabbed the top tarp and slid in next to me, on top of my bag. "Let me sleep with you. I'm freezing," he said. I could smell smoke and booze in his long beard. He was wet and dirty and smelled like wet wool. He was rubbing his muddy wet boots on my bag. I turned around, my back to him, and jumped up, in my long underwear.

"Get out of here, Jack, I'm trying to sleep," I said.

"I want to sleep with you, please? I lost my sleeping bag on the freight train." He sounded drunk.

"No, get out of here. Go sleep under the bleachers."

I would talk my way out of it. Robin growled as he stumbled past her. I made her sleep under the tarp with me. I was really wet, much too wet to get any sleep, with my thoughts turning back, over and over again, to that clean white and blue room at the Royal Inn.

In the morning, I rolled up my stuff and saddled up Cowboy. I would go and join the others at their camp, no matter how far away it was. That was it for Yukon Jack. I never saw him again. Probably drinking his weight in half-and-half, on the road to the Yukon Territory.

We moved over to Kelly and Jim's place, on the edge of Dillon. It was a prefab type house, a little taste of suburbia. Cowboy mowed the yard for them. The mules and Red helped out too. We stayed two days there, sleeping on the floor in the comfort of their home. Deb and I made the boys dinner. We had steaks, potatoes, salad, the works.

We were all starting to feel the call of the road again.

"I'm going back out to the Rest Home to see Frank again," I told my three partners. I had been down to see him the day before and wanted to talk with him some more. He was waiting for me. I promised him I would come back.

I saddled up Cowboy and rode downtown to the Rest Home. I could see ancient, white-haired people in every window. A very small woman, who looked like she was over a hundred years old, stood at her window and waved to me. Her smile was denture white. Her eyes sparkled. She stood there, waving, for a long time.

Inside, she was the first one to greet me in the hallway. She walked up to me with the help of her walker, taking halted steps until she stood directly in front of me.

"The Appaloosa sure is a handsome fellow! I had one that

looked just like him when I was a girl in the Palouse. Strong and as fast as the wind he was! Can your horse run fast? Can he?" She adjusted her sweater, a white one with pink threads running through it, held there with pearls on a string.

"You had a horse that looked like my Cowboy, why I didn't think there was another like him!" I said to her. I couldn't take my eyes off hers, blue and sparkling. Even though her body was ancient, those blue eyes of hers showed her heart, and sparkled at me with alarming brilliance.

She grabbed my hand. Hers were all bones, covered with cold skin. They were soft to touch.

"My goodness, your hands are so strong," she said to me.

"From holding onto the reins and the ropes," I added.

"Are you here to see me?" She was serious now.

"No, I wasn't exactly, but I am glad to see you," I told her. "I came to visit Frank down the hall. He's going to tell me some things about Dillon."

She stood and watched me walk down the hall with my tape recorder.

"I'll watch your horse for you," she said, standing there, teetering.

Frank was waiting for me. He had dressed up a little bit. He had on a Pendleton plaid shirt and newly pressed slacks. He looked really nice, and turned to me and smiled, putting out his hand and grabbing mine.

"Sit down here, little lady," he said to me, patting the bed across from his chair. "That is one beautiful Appaloosa you've got tied up out there! Are you getting about ready to leave us?"

"Yep, Frank, we are leaving in the morning. Would you mind telling me a little bit about this area before I go?" Just then the aide came in and brought Frank some pineapple juice. He raised it to his lips with shaky hands, spilling it down his shirt. I grabbed a napkin and mopped up his shirt.

"What would I do without you?" he said, laughing. "Well, I'll tell you what. This is what it was like back then, when Dillon was a big boom town. My first school was in the church, out in Bannack. It is still out there! It's one of the only buildings left standing! It's only twenty miles over there. I remember Bannack since I was six."

He stopped for a minute and said, "You had better run on over to the window and see how your horse is doing out there!" He took another sip of his juice, spilling more of it.

"At one time there was a million dollar payroll. There were eight saloons, three churches and two stores. My dad's saloon is still standing over there. We lived next to the saloon in the jail building."

He stopped and looked down at his lap, looking for something.

"At one time there were three dredge boats in Bannack. And you know what, little lady? There is more gold left than they ever took out. If they could only dig down into the bedrock..."

He was knocking on the table, thinking about the bedrock, and the gold that remained there.

"It frustrates me to think of all the gold that is still there, and I am stuck in here."

"I bet," I added jokingly. "Why not tell me how to find it?"

He laughed, and wiped his mouth with the edge of his shirt sleeve.

"I remember Dad taking me in the saloon all the time. When I got a little older, I put three days and nights alone in the jail. I had run away from home, and was thirteen. Dad left me there for three days with no bread and water!"

"What are some of the best memories you have, Frank?" I asked him.

"I don't remember too many stories." He stopped, and I watched as the light lit up in his eyes. The light was filtered through eyes the color of the waves under cloud cover, a grey jade.

"I left Bannack when I was fourteen, but I never lived out of Beaverhead County. I done a little cowboyin', but not too much. I worked on ranches, though, since I was fourteen."

"What was your school like?"

"My first school was in the church, since there wasn't a school building yet. Things were still pretty wild around here back then. There were still lots of Indian families comfortably settled on the river, living there in peace. I went there for the first, second and third grade. My first teacher was Elizabeth Price Jones. I will never forget her as long as I'm alive. She was beautiful and brave and came out to Montana from back East somewhere. She was a good teacher, and could teach all the children, all ages." He took a sip of his drink.

"When did you come West?" I asked him, still thinking about the angel teacher of Bannack.

"Oh, my brother brought me west to Montana."

"How old were you?"

"Oh, I was a little boy, and I'm a little boy yet." He looked at me mischievously. I half expected him to reach over and kiss me. Instead he held his hands together on his lap. They were pretty shaky, but still had a lot of strength in them.

"Montana was and always has been a great state. Even in the Depression we always had plenty to eat. We grew all our food, in a big garden. We always hunted for grouse, rabbit, deer, elk and occasionally bagged a bear." I felt sad when he said this.

"I stayed down at the rodeo grounds, you know," I said enthusiastically.

"Wonderful! I bet it was a good place for the horses and the mules, but what about you? Don't you ever want a real bed?" He pointed towards his bed with a shaky index finger. It was perfectly made, with the corners of the blanket boxed. His granddaughter smiled at us from a gold plastic frame on the bed stand.

"If I think about it too long," I answered, with a smile.

"Yeah," he continued. "My family moved here from Canada. My father was French Canadian."

"Why did you come to Montana?"

"I was born in Wyoming. We stopped by to visit my aunt in Horse Prairie. My father took up a homestead. Through a grant, if you served time in the Army, you got this grant land from Hudson Bay Company. He was in the sheep business up there. I lived up there on Horse Prairie from 1904-1910."

"Has Dillon changed a lot since the old days?"

"Dillon wasn't much of a town back then. Mostly ranches. I never did farm. I just ran around."

"Did you travel a lot?"

"I worked on the Pierce Ranch one winter, in 1910. I've been here in Montana forever. I've got great-grandchildren like grasshoppers! There are four generations of Thompsons. My father worked on the Pierce Ranch too, for many years. Old Mother Pierce was my aunt. There's been a lot of kids born since then!"

"Used to pitch hay, ya know, feed cattle all winter, and in the summer I'd ride on the range, free as a bird, chasing cattle."

"Did you used to pack into the mountains?"

"Oh yes, we used to pack."

"Did you use mules?"

"You better believe we used mules to pack. Those little burros could go where a horse couldn't go. You could hardly walk there either. Those burros could go anywhere!"

"How many children did you have?"

"No children. I never married. I didn't have time to settle down. So I just call my brother and sister's kids my own kids."

"That's the life. It seems you were, you were happy that way?" I stammered.

"Oh yes. It's been a good life." I watched the jade waves breaking in his youthful eyes, shining out at me from a very old, worn face.

"Do you like the rest home?"

"Well, I like it to an extent. But I don't have my privacy. It's hard to carry on a conversation with most of these people. Most are pretty much gone," he said.

We sat quietly together. As the sun filtered through the white curtains, summer whispered to me to come back outside and get back on my horse and ride away. To leave this sweet old man, to get back on the road.

"At eight o'clock I'm going to a country western concert. It's live music, guitar and piano. We have that once a month." He looked thoughtful. "I just make the best of life, because I'm the last one alive in my family. They are all gone but me."

It was time to go. I found myself edging towards the door backwards. I said goodbye, hugging the old man in my strong arms. I didn't talk to anyone else on the way out. I just smiled and headed out the door, passed the wheelchairs and walkers. Cowboy looked eagerly in my direction as the big door swung open, and I was back in my saddle again. Everyone watched from the windows and the doorway as I rode Cowboy down the road and out of sight.

Finally, we were packed up and we were leaving Dillon. Our friends, Kelly and Jim, stood in the road and waved as we

disappeared over the rise and down the Montana trail that lay ahead of us.

B. Shields '94

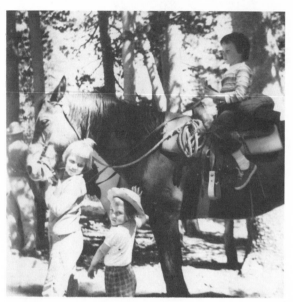

*Debbie Foss and Jill Tipton lead Jody's horse
to the High Sierra Trail. 1959.*

*High Sierra swimming hole. 1959.*

*Jody, Star, Laurie and Sarah the pony. Christmas 1968.*

*Stanley Rat, La Cañada, California. 1968.*

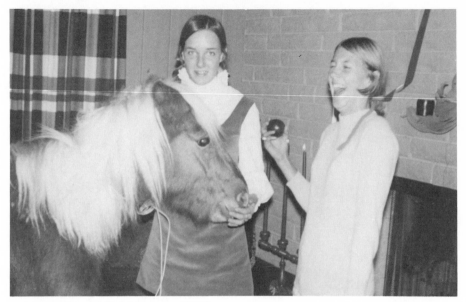

*A pony in the living room. 1969.*

*Don and Marilynn Foss. 1969.*

*Sarah Jane. 1976.*

*Ready to go.
Park City, Utah.
1976.*

Dave Thompson, High Uintas.

Dead Horse Pass, High Uintas, Utah.

*Dead Horse Pass, High Uintas, Utah.*

*A lakeside camp, High Uintas, Utah.*

*First day on the trail.*

*South of Cokeville, Wyoming.*

*Shadow-rider.*

*Debbie and Ray Goodrich. Cokeville, Wyoming.*

*Ray Goodrich. Cokeville, Wyoming.*

*Jody Foss*

*Robin.*

*John Najar*

*The Grand Tetons, Jackson, Wyoming.*

John, Robert Wuthrich, Cadillac Annie, Jody, Cowboy and Gary. Henry's Lake, Idaho.

Log cabin camp. Henry's Lake, Idaho.

*Robert Wuthrich. Henry's Lake, Idaho.*

*Big Red and Annie. Dillon, Montana.*

*Debbie Foss*

*Montana road.*

*Moose Bar,
Dillon, Montana.*

John Najar

*Making tracks, Montana.*

John Najar

John Najar

*John, Jody and Debbie. Home sweet home on the Idaho-Montana line.*

*Debbie Foss*

*Rest stop.*

*Stevensville
old-timer.*

*Montana dreamers.*

*Paradise old-timer.*

*Mules in Paradise, Montana.*

*Bud and Florence Roe, Trout Creek, Montana.*

*Clark Fork River.*

*Even the smallest rider can handle the gentle Sarah Jane.*

*Crossing the Clark Fork, Clark Fork, Idaho.*

*Idaho outhouse.*

*Pend Orielle reflection.*

*Cowboy and Jody. Clark Fork, Idaho.*

John Najar

## *Across the Great Divide*

The ride out to Bannack was a two day trip through dry, hot sage country, straight yellow dirt roads, silence, no cars. There are more rattlesnakes out here than in any other spot in Montana. Gary shot one today, and we skinned him and roasted him over the fire for dinner. Like everything else, it tastes like chicken. There is something almost scary about eating snake, I don't know what it is. This is their country and we are passing through it as strangers. The rattlesnakes sunned themselves on the road, and when startled by the animals, would start to rattle. I couldn't believe how easily Gary took his gun and killed the snake, something I couldn't do. But, when offered hot barbecued rattlesnake right off the campfire, I didn't hesitate. The hunt, we leave up to Gary.

We camped by the river in the willows, in the same spot the Bannack Indians camped in the summers, as late as 1930.

"This is the spot where gold was first discovered on Alder Creek, and the remains of the first dredge are still here," an old-timer told us.

We rode into the old mining camp.

"I can feel the spirits of the people who lived here, can't you, Deb?" I asked her as I stopped Cowboy, tying him up to some willow branches. I could see why the Indians lived there, until the settlers made that meadow a cattle ranch. The tipis are no longer there, but the trees are. They know all the stories. I hung my saddle on the old dredge, and sat against it and listened to the birds, restless in the willows as the rain disturbed their sleep.

After a long day in the saddle, in the rain, we were glad to see our friends, Kelly and Jim, show up in their truck. We had stayed a little too long in Dillon, and we all had grown soft in the few days we stayed with Jim and Kelly.

They came out to have dinner with us. We got a nice fire going, and the potatoes were wrapped and ready to be thrown into the fire. It started pouring.

"Why don't you guys come with us to town, and we'll bring you back in the morning?" Jim asked. We decided, after a few minutes, standing there in the rain, to go back to Dillon. We covered the panniers and hid them in the bushes, picketed the animals, and jumped in the station wagon. The heater was blasting hot air onto our frozen legs, and we were warm in minutes.

Jim brought us back at five a.m., and the horses and mules were more than ready to be moved. They had cleared the area where they were picketed and were ready for a change. We moved them, made a fire, and prepared our gear for the day's journey. We rode a long hot day in the sun, across Horse Prairie.

We arrived at the "Horse Prairie Hilton" at Grant, population six. The folks who run the place are cowboys with a three-year-old named Justin. We took our lunch break at the "Right On Country-fied" store next to the Hilton, a big old building with rooms for rent. We had a beer with old Monte, an old-timer who lives down the road.

"What ever inspired you to take off with a bunch of green broke Appaloosas?" Old Monte asked us while we sliced cheese on Home Pride Wheat.

"I don't know," I told him. "Just a thought that wouldn't go away, I guess."

We left the Horse Prairie Hilton, laughing, galloping in the evening sun. Soon it was gone and we were still miles from the Pierce place.

Tommy Pierce lives with his wife and two young kids in a new house on the front forty acres of his dad's spread. Tommy had lived there forever, out on the Montana prairie, and the ranch house was a beautiful old place.

Old man Pierce came down to Tommy's place and started talking.

"Chief Tendoy was one of the best loved of all the Chiefs in this part of the country," he told us, as he poured sugar in his tea and stirred it slowly. "The Indians used to go up to Red Bluff. It was there that they spent time in silent communication with the spirits. You'll pass by there, the way you're goin'."

He told us stories about the Indians, and we passed Red Bluff the next morning. Even Lewis and Clark had written about it in their journals. It was a sacred place.

As we passed Red Bluff, I could feel the hair on the back of my neck stand on end. We rode by in silence. The evening sun made the rocks bright orange, and the dark pine trees below them. Sage, juniper and yellow daisies dotted the sand. The wind whipped through, singing to us as we rode along, none of us saying a word.

John and I rode alone and Deb and Gary went ahead in the truck with Dennis. They carried a lot of our gear in the truck, so John and I could freely gallop on the road to the pass. We packed nothing but peanut butter and jelly sandwiches and our water bottles. The two mules were frisky, and were glad to be free of their packs for a day. They loped along behind us, on big cotton ropes.

Tommy Pierce stopped by in his truck. We pulled our pack train to a stop.

"Hey, you guys want some smoked trout?" he yelled out the window.

"Sure," John said right away. He jumped down out of his saddle and grabbed the bag of trout from Dennis. We were always hungry, and anything that varied from our usual fare was a treat.

"It'll keep us going until dinner," I said to Dennis, as I took a big bite of the delicious smoked fish. We ate it in earnest. Of course, we would try to save a piece for Gary and Debbie but we weren't promising anything. The fish wouldn't be easy to resist, as we rode up the pass towards the Divide.

"Let the mules go free, John. They'll follow us," I said to him. They stopped to eat, then ran to catch up, never getting more than fifty yards behind. John and I rode for hours. We could feel the spirits of the old adventurers who travelled here before us.

This was the trail of Lewis, Clark and Sacajawea. It was the road of the Lemhi and the Tendoy, and had been a main route for centuries.

We rode up the Divide in silence. It was dry country, with little pine and lots of sage. Big butte rocks lined the trail in places, and we couldn't help but look straight up while we rode along. We sometimes felt like the spirits of a long ago time were looking at us as we passed. Neither one of us said a word for a long time.

We reached the top about four p.m. and looked over to the other side. Years ago, the princess Sacajawea had looked down in that valley and saw her family, her tribe. Lewis and Clark left her with them shortly after.

John pulled out his water bottle. "Want a swig?" he said.

"Sure," I answered. We sat there, on Red and Cowboy, looking at the valley below us.

"That's Idaho down there," I said to John quietly. "And look, there's the Robber's Roost road." I pointed to an overgrown rut in the hillside that could barely be seen through the weeds. It ran parallel to the gravel road. It was the route Lewis and Clark had taken over the Divide in 1805.

We found Gary and Deb in the meadow, at the confluence of the Missouri River. Far from the river boats, far from the transport docks and booms, we were at the source of the River. From here it found its way down through the Rockies to the flatlands and out to the sea.

Lewis and Clark had followed the river all the way from St. Louis to where we were camped. The Missouri flowed out of the rock, nothing more than a crystal clear trickle. We took our cups and drank from the spring. The water was cold and sweet.

We had a feast. Gary had killed a sage hen. Deb and I plucked out the feathers and prepared the hen for the pan. Neither of us had ever plucked a bird before.

"You're kidding, right?" Gary said to us.

We had trout, soup, pancakes made of cattails and wild raspberries, coffee, potatoes, wild onions and gravy, and the sage hen.

We were on the border of Montana and Idaho, and it was a

hard camp to leave. The spirit of the place was so strong. Every time I looked over at the spring, I could see shadows there by the water. Debbie saw the shadows too — ghosts of travellers, explorers, Indian princesses. We went skinny dipping in a pool below our camp. We watched the stars late into the night, had eaten like kings and queens, and wanted for nothing.

We followed Agency Creek on Wednesday, thirteen miles down through the trees to Tendoy, a tiny Idaho town with just one gas pump and a store.

We were enjoying the sunshine, basking in the simple pleasures of civilization, like sitting at a picnic table with the sound of a country radio singing a Willie Nelson song inside the store. The mules and horses were grazing under the trees. We pulled out our lunches.

"Debbie Foss, telephone is for you." The woman who owned the store came out, wiping her hands on her dirty apron. We all looked at each other in amazement, stunned to think anyone knew we were sitting at this picnic table, in this remote spot out in the middle of the Idaho mountains.

Debbie came back from the phone call.

"It was O.C. Budge from Channel Two in Salt Lake City. He just happened to call the store, knowing they would have seen us if we had been by. He's in Salmon, and wants to come interview us." She still looked a little shocked by the unexpected phone call. We'd been in the wilds for weeks, and this O.C. Budge had tracked us down with one call.

He had driven all the way from Salt Lake City, in Channel Two's motor home. He invited us into his mobile studio, complete with cold beer and Ritz crackers.

"O.C. stands for out of control," he told us. He threw beers to all four of us as we stood there, reaching out for the cold aluminum, dripping with water from the ice box. He had a great smile. His potbelly was okay on him, his jeans hung low and his perm was blond.

We were feeling dirty all of a sudden. We were so used to living outside that a carpet under foot seemed strange to us. Our world changed like that; from riding along the old road of Lewis and Clark, staring in awe at the old wagon ruts running down the gulch, to eating cheese and Ritz crackers in a white carpeted mobile television studio.

"Well, after you get finished with these cold ones and the snacks, we'll get to the filming. We plan to run this next week, so we have no time to lose," he stood there, smiling at us, especially at Debbie, who I could tell had already captured this man's full attention. The color clip showed us riding down the road, bordered with majestic pines and willow trees, just going along, our own pace, free for months in the wilderness. The camera seemed naturally attracted to my beautiful sister, and the four minute short seemed to be two minutes of her flipping her long luxurious hair out of her face, smiling at O.C. directly into the camera, and talking about our rediscovery of the American West and how we never wanted to go home again.

Our stay at Indian Creek Guest Ranch was beautiful. On the way in, we were riding down the road and right in front of us was a ten-rattle rattler, coiled and ready to sink his poisonous venom deep into the tissues of our legs. Gary's gun rang out and with one lurch, the snake was dead. He skinned it, put the snake meat in a plastic bag in his pack, and wrapped the skin around his cowboy hat.

The ranch is a dream place, sitting on the edge of the roaring creek, in the arms of the forest, on the edge of a meadow, under the bluest sky. We set up camp next to the chuckwagon, and Lois Briggs had us in for dinner. We had barbecued spareribs, baked potatoes, hot homemade rolls, coffee, salad and wine. A regular guest at the Ranch was a physics professor at Notre Dame in South Bend. He is the one who discovered the base serum for penicillin. He invented the molecule for the Styrofoam cup, and an unburnable plastic, and is in Who's Who in the World, and has four hundred patented inventions in the U.S. alone. It was an interesting evening, following a long day in the saddle, all the way from Salmon, up the dirt road from town.

It was twenty degrees outside when we went out on the porch and headed out into the dark night. Indian Creek was rushing wildly, singing, leading us back to camp. We stepped out of the warmth of a house full of food and music, into a world of a powerful creek roaring down the gorge. We walked back to our home by the river, slid into our sleeping bags and listened to the sounds of the forest.

Sarah Jane and Annie were picketed in a little meadow above Indian Creek, under a huge white pine. Red and Cowboy were out in the back of the pasture. We were heading into some very remote country, between Indian Creek and Darby.

Mary, John's girlfriend, came into Salmon on the bus and planned to walk all the way to Darby with us. She was trusting us, and hoped we knew what we were doing. She had never camped out overnight before and was more than a little bit worried about losing the trail. We tried to assure her we wouldn't get lost; that with our maps, we could surely make our way to Darby.

Tin Cup Spring, up on the High Divide.

We are on top of the world, at the very source of a river, that flows on from here to the Pacific. We are camping near Little Tin Cup Spring. It is so small, the only way to get to the water is with a tin cup. Each cup brings forth various things, not just water. Pine nuts, guppies, sticks, a little dirt.

There is something holy about this place. We are one-eighth of a mile down below the ridge of the Bitterroot Mountain Range, and the Idaho-Montana border. We climbed very high today on the trail, to almost ten thousand feet.

Like our camp up on Lemhi Divide, there is such a good feeling, sleeping between two states. The trees don't recognize the border; they spread their arms out to each other, blanketing the mountain.

There is not a big welcome sign, "Welcome to Montana" where families stand and smile while Dad snaps the Nikon. Instead, we climb, the horses snort and puff, the mules shift into second gear, and we know on the other side lies Montana. The welcome is a vast valley below; more mountains to ride through, more rivers to swim in, and the biggest sky above us.

We followed the ridge in the direction of Irishman's Rock for two miles. As we approached the place where we thought the trail should be, we searched the woods and sure enough, there it was, and down we went, seven miles straight down a tiny trail through the lodgepole pines. I was glad to have a good saddle for that ride.

We took a nice break around four at the bottom of Mine Creek Trail. We ate dried fruit, peanut butter and bread and of

course, fixed up some cowboy coffee. As we sat there in the old hunting camp, we listened closely and could hear the sound of a truck, far off in the distance, getting closer.

Debbie had gone down to Jackson to meet up with her husband, John Nielson, and they had found us, just in time for dinner. They brought supplies, and we had a huge spaghetti dinner. The next morning, John took off in the car, heading back to Park City, with our map.

We weren't sure if we had missed the dirt road to Alta or not, but we kept going. John Najar and Gary were laughing; it would be quite a surprise to learn we had ridden twenty miles out of the way. We passed some familiar names on signs; some I remembered from the map.

"Maloy Gulch?" I said to John. "That rings a bell."

But still I wasn't sure. Mary had already chewed off all her fingernails, after spending four days with us, killing rattlers, climbing ridges, looking at disappearing trails in front of us, out in the middle of remote central Idaho. We tried to convince her that we were not lost, just confused.

John Nielson came and found us, saying we only had three miles to go. He had decided to stay around another night. After another delicious spaghetti dinner, I lay awake by the fire for hours, listened to a wolf howling, off in the distance. The eerie sound echoed off the canyon below.

The trail that had brought us into the valley was the most beautiful of all trails so far. The West Fork of the Bitterroot Valley was full of chokecherries, elderberries, strawberries and huckleberries. No wonder the Bitterroot Indians lived here. We had some rain, too, but mostly it was just cold. All the trees in the valley are beautiful shades of reds and yellows.

I could almost see the Indians, travelling through these forests along the river, with the travois; babies, dogs, horses, men and women and children, walking on the river bank. I could see them there, almost hear their voices. We passed by the Alta Pine, a pine tree that is guessed to be close to five hundred years old, the oldest ponderosa pine in Montana. There is a large triangular cut in the bark; the Indians put it there long ago to mark the trail to buffalo hunting country.

This was the prettiest country I had ever seen in my life. I was a babe, at home in the woods, and Mary was a babe who desperately wanted out of the woods. She would catch the bus back to Salt Lake City, when we got to Darby in the Bitterroot Valley.

## The Sweet Bitterroot

Coming down the hill into Darby we were stuck in one heck of a rainstorm. It passed right over and dumped on us on its way to town, gathering itself together, in great charcoal billows, pregnant with rain. We watched the rain begin, and rode along the dirt trail, filling our nostrils with delightful scents of the forest. I was sure glad to have my chaps with me; the thick, dark leather kept my legs really warm and dry.

Gary has added a new dimension to the ride. He is turning out to be the perfect partner for us; easy going, slow talking, ready on the draw, protecting the three of us from rattlesnakes with his gun, and bringing some fine birds to the skillet. A few months ago, if you had asked Debbie and me if we would eat a rattlesnake, the answer would've been "No!"

It was a happy day today, and I will remember it until I am a very old lady. Galloping along through the deep grass in the rain. Sarah Jane was running along, kicking up her heels, as if her pack weighed nothing.

Sarah and Annie are two of the best mules in the West, and have never failed us. Only once, when Sarah went galloping off in search of Cowboy, but can you blame her? Mules hate to be separated from the herd. It doesn't matter how much they like you, either. We've found that out.

Annie takes life very seriously. She is smaller than Sarah, a cinnamon brown mule with black ears. Now I know why they were laughing when they sold her to us, in trade for Chief and a hundred dollar bill. Luckily, John still had one! She has an incredible flatulence problem. And when she lets her gasses go, the entire pack train panics and bolts forward, which can cause a major derailment. She is embarrassed by this fact, and takes life very seriously, not smiling much for a mule, looking sheepish and slightly embarrassed much of the time.

We rode in to Darby, a block long and twelve buildings wide.

Darby is a small Montana town, and one of the friendliest places we've been so far. Everybody that passes us smiles and waves. Out of the wilderness and into civilization we ride, once again in search of the pleasantries of town.

We parked the mules and the horses in Mack's Barn, a large red structure that could be seen up and down the valley.

"It's old and worn, but still strong," Mack told us, as he opened his grain room and bagged up some oats for the horses and mules. "It's been a good barn. I have been farming this small patch of ground for forty-five years. The Bitterroot Valley has always been my home. Wouldn't know where else to go. Oh, you better believe that we get our snows in this valley, but we forget about it every Summer," he said, laughing to himself.

Robin immediately made friends with his dog Cinder, another Labrador, and we watched them run together in the field while we talked to Mack.

Farley, Deb's dog, had ridden up from Utah with Deb's husband, John. Farley was a little furry black and white dog, with big, sorrowful eyes. He was having the time of his life in that Bitterroot Valley alfalfa field. He would stop right on the edge of the stream, as the other two dogs sailed gracefully through the air, their ears flying. His legs were too short to get him across the stream. Robin and Cinder were jumping circles over the stream, and Farley would catch them momentarily before they set sail once more, then watch them anxiously from his post on the stream bank. He was a smart dog. Knowing his limitations, he wasn't going to try the jump. The dogs fell sound asleep by the campfire, and didn't budge until morning.

I looked up at the mountains, framing in the narrow valley. I looked around at the green fields. The alfalfa was almost ready to be harvested, the second cutting of a four-cutting hay season. The apples, the plums, the berries, hung precariously to branches, threatening to drop in the heat of the Montana afternoon, turning sweeter by the moment. It was a good day.

Everybody went off to take showers, but Gary and I decided to sit in front of the bar on the rickety wooden porch and watch the afternoon storm come in. A cowboy, with "Jesse" scrolled across his shirt, came out of the bar and handed us each an Olympia beer.

It took him awhile to understand we had come from Utah on horseback, and he still didn't seem to really believe it. Gary and I stretched out our weary legs and listened to the rain, beating out a rhythm on the tin roof above our heads. He ambled back into the bar. A big lumberjack named Pat came out next, carrying two hot ham and cheese sandwiches for us, thrusting them toward us in a gesture of warm hospitality. Gary and Beauty and I sat there on that little wooden bench for a long time, and watched the mountains change color. We savored every bite of those juicy, delicious sandwiches, and Beauty looked at us hopefully for a long time, even after the sandwiches were gone.

We packed up and headed up the valley, after coffee and eggs at the local cafe in Darby. I can see why this valley is one of the prized locations in the whole state of Montana and beyond. It is fertile, and they say that winter isn't so harsh as in Dillon and Bozeman. The fruit orchards cover acres of valley ground, and we could not have timed it better; we seem to be the grateful recipients of the best of everybody's garden.

In Hamilton I met Francis. She was sitting in the window of her room in the Bitterroot Valley Rest home; I went down there in the morning while Deb, John and Gary went to the laundromat and the store, and spent most of the day in the company of the ancients, listening to their stories. From the rest home windows, the view of the mountains is majestic.

"My big brothers would carry me part of the way to school," Francis told me, "because it was a long walk for us, and I was too small to keep up." As she spoke, she reached a shaky hand up to her white hair, searching with bony fingers for a bobby pin that was no longer there. I had heard it fall to the floor, and searched under the bed until I found it for her.

She continued: "We didn't go to school for nine months because of the farming. It was 1901, and the most important thing was the homestead, not schooling. Schooling was secondary to the farming and plain old survival. Schooling was a luxury then for us farm kids.

"Angels came to us," she continued, "schoolmarms from back East, with stern faces and stiff dresses. And with them, they brought their own ideas of what we kids should learn."

"What were your chores?" I asked her. She gave me a funny look.

"We had to do all the regular chores farm kids had. We had to of course weed gardens, get in the wood. We hauled water and cleaned the cabin for Mom. The boys hunted for quail, deer, grouse, sage hen, rabbits, anything they could find. We milked the cows, the goats, and fed the chickens, collected eggs, went berry picking, and picked the apples and peaches and pears off the trees we had planted.

"But we had lots of good times, too, because we made our own good times. My brothers would make skis out of the barrel staves. It wasn't too hard to get hold of a big old oak barrel then, you know! Everything was do it yourself then, you know, that's the way it was." Then she added, thoughtfully, "Not like now."

"Did you make your own butter?" I asked her.

"Of course, how do you think we raised eleven kids? Of course we made our own butter. Everything was do it yourself. There were eleven of us. My folks were good farmers. See, my dad worked in the logging camps in the winter."

"This was new, unbroken country, you see. It belonged to the Indians then, and it was clear to the settlers that the Indians knew how to live on the land." She stopped and closed her eyes for a moment.

She continued: "The early settlers called the town of Darby 'Doolittle' after Jimmy Doolittle. And then they decided to call it Darby after the Postmaster. That is the way all the towns got their names; from whoever was around at the time of the naming. They were going to call it Harrison, but when Washington wrote back and said they couldn't have that name, Darby decided to name it after himself, and it's been Darby ever since. It's burned down a couple times, but it's always raised up from the ashes." She laughed, and suddenly looked out at the mountains. "Look, the light's changing on the hills," she said.

"Darby is a good town," I said to her. "Do you know Mack? We stayed with him. We slept in his barn and the horses slept in the pasture. We came up Indian Creek, and then down the West Fork of the Bitterroot River, and on up here to Hamilton. We came across Lemhi Pass!"

Her eyes lit up at the mention of the river and the pass, as if

I had mentioned the names of old, long lost friends. She looked away from the window.

"I was only thirty-two when my husband died. My sixth child was born four months after he died, so you can imagine, it wasn't easy for us. The children and I always stuck together though, and we made it through together." She stopped. I knew she was thinking about her husband. She reached up and wiped an unexpected tear from her eye; it had surprised her.

"I worked at the newspaper. I was a reporter for the Republican, it was a weekly. I was the editor after the old editor died. I could write anything, any old chore! You don't get rich on it, see. But it's a good life, it's all about people. You see, people are the most interesting thing about the world." She stopped and smiled. She was old now, and her hands could no longer negotiate a typewriter; that was obvious to me. Her hair, like spun silver, was arranged in soft curls like a loose fitting hat on her head.

"I wonder why the people in Montana are so friendly," I said to Francis. "Everyone we have met in this state has been so wonderful to us."

"Why, it's still the Old West," she said to me, smiling, grabbing my hand, and bouncing it up and down in hers, playfully.

"Oh, you know that song, out where the handshake is a little stronger, out where the smile lasts a little bit longer, out where the West begins....." she sang the words in a sweet lilting melody.

"Oh I used to sing, but that was long ago. Oh, I was always a country girl singin'. The teachers in district school taught us how to sing. That was the great thing, they taught us how to write tunes. No real training, but we sure could sing, yes indeed!"

"Did you know cowboys?" I asked her as I stuffed some Fritos into my mouth.

"Did I know cowboys! The cows were driven up from Darby in the spring, and sure, I knew the cowboys! They were the real thing, the real McCoy! They sat proud in their saddles, wore shaggy chaps and worn-out hats, but they were real good looking to me. They were good men. Why sure, they had their Saturday night parties, but they earned 'em! They are the ones that really built up the country. It was the Bitterroot Stock Farm!" she continued. "You can imagine how the Indians in the valley felt about it. Now there isn't so much of that anymore, driving the cows up the country and all. Of course, the Forest Service controls much of the range now, you know. The cowboys were good men. It's different now from what it was then. It took more than a belt buckle back then to be one."

I offered her some Fritos and she pointed to her dentures, flashing them at me, winking with her good eye. The other one, I noticed, was foggy and didn't look like it was doing much for her.

"Did they used to come to town, and ..." I stopped talking while she continued.

"Sure, that was what the town was for! Sure, they came to town! But they drove the cattle through the back of town, on a little side road, through the woods. They couldn't bring them down the Main Street."

"Oh I always thought they did." Everything I knew about the cowboys I had learned from television.

"No, they wouldn't dare do that." I could tell she was thinking how time had changed things.

"How did Hamilton get so much bigger than Darby?" I asked her.

"Well, it's really the youngest town of the valley, did you know that?" She continued. "Marcus Daly came here, you know. No, he wasn't a big cattleman, he was a mining man. He went over to Anaconda and built the big smelter up there. He was born in Ireland, like so many of them, and he worked on a pig farm. He quit his job when he was fifteen and shipped West. He was all over Utah, California, and then he headed on up to Montana. He got into mining as a young man, and bought up two or three sawmills, and twenty-two thousand acres for his stock and family. He built all the business buildings. He put everything into it that he could, you know! He always kept the stock farm, and a mighty big payroll, and kept the mill going too, you know. But he died then, in 1900."

"But then the timber begin to fade out. I came down here in 1922, and they were taking the mill out then."

Just then her friend came and stood in the doorway, raising her cane, pointing it in our direction.

"She's not wearing you out, now, is she Frances?" She seemed to be kidding. Francis waved her away with a few rapid motions of her bony hand, and pointed at my tape recorder. "This Bitterroot Valley has had its ups and downs. They tried to make an orchard deal out of it, you know. It was back in 1910. They found it wasn't a one crop valley. It was a mistake. But that's what promoters do to the country you know. But we still grow apples," she said proudly.

"I know," I answered. "We have seen every kind of fruit and berry in the world in this valley."

We sat in silence for a minute or two.

"It's been a good life, I know. I married when I was nineteen. He was terribly handsome and the son of a doctor. We went over and worked for the Forest Service on the Clearwater in Idaho. But that's about all." I could tell she wanted to change the subject.

"Where are the Indians now?"

"Well you see, in 1898 the Indians went out of here." She looked seriously at me. Her expression turned grave.

"See, there was this thing called the Garfield Treaty," she continued. "The Indians abided by that, but Chief Charlot refused to go, because his name was forged to the treaty. His father, Chief Victor, was always against it. Things were getting really rough for the Indians in 1891 when so many people came in and all, and the white man's way was not their way, and so a lot of them went on up to what they call the Jocko Reservation."

"They yielded. It's called the Flathead Valley, but they were not the original Flatheads. That is a misnomer. They were the same as the Kootenai tribes. The government gave them four million dollars as payment for the Bitterroot. Four million dollars! My goodness. It's worth four billion, at least!" I saw fire in her eyes. She was really getting angry for such an old lady.

"Of course, they have always cheated the Indians. It's been easy," she said. "The white man has always cheated the Indian out of what was his. It was always Indian land. It belonged to them. They never fought the white people like the other Indians did. Tendoy was quite a peaceful General too. I can't remember. I'm getting a little rusty on my history. But I think he was killed in one of the fracas with the army."

She stopped and sat quietly. I could feel her anger subside and she calmed down. She took a deep breath and a sip of water.

"The only time we would see the Indian was in the autumn, during hunting season," she told me. "See, when my folks came in '88, the Indian families were all up here, living in the meadows at the edge of the river. They would go up the East Fork to hunt. With the travois and the mothers with the babies on their backs, with all the horses and pack horses, they would go up there to hunt."

"1841 was when the Jesuits came. In 1941 we had the Centennial celebration, and I saw an Indian woman cooking on a campfire, and all the kids were running around barefoot. This was right by the church, by St. Mary's."

She was smiling again, her memories of the Indians brought her pleasure, I could tell. "They are earth people, they are good people, the Indians, and they lived close to the earth, to nature."

"Chief Victor was a statesman. So was Charlot. So was Joseph," she continued. "Chief Joseph was a statesman. They didn't have the training that the statesmen had that came from Washington and made up the treaties. They believed in sticking to their birthright. This was their land! I've learned a lot since I was little and I saw Indians, and was scared to death. We didn't know anything about it, then. We didn't know enough about them, you know." She looked down. I felt her regret.

"Did you have a horse when you were young?" I asked her.

"No, but my brothers did. But, I guess women's rights weren't..." Her voice trailed off.

"Of course there was the horse and buggy, and I would drive the teams. Then I became a forest ranger's wife, and went to Idaho after the fires were over, this was in 1910. I went by Spokane in October in the train, to Kooskia, and I got on the horse with my husband, and I was four months pregnant. I rode the mountain trails and loved it. But that was the life we knew."

"When the forest fires came, there were no airplanes to drop stuff, you know, there were just the horses and the pack mules and a foot man."

I could hear the sound of people slowly heading down the hall, their canes, walkers and wheelchairs making a racket on the linoleum, the sounds echoing off the walls.

"It sounds like dinner time," she said to me, smiling.

"Well I guess I'd better go," I answered, and walked with her as far as the dining room. I watched her sit down at a long table with about twenty other women. She blended in with them; a sea of pastel sweaters and silver hairdos.

I decided to ride alone ahead of the rest, as far as Missoula. I wanted to catch up with Joe Smith, an old high school friend from La Cañada, who was playing football for the University of Montana. Joe and his family had forty acres up Rattlesnake Gulch outside of Drummond. Joe Smith was one of the kindest men I had met in my life, and I had never heard him whisper a bad word about anybody.

Robin and I headed out early in the morning, before the sun was breaking over the Bitterroot Range. I rode Cowboy along the highway, on the frontage road, loping along, free and easy. The only sound was that of his hooves on the dirt. The world woke up and it was a day full of car and truck noises, as I rode up the valley, around Missoula, never taking my eye off the big M on the hillside above the school.

I tied Cowboy out in front of a little restaurant, directly across from the University. He was happy to graze on the well-tended side lawn. I ordered coffee. Robin was waiting patiently, as always. I had promised her something from the cafe.

"Sorry to bother you, but my name is Chris and I am from the station, the local TV station. Would you mind driving down to the studio with me? Could you leave the horse here?" Chris was about twenty-six. His belt buckle was a huge trophy buckle, probably something he won in a rodeo before he became a newsman.

"Sure, why not?" I told him.

Robin and I hopped in the van with him. I took my saddle bags off Cowboy and left him in the side yard of the restaurant. He would be entertained there for hours; the long green city grass had never seen the lips of a horse before. He didn't even look up as we drove away.

Robin sat next to me, at my feet, with the old white Alamo that Ray Goodrich had given me, sitting squarely on her Labrador head. She took the interview very seriously, and stared solemnly at the cameras. Later on, we got to watch the tape. We looked like a couple of real characters up there on the screen. You could see the miles on both of us.

I never did find Joe. He had gone up to the cabin for a few

days. I met up with Deb, John and Gary at the fairgrounds, and we went from there over to the Hogan's house on the edge of town. Lynee Hogan was a friend of mine from Whitworth, and even though she was off in Stowe, Vermont, waiting tables at the Trapp Family Lodge, her parents made us welcome at their home.

The mules and the two horses were happy in the corrals, and Mr. Hogan fed them some good oat hay. We dined at a real dining room table, and had a very delicious dinner with the Hogans. I slept in Lynee's bed, in a room she had long ago left behind. To its walls were taped pictures and team flags and poems she had written on notebook paper. The bedspread was frilly, and the pillows were all cased in pink flannel and lace. I stood and looked in the gold mirror above her dresser for a long time. The high mountain sun had tanned my skin and my eyes stared back at me like bright pools of water. I smiled. I loved this road.

After two days with all the trimmings, we were ready to go again.

## *Close to Paradise*

We woke up to the smell of coffee on the old electric range downstairs in the Hogan's kitchen. I opened my eyes to Lynee's pink bedroom. Surrounded by lace and linens, I felt like a twelve-year-old again. A worn teddy bear looked at me from across the room. Lynee probably hadn't even said goodbye.

I stayed there, in the canopy bed, under the checkered quilt, in a state of bliss, the smell of coffee and bacon filling the air. This was the cleanest moment of the trip I had experienced, and yet my outside life was close at hand; I could see the mules and the horses grazing in the pasture, framed by the frilly curtains. I lay back on the giant lace covered pillows and watched them for a long time.

I got myself back up on my feet, remade the bed, and pulled on my jeans. Lynee's mom had washed them for me; I could hardly pull them on. They were still warm from the dryer. She had brought them in that morning, while I was off in dreamland, in a high mountain meadow on the Great Divide.

"I'm warning you," Lynee's father said to us that morning as we were packing the mules and saddling the horses. "The road between here and Highway 200 is a real killer! It's a dangerous little stretch of road, I tell you. I don't think there is a shoulder whatsoever; the canyon is narrow and the river bottom is rough and rocky. I don't see how you can possibly stay off the road."

"So what do you think?" Debbie asked him seriously. John, Gary and I stood there, silent, thinking. None of us wanted to take a ride in a stock truck, and yet this local man was advising us to let him take us up the road past the narrow part of the highway.

"I think you should let me haul you beyond the dangerous part." He was looking at us, stern and serious. He wore a nice white cowboy shirt with special pearl snaps. Mrs. Hogan walked toward us, carrying a large bundle full of cakes, cookies and fruit for the trail. "Please let me do that," Mr. Hogan continued.

We didn't have to think about it too long. Before we knew it,

we were travelling at forty-five miles an hour up the highway. We rode in the back of the big red stock truck with the animals, all of us except Deb. She rode up in the cab with Mr. Hogan.

"Just think, John," I said in a loud voice over the wind, "this forty miles would have taken us a good three days."

"Or four," John added. We looked out of the stock truck slats, far down into the rocky canyon, chiseled by the river. As always, John was preparing a Jif and Home Pride sandwich with his Swiss Army knife, dipping it into the jar for another layer of peanut butter. We were on the road to Paradise, Montana. We sang anything that came to mind, and rode with our heads out in the wind.

Mr. Hogan dropped us off on the side of the highway in the Valley of the Clark Fork River. The Clark Fork and the train track dominate the valley, surrounded by mountains covered with the thickest blue spruce and huge old pine trees, mixed with cottonwood, tamarack and willow.

We spent the night across from the Pair-O-Dice Saloon, a clapboard building from another time, with a neon sign that said

Pair-O-Dice, and had big dice rolling down towards the parking area in front. The horses and the mules were practically buried in the pasture grasses. We picketed them to fenceposts, and let Sarah go free. She was in mule heaven.

I can see why they call this place Paradise. The Canadian honkers flew over, heading south. We saw eagles and hawks, circling around us and then disappearing over the ridge next to the river bank.

I walked down to the river's edge, and sat there, cross-legged, on the reed grass, and watched as the swift moving Clark Fork flowed in a rapid, steady motion past my naked feet. I sat there for a long time; it felt so good to be barefoot, the sun shining between my toes. There was no sound at all; it was quiet down there, until I heard the Burlington Northern, heading towards us from Missoula and beyond, clacking along the track. The train signaled its arrival with a loud whistle at each road crossing and town all the way up and down the valley.

We sat in the smoky Pair-A-Dice until eleven, and watched the full moon light up the valley grasses, the wide river, and the mountains beyond. The neon sign in front cast a red and yellow glow on the parking lot outside, as we looked out the dirty glass, patterned with greasy fingerprints. We could see Sarah's shiny white coat in the moonlight. We could see our herd, thanks to her, a white beacon in the field.

We came out of the Pair-O-Dice and walked silently back to our camp by the river. The moon looked huge. We were spellbound by the beauty. The whole place was so quiet, we could hardly believe it. There were very few cars on the highway, and we could hear them for miles before they went by.

Deb and I walked down into the meadow to talk to Sarah Jane. She was literally glowing in the moonlight. We scratched her ears, on the inside, the way she likes it.

"Look at her," Deb said to me in a whisper. Sarah had her big head in Debbie's lap. She loved to have her ears scratched. It was Sarah's very favorite thing, besides rolling after we took her pack off at the end of a long, hot day.

"She loves that," I said. We both wrapped our arms around our Sarah Jane. She nudged us gently with her head.

It was another good camp, with all the essentials close by; pasture, shelter, and plenty of water.

Deb got us out of the sack at an early hour, tempting me to rise with a hot cup of coffee from the Pair-O-Dice.

"Creamora and sugar," she said to me.

We rode fourteen miles, up the old road. This is the best road yet for making good time. Fifteen miles seems like nothing out here. When we were in the high mountain country, fifteen miles would take us twice as long. The road is big and wide and soft on the animals' feet.

We saw the little chalk "P" on the hillside above the town. Two men, one very short and the other one very tall, were stacking wood in the sheep pen at the fairgrounds. They both had on overalls and big black mud boots. Their hats were day glow orange with furry flaps over their ears. They were dressed identically.

"I saw you on the news the other night, with that dog, wearing a cowboy hat," the short man said to us. "Is there anything we can do to help you folks?"

"Do you know where we can camp in Plains?" Debbie asked him, standing there with her arm over Sarah's neck.

I took a swig of my canteen, and handed it to her. The water was warm, but tasted pretty good anyway.

"Camp by the river," the tall man suggested. "There is a beautiful place with plenty of firewood, and a nine acre pasture for the horses and mules."

We let them go free. They ran, bucking and kicking up their heels, down to the richest part of the pasture, and we didn't see them again until morning. I think they could've stayed in that pasture for the rest of their lives, trying to eat it all. We really lived it up and splurged on dinner salads and guzzled coffee and cream at the Mint Cafe. We stayed there for hours, putting a serious dent in the restaurant's saltine and coffee supply. Nobody really seemed to mind. There were only two other people in there all night; a man about eighty, tall and skinny as a string bean, in a pair of faded old overalls and black boots, and another guy who looked like he never left the cafe.

He was a fixture. He sat at the counter, hunched over a cup of coffee that was always full, the smoke from his cigarette rising into his unmoving, pock-marked face. He lived out behind the restaurant in a tiny cabin with one light bulb hanging down in the center of the room on a piece of chain.

"His name is Frank," the waitress said to me. I looked up at their bumper sticker on the mirror behind the counter, next to the boxes of breakfast cereals and syrups. It said: "If you want it your way, go to McDonald's!"

It was another beautiful, starlit night. The animals ate so much clover, they could hardly move, and stood still for hours so their stomachs could settle, and they could eat more. I woke up just as the moon disappeared behind the ridge, and the twilight turned the mountains, dark green in the shadows and crowded with proud stands of pines and cedar, to shades of orange and yellow. The sun started to brighten the sky, and the frost on our bags melted, turning to dew. Mornings were cold and wet.

In the early morning, I got up, even before Deb, and walked over to the Clark Fork Valley Rest Home. I tied Cowboy up out in front, next to a deep patch of grass.

It was there on the porch of the rest home I met Cora.

"I am eighty-five years old now," she told me.

"Have you lived here in Montana for most of your life?" I asked her.

"We came from Ontario, Canada, and my family moved to Moosejaw, Saskatchewan, in 1903, and a few years later to Havre, Montana." She looked up at me and smiled.

"Am I ever glad to talk to somebody like you," she said. "It gets lonely here for me."

She remembers it all as if it were yesterday. She talked about her old homestead, and her eyes were sparkling with memories. But then, the tears would come and she'd change the subject.

"I see it all so clearly," she said slowly, closing her eyes. "The homestead in Moosejaw. We had a beautiful grove, an orchard, full of the best tasting apples in the valley. Everyone would come, from miles around, in their buggies and wagons to pick our apples. We had big parties, with the families from all over the country. My father was a very friendly person, who shared what he had with everyone else around. Everybody loved him. My mother was shy; much quieter than my father, who always had us kids laughing. Mom kept our little cabin neat as a pin. She worked all the time, never putting down her broom or stirring spoon."

She stopped for a minute and wiped her eyes. "I remember the rides with my father in the sled. We'd hitch up our buggy horse, or the big red mule, and slide at great speeds towards town in the sled. He had skins and furs to keep the chill off. He had a little flask of something he enjoyed under the front seat of the sled, and as he drove us toward town, he would sneak a drink of the flask. For me, he had a box of candies he kept in a little cigar box under the seat."

"You have a mule?" she asked me.

"Yep. And she's a beauty," I boasted.

"Mules are smart," she told me. "I remember that old Red. He was always in our corral, as long as I can remember back. He was really good with the little kids, always watching his feet. We'd crawl up under his belly and lay down on the ground underneath him! We grew up playing around that old red mule's feet, and he never ever stepped on any of us. The cowboys used to make fun of my dad because he preferred to ride the mule. He loved that old mule."

She stopped and smiled, thinking. "You know, things are so different than when I was a girl. People now would never consider driving a buggy to town, or at least not many of them. Everything in the old times depended upon the horses and the mules."

"I remember my dad telling me a story about an old mule they used to use during the wheat harvest. Around harvest time, all the mules were put to work — sometimes close to forty of 'em. This one particular mule, I don't know what his name was, hated to work with so many other mules in the hitch. He'd disappear down into the gully behind the ranch, trying to avoid work."

"One year, he really lucked out. He was down in the gully, the night before all the work was to begin. He got sprayed by a skunk down there, real bad, and no man would get close to him. Nobody wanted to put his harness on, since this mule smelled to high heavens! Even the other mules stayed away from him. He got to stay in the pasture, while everybody else went to work, and he liked it that way. Year after year, the mule would make sure he got sprayed by a skunk the day before harvest. He never worked again." She laughed. "At least, that's the way Daddy told it."

Then, she continued: "I remember the parties we used to have with the Canadian cowboys. It was 1910. All the boys I knew were cowboys, and were either working the hay or tending the herds. My sister and I were favorites at the dances. We both loved to dance with the handsome cowboys, in their party clothes. Most of the time they were scruffy and dusty, but when it was time for a dance, everybody got cleaned up. Some of those cowboys would ride their horses fifty miles one way to go to a dance in town. They'd all ride together, from ranches all over the area. It was a big event, and everybody came to the dance, everybody. Even the oldest grandma would come, and watch the dancing."

"Moosejaw was named by my father," Cora told me. "A man was passing through, and lost a spoke of his wagon wheel, and needed help repairing it. My father's friend had a moose skull hanging above the buggy shed door. The two of them repaired the wheel with the jawbone of the moose skull by lashing it on to the spokes and hub of the wheel. That was when my father suggested they call the stop Moose Jaw."

She went back to her room to rest and I sat in the hospital lunch room with a cup of coffee. There were pansies on the table in front of me. They were too beautiful to leave there on the table, so I took them in to Cora.

"Cora, I brought you some flowers."

"Oh thank you, honey. Where did you get them?"

"In the lunchroom!" I answered a little sheepishly.

We said goodbye. I got on my horse and rode on. She stood out in the road and waved to us until we were out of sight, over the hill.

Sandra Gingery waved us down at her mailbox. She had been waiting for us to ride along her road for two days now.

"I saw you on T.V. Come on in and have some lunch. Your horses can have some oats, too," she said. She stood there and watched us as we tied up the animals to her sturdy cedar fence.

We went into her kitchen: Debbie first, then me, then Gary with John behind him. Beauty and Robin stayed by the door. They were glad for the break; both of them crumpled in heaps, sharing the porch mat. Sandra had everything ready for us. She was a horse lover, always had been. She was a mother now. Her rambling days were pretty much over.

"You know, I was gonna take a ride just like the one you're on, with my friend Luann, back in 1967. Then I met Bob, got married, and got pregnant. So did Luann." She looked down and studied the plastic table mat, with the picture of Old Faithful on it, and started wiping it off with a dish towel without thinking about it.

She served us tuna fish sandwiches and soup and home baked cookies for dessert. She walked us back down to the horses and the mules, and put us back on our way towards Spokane.

Sandra reminded us that we were running out of Indian Summer and soon Winter would be coming into the valley with her bulky coats of snow. She packed our saddlebags with homemade cookies and dried fruit. We thanked her and waved goodbye, and rode on with our bellies full of sandwiches and cookies.

There is always a certain time in the afternoon, when we are practically walking in our sleep, and everybody is real quiet, with Gary out there looking for grouse, or anything else he can find for dinner. The afternoon sun beats down, and the animals are in a steady walking rhythm. We don't stop walking for ten miles or so. The hours pass like pieces of lumber in the swift flowing Clark Fork River.

We made it to the Thompson River and set up camp on the banks, eight miles away from Thompson Falls. I saw a black bear climb the hill between two trees.

"Look," I said to the rest of them, but the bear was long gone before anyone else saw it, except Sarah Jane. She saw it right away.

Those brown bears can really run, and usually do. They like to get as far away from people as they can. Usually the feeling is mutual.

The train whistled and a light on the front cast a bright glow across the trees. I looked up and could see the silhouette of the horses and the mules in the light.

I waited for the big, loud whistle of the train and the rumble in the ground as it went slowly down the valley. Ever since we left Missoula, we have been keeping company with the Burlington Northern. It is always so strange to think that these trains, only an hour ago, left the big yard in Spokane or Missoula. The whistle blows in each town, and echoes off the mountains, ricocheting back and forth across the river.

I woke up Wednesday morning to the sound of Cowboy crying loudly. I had been mixing the sound in with my dream, so I hadn't realized he was really in trouble. Red, Annie, and Sarah Jane had wandered off, in search of better pasture, down the bank. Sarah had left a whole patch of thistles, untouched. Red pulled hard, like a work horse pulling logs, and took his picket line with him to find the two mules.

There was Cowboy, deserted, trying desperately to free himself of his picket rope. He got so frustrated, he jumped in the Thompson River, and wound himself around a chokecherry bush.

Jumping out of my sleeping bag next to the fire, in my bright yellow underwear, I jumped up on his back, unhooking his picket rope. He was like a stick of dynamite, not too far from a flame. He tore up the hill and headed down river. I was busy trying to keep my bare feet off the thorn bushes, rubbing the sleep from my eyes, trying to keep from slipping off his back.

He was leaping down the road, each leap bigger than the last, as he gained speed and traction on the ground beneath his hooves. I held on to his neck and kept my head down, my fists clenched tightly around his mane, holding on for dear life.

Cowboy found the mules and Red almost immediately, and came to an immediate halt when he did. I ended up on his neck, straddling his ears, and managed to slide back without falling off. They gave me a little chase, and finally I caught up with Red, roped him, and led them back. I came back to camp, leading the bunch of them. Deb made me a nice hot cup of cowboy coffee, and we laughed as I told them the story a couple of times.

Sarah loves plums. All mules do, but she seems to savor them more than the others. The fruit is so plentiful it is falling off the trees, much to Sarah's delight. When she eats a plum, she puts her nose high in the air, so she doesn't spill any of the delicious juice. She keeps her head up in this position for several minutes, while she works the plum seed until it's clean, and then she drops it out of her mouth and begs for another.

Thompson Falls was only eight miles away. We rode in past the mill, and there was Peggy Eldridge in her car, waiting to take us to her corral on the hill. On the way up the hill was a perfect apple

tree with some of the sweetest apples I had ever tasted; we were hungry, too. I had made some apple sauce for breakfast, over the fire, but it had a very strong smoky taste and we couldn't eat much of it. We know we are getting close to Washington, living on apples, plums, berries, cherries, peaches and pears.

Thompson Falls is one street with two cafes, six bars, a park, five churches, train tracks and a few other businesses.

We did our laundry, and I went off to the Rest Home. I met Francis.

"I came to Thompson Falls in 1919. My dear husband, they called him Fat Charlie, traded with the Crows for horses, and sold them back in Massachusetts," she said. "For years I watched him load the box cars with the most beautiful, wildest looking horses, all headed for Back East. The horses were sold for a higher price than Charlie had to pay, that's for sure."

She stopped and thought for a moment. "You know, I'm already ninety-one years old. I don't know where the years have gone. I remember turning forty like it was yesterday. Life has been good to me, and I have a lot of living to do yet. My life is still full of family and good times. Of course, sometimes I really miss living with my husband, but he's been gone for a few years now, and I'm just starting to get used to it."

We came back in the morning and said goodbye to her. We took her picture, standing in front of the mules. She took me aside and gave me a twenty dollar bill.

"You look like you haven't had fried chicken for a long time," she said, pressing the bill into the palm of my hand.

"You are right about that," I said to her as I put my foot in the stirrup and my hands around the saddle horn, lifting myself up on to Cowboy's back.

We travelled on, taking a back road from Thompson Falls; the dirt was dark and wet on the road, easy on the animals' feet. It was a long day, along the Blue Slide Road. It wound its way up the hillside, overlooking the Clark Fork River way below. The Blue Slide was a sheer rock face, way below us, throwing the most extraordinary reflection on the mirror-like waters of the river.

By noon we had ridden by a couple of ripe apple trees, and rode on with our saddlebags full to the brim. When the sun went down, we were still in the saddle. Finally, off in the distance, we saw Trout Creek, a tiny lumber town between Noxon and Thompson Falls. There were no more than twenty lights in the whole town, and still, we felt warmer once we saw them. We were hoping the cafe would still be open by the time we took care of the mules and horses.

We were always happy to see town, and always just as happy to leave it again. We had ridden twenty-seven miles. Coffee sure sounded good, and salad did too. We were all very hungry and tired, more than ready to call it quits for the day.

I can always tell when the horses and the mules are ready to quit. Cowboy no longer listens to me when I say, "Head up, Boy." He grabs at every blade of grass he can possibly reach. Sarah Jane slows down, and starts looking for camp. When she finds a place she thinks is good enough, she'll stop as if to say, "This is fine with me."

We stopped a car to escort us across the bridge into town. It was a very dangerous bridge, and only a month ago a horse was ripped from underneath a thirteen-year-old boy, and was dragged to death on the front bumper of a logging truck. We hurried across the bridge, pushing the already tired animals. We could see the cafe was still open. The old neon sign flashed "coffee" and "breakfast". Our stomachs were growling.

We rode up to Bud Roe's trailer. He had invited us to stay; they had a nice two-acre pasture that needed trimming. I knocked on the trailer door, and was greeted by a thin man with a warm handshake. His wife, Florence, stood beside him, opening their trailer to us, making us feel welcome with coffee and donuts. Florence was a country lady who grew the biggest vegetables in the valley.

"You can pitch your tent out by the barn," she told us, smiling. "You know, it's not every day we get a pack train staying with us."

Florence gave us this huge cabbage; it still has its place in the blue stuff sack. We gave the mules and horses some oats, and hurried off to get to the cafe before it closed for the evening. It was ten minutes to ten. It had been a long haul, twenty-seven miles. We made it inside the cafe in time to order. They were still serving, until ten. We were stiff and tired, after twenty-seven miles, and now here we sat in chairs at a table in a dining room.

Gary said, "This feels really good to sit here, don't it?"

We all agreed. We walked back after our usual low budget meals and fell asleep almost immediately. The mules were still busy getting their pasture meal when we went to bed. They, too, soon fell asleep.

I am riding Annie, our mule, and leading Cowboy. We are west of Trout Creek, Montana, only fifty-five miles from Sandpoint, Idaho, and a hundred and forty miles from Spokane, Washington. That seems like nothing to me now. We are anticipating our arrival in Spokane, in only twelve more days. We've been on the trail for eighty days.

The final days of the ride are passing too quickly. The days are so short now! The skies are a clear deep blue, the air is warm and the trees applaud autumn with a large variety of colors. On my right, I am passing bright yellow aspens, and on my left, a green meadow and red tamaracks.

Here comes the wind. We have gone a thousand and one hundred miles so far.

It feels so good to be back in the Northwest again. Not until I reached Paradise, Montana, did I feel like I was almost home. And now, the Clark Fork is opening up into the Noxon Reservoir, then Lake Pend Oreille, then it becomes the Pend Oreille River and flows north towards Canada. We'll ride through Priest River, Newport, and then we'll head south towards Mount Spokane and our final destination.

On October seventh, Thursday, we will be riding our last miles together.

I have grown so accustomed to sleeping out under the stars, on my saddle blanket. There are so many fruit trees, and greens, we live on the food we come across along the way. It is a good thing too, because I have only one dollar left in my pocket. My folks have sent a five dollar bill to every post office. Mom sent me long-johns, a warm T-shirt and some dried apples.

Living outside like this, I feel healthier than I ever have in my life.

## Lucky Coins For a White Mule

Noxon, Montana.

We are feeling so at home in this sweet river valley. People live here, for the most part, for the hunting, the fishing in the Clark Fork, and the wilderness. It is far away from anywhere, except Paradise. Debbie and I ride along, eating off the trees as we go, laughing for no reason. It's almost as if we are suspended in this world of the trail, and the golden road lies out before us, and we go down it, without a care in the world. I have never felt so free in my life.

I wonder what it will be like to be back to normal life after this. I am excited to get there, but I will be sad too. It will end, and we will then be off on our own again. It makes me lonely to think about it.

Riding towards Noxon, we looked way down the road and there sat a big black pickup. We knew it was Jo and George, the horse loggers we met up at the Wayside Bar. George asked us if we wanted to come up to dinner at their camp.

We picketed the horses in the field at the base of the mountain, and George and Jo hauled us up to their camp in the back of the big black pickup truck. We drove into a driveway, up the steep logging road, and we were "home".

They have a homemade trailer. They haul their water up from town in big plastic jugs, and have a little outhouse out back. There is a big canvas crew tent with a potbelly stove in the middle of it. Astro turf lines the floor. The tent is lined with little cots, each one with its own blanket. This is the guest house, and this is where we will stay tonight.

Out in back of the trailer is a lodgepole corral, home for the giant team of Belgian Horses they call Queenie and Ted. Chip, a bay Quarterhorse, is Bulldog's favorite bulldogging and cutting horse. He just roams the camp, finding open sacks of oats, knocking on the door of the trailer with his hoof, and itching his rear on the rough bark of the white pines surrounding the trailer.

The wood smoke rises from the stove pipe, puffing up into the pine trees towering above me. I stop outside and stand there, breathing deeply. The smell of pine, alfalfa hay, chainsaw gas, and wood smoke fill the air.

This is a special home. It is a makeshift place, and one of the homiest places we've been. They just welcomed us in, as if we were old friends.

George had spent his life with his nose to the grindstone to feed their twelve kids; six of Jo's and six of his own. He had been married before, and had lost interest after the first kid. George and his first wife didn't get along too well. She would "wallop" George, and the last time she did, she threw him down the stairs and he landed on his nose, breaking it for the third time. That was the last straw.

She threatened to leave. George said he would have a car for her by ten the next morning. He ran down to the bank and made a deal with the banker, who knew George's wife. He gave him the money for a Sixty-five Pontiac with two spare tires, so she wouldn't get a flat, and come back. He had the car for her by ten, just as he had promised.

She had bought a set of Samsonite luggage the year they started having babies. In a period of ten years, she hadn't gone on one trip with the luggage, but it was worn to the nubs because she had packed to leave so many times. But this time she had a car. She packed up, and never came back.

Jo was married too. George rode up on his horse, the first time she ever saw him. He was drinking a carton of milk to overcome a terrible hangover.

Jo thought he was the cutest man she had ever seen. Jo's husband was out of town, and she needed a stove. George found her one. The husband came home, and hit George in the nose as he was pushing the heavy propane stove into place. George lay down on the floor, said good night and went to sleep.

Jo moved in with George, and then they had twelve kids to raise. That was fifteen years ago, and they still get a twinkle in their eyes when they look at each other.

They had a wedding with all twelve kids present.

Last night Jo made us meat loaf, mashed potatoes and gravy,

salad with Thousand Island dressing and cupcakes for dessert. George played the guitar and drank Black Velvet. We all sat around in the little trailer, with the dogs out in front and the horse Chip at the door, laughing and trading stories with these people we had just met the night before.

They had worked away all those years, until this summer, when they gave up their house, put all their stuff in storage, bought a team, and started logging for Washington Water and Power. They allow no machinery on their contracts; only horses are allowed to log this land.

"In Oregon, the horse loggers are required to keep diapers on their horses!" George told me, seriously. I thought he was kidding when he told me that. After dinner, George went out to the big canvas tent, our home away from home, and lit a fire in the little potbelly wood stove. It warmed up the tent almost immediately. The dancing fire splashed big shadows of gold on the dark walls.

We threw out our sleeping bags on the cots and closed our eyes, properly fed and dead tired. During the night I woke up and had to go to the outhouse. I knew it would be torture to wait until morning. I considered how unfamiliar I was with the positions of the stumps directly outside the tent, and that I was sleeping in my birthday suit, wearing only socks. Still, I knew I had to get up.

Debbie, John and Gary seemed to be very much asleep. They were all three snoring in various tones. I felt the warm, slick fur of Robin under my feet, but before I could recover, I tripped. I swung around, stepped gingerly and fell over at the same time, trying to be quiet. I landed on the top of the red hot wood stove, the bare skin of my precious behind burning off, not unlike a branding iron as it touches a cow's hide. I squealed, jumping up as fast and quietly as I could.

I looked at the burn in Jo's mirror in the trailer. It looked like train tracks heading out of town.

I have been riding Cowboy with my right cheek slightly askew in the saddle ever since. It's not an easy place for a burn to heal, in a pair of Levi's, on the back of a trotting horse.

I woke up that next morning with my sleeping bag pulled up around my head to keep the frost off my ears. The fire in the potbelly stove was long since cold. The early morning sun made its way through the cedar, through the canvas, casting a welcome light on my sleeping bag. I rolled over on my back, and was immediately reminded of my brand.

I heard a chainsaw start up, and could hear George talking to the big pair of Belgians. He was already out there, in the trees, working the giant horses.

I got dressed and walked down the road and into the trees where they were pulling out logs. The horses' breath billowed out in great white clouds in the frigid early morning air. George gently gave the order to the team to pull forward, to stop, or to drag the log out to the pile, and they always responded to his gentle, quiet commands. George looked so good out there with the team, pulling logs out, one at a time, on the end of a big heavy chain attached to the team's harness.

The use of the big horses in the woods for logging purposes is common in the Northwest; some contracts require that the trees can be cut, but no use of heavy equipment can be utilized. With grace and skill, the giants maneuver the logs to the loading area.

I headed back up the logging road to the white trailer. The smell of coffee filled the air. Jo welcomed me into the trailer with a big mug of hot java, smiling and saying, "Do you need some milk?" She came towards me from the ice chest carrying a large carton of milk, with a big smudge of chain saw grease on the side.

"George must've poured himself a glass of milk," she said casually.

She said, "Say when," and doused my hot cup of coffee with a big slug of milk. Grease from the bacon danced merrily above the tiny propane griddle. The bacon was almost done. On another little burner she had eggs frying, and in another, pancakes.

She was doing all this, and smoking a cigarette. I just sat there and watched her. The trailer was so small, there was no need to offer assistance. The best thing I could do was just stay sitting down and out of her way while she whipped up this incredible Montana logger breakfast. Delicious breakfast smells filled the trailer. The lightweight aluminum door with the holey screen flapped open, and outside the sun was getting higher in the sky, shining into the dark cedar forest.

George and Bulldog started up towards the trailer for

breakfast. The sun filtered through the thick cedars, and I could hear them talking. George was laughing.

Bulldog had worked with George and Jo on many horse logging jobs. They spent long hours at the Formica fold-down table in the trailer with a bottle of Jack Daniels and a deck of cards. Bulldog, true to his name, was straight faced and hard as steel until you got him to smile. He was built square as a tree trunk and was just as rough on the outside.

George was good looking, friendly at first glance, with his eyes shining mischieviously. The two of them together were quite a pair. It was obvious to me that Jo was just as pleased as she could be with the job she had of feeding these two in the morning. Bulldog was almost always there for breakfast.

"I heard you won the white mule by flipping six lucky quarter heads," he said to me seriously, not the mere hint of humor in his countenance. I was duped by Bulldog; he knew he had me in the palm of his hand. I looked at his ripped undershirt with the oil stain down the front.

"Yes I did," I answered, with pride in my voice. "We all three owned Sarah Jane together, and now that the trip is almost over, we couldn't exactly divide her up." A forerunner of a smile crossed his lips, but if I hadn't been looking right at his stubbled chin, I wouldn't have noticed. He had something up his sleeve.

"Well, you had better go down and check her out. I was just down there with the mules and horses in the pasture, to see how they were doing. The white mule has lost all sorts of hair, see, it's all in a big pile around her feet. She must have an awful high fever to be losing hair like that. I don't know what to tell you. I have never seen anything like it." He stopped, and tried to look pathetic.

With that, I decided to go down and have a look for myself. I slurped down the last of my now tepid coffee, and jumped in the front of Bulldog's big Chevy pickup. I needed climbing ropes to get up into that thing. It was lifted way up off the ground, on huge tires.

We headed down to check on poor Sarah in the meadow. She had only been all mine for twenty-four hours, and now she had a high fever and was losing hair. I couldn't believe it.

We pulled up into the meadow. Bulldog said, "She's over there," and started out towards her. I followed behind him, silently saying a prayer that Sarah's fever would break and she would be fine again.

As we got closer I could see her tail had changed considerably since I had last seen her in the evening twilight. It was cut into the shape of a Christmas tree, in perfect angles. Bulldog had taken the scissors to poor Sarah, leaving her with the sign of the kicking mule. Sarah's belled tail stayed that way until the next summer, and people and animals alike stayed clear of her rear end.

Bulldog taught me some things in the short time we spent in his company on the mountain. Everything was said in a very serious low voice, with a look of pure tomfoolery and mischief, as if life was to be taken lightly. This attitude seemed to be the tone of the life in the horse logging camp. Bulldog, George and Jo were happy there, buried deep in the old growth forest.

Every day, when those two men woke up, they knew their horses stood snortin' out in the corral, waiting patiently for a flake of alfalfa hay. Their huge hooves shifted around the small pen, crushing the earth beneath them. These were the gentle beasts of the plow and the wagon, the thresher and tiller, pulling logs out of the forest with heavy chains. Waiting for their breakfast, they looked like overgrown, expectant ponies, their soft eyes shaded by thick, blond eyelashes two inches long. They made my horse Cowboy look so small in comparison to their soft, round bodies, dappled with darker spots the color of honey, over their cream colored coats. I stood looking at them for a long time. Clouds of steam rose up into the air from their huge nostrils, the cold air freezing their breath almost to crystals.

## *Up the River and Down the Open Road*

It was time to leave the horse loggers and head west towards Idaho. We were only miles from the border, near Heron, and from there it was only another forty miles into Sandpoint, Idaho, around the blue crystal lake called Pend Oreille. Autumn hung to the air like a sweater. We all knew that the road was growing shorter, as were the days. It was cold at night, often down in the thirties.

We knew that Sandpoint was a big town, the biggest on our route since Missoula. We were savoring each day on the dirt road, crossing the hilly country on the banks of the swiftly flowing Clark Fork River. The apples dripped to the ground from ancient, overladen trees. We feasted on plums, the sweetness dripping down our faces, and sticking to our teeth. I could always make Deb laugh by blacking out a tooth with a piece of plum skin.

On the dirt road heading west, Debbie dropped her wallet somehow. She lost some money, but frankly, we both were so broke it didn't matter. We had at least enough cash for a cup of coffee and a dinner salad. We soon forgot about the wallet, and left it there, on the road somewhere, after Deb rode back a few miles to see if she could see it on the road. We all waited, napping in the sun by an old deserted cabin while she ran back on Sarah Jane. Not finding it, we headed on into Clark Fork, and found a ten-acre pasture and a good place to camp by the river. (Months later, the wallet was returned to her, back in Park City, and it still had the money in it.)

The sunset that night lit up the sky in purple, red and orange. We built a little campfire and cooked up some dinner, watching the last purple disappear from the western sky. The full moon was coming up. It was as if the moon had sailed close to earth; it was so huge, the color of polished ivory.

I ran down to the swift flowing river. The moon dashed brilliant light over the eddies and rapids. Huge eagles flew out to the slough, together, screaming to each other as they flew. The lights of the little burg of Clark Fork sparkled across the river. I listened closely, and could hear country music coming from the Out of

Bounds Bar.

Someone was burning brush in their back yard on the other side of the river. I sang out to the river, from the place I was sitting, with my legs hanging out over the water. Sitting down on the bridge, over the swift water, I sang out a beautiful song, and listened to the tone of the melody, the words and the tune, and found myself lost in another world, far from the campfire and dirty iron skillets.

Looking up at the wooded hills above the little town across the river, I could see the soft folds of the hills as they became canyons and mountains. Directly north was Canada, beyond the Yaak River Valley as the crow flies, no more than seventy miles. I sat there for more than two hours.

Deb and John and Gary had gone into town to the Broke and Hungry Cafe. I checked on the mules and horses in the pasture, grabbed my coat and headed across the bridge with sleek Robin at my side. I could feel the warmth of the wood stoves in the houses, as I passed silently and alone on the dirt road into town. Everyone had huge piles of firewood, and they would need every stick of it this winter.

I could see the neon "Bud" sign, and another "Beer" sign, flashing in the window of the Playhouse Bar. I went in, sat down on one of the seats at the bar and ordered a cup of coffee. Everyone in there took their turn at welcoming me, checking me out, asking me about the long journey from Utah. The next thing I knew, there was a cigarette puffing cowboy, looking at me from the corner of his eye, sitting on the stool next to me.

"You rode a green broke, pintailed, high strung nitwit cayuse Appaloosa all the way from Utah?" he shouted at me.

"Yes I did," I said.

"Well I'll be doggoned. How's yer behind?" A peal of laughter followed, as the cowboy spun around and fell off the stool.

I headed on out into the night to find my trail partners. They were over at the Broke and Hungry, sitting there drinking tea and writing postcards, settled in a booth as if it was theirs.

As I approached the table, I could smell the woodsmoke in their clothes and hair. It smelled strong and mixed with the smell of horses and fish bait. A ripe group we were, and only in the company of the characters of the towns did we ever realize how really smelly we were, and that as we travelled each slow mile, we were becoming more and more a part of the landscape around us. With the plum juice dripping down our faces, Montana red dirt on our cheeks and the dust of many a mile in our braids, we had been living in our own world on the trail; a different reality. Thoughts of the journey coming to an end made us feel sad, nostalgic for something we were sure to miss terribly: our free life on the open road.

Little did I know that Clark Fork would become my town, and I would buy a place eight miles back towards the Montana line. We had passed the most beautiful squared log house, in an opening just up from the river.

"I want to live here!" I yelled ahead to Deb, who had blazed the way past the cabin and on up the road.

"You do? Well, the people probably won't mind," she said cynically. We laughed. We had passed so many picture perfect homesteads in the region we had said that a hundred times. But this cabin must've been special, with its huge cottonwoods and pines, apple trees, and massive log barn. It was eight miles to Clark Fork, down river to the town of five bars and five churches. Northern Idaho made a lasting impression on me, and I returned to live there, on the shores of the Clark Fork, with Sarah Jane, Robin, and Cowboy the Appaloosa.

We said goodbye to Montana. Now we were riding in towards Sandpoint, right along Highway 200. We had literally been on dirt since Paradise, and the pavement was a reminder of the world awaiting each and every one of us.

Sandra Gingery showed up with a piping hot beef stew and an apple pie. We camped down next to one of the trailer parks on Lake Pend Oreille, and watched the sun disappear as we devoured a delicious dinner. They stayed awhile at the camp, and we had some laughs before they headed back to Montana.

As we rode into Sandpoint, in the railroad easement, along the shores of the deep blue Pend Oreille, we started to realize the days were getting shorter more rapidly than we were getting used to the idea of quitting this range rider life of ours.

"What do you think, Jod?" Deb asked me, as apple juice from an apple she had just picked while passing an old tree dribbled down her chin. "What do you think about getting there?" I knew as well as she did we would reach Spokane in about ten days.

"What will it be like to have a bathroom inside, and food in the fridge?" I asked her.

Ninety days is a long time to sleep under a blanket of stars. We had grown used to our rugged life in the great outdoors. The bathroom was the nearest bush. Our packs had dwindled down to practically nothing; we had only one pack animal now, since we could make better use of Sarah Jane as a riding mule for Deb. We had become accustomed to cooking our food on a campfire, and finding our fruit on the trees we passed. Our bodies were strong and we were tan as saddle leather.

"I wonder what married life will be like!" she said, and laughed.

"I'll tell you what I'm going to do," said Gary, with a grin on his face. "I'm going to have a big steak dinner. I'm about to go crazy just thinkin' about it." His knife was whittling away at a soft pine stick.

"I don't want it to end," said John to all of us. "We will never be able to go on this trip again. I'm going to miss you, Jod." He wiped a tear away with his hand. His red curls were shining in the late day sun. He brightened. "But I can't wait to have free access to food again. And to eat spaghetti until I can't walk away from the table."

John had lived for ninety days on Jif and Home Pride Wheat bread and spaghetti. He could put away spaghetti like no one we had ever seen in our lives. At around four-thirty every day on the ride, I could swear he was going to faint from weakness. Debbie and I would come to his rescue with a peanut butter sandwich to revive him for the rest of the day, pulling him through until the evening grub was sizzling. His horse was much like him, even looked like him; he was very sweet, with no real bad habits. John loved Red, but had lost his favorite horse back in Tarpin Meadows, when we said goodbye to Chief.

John had on his only pair of cords. They were well worn, especially on the top of the legs. His down vest was dirty, and so was his plaid shirt. He was a great partner.

His girlfriend, Mary, had been scared when we got lost for two days. That was the end of it for her. I can still hear her crying that night up on top of the Divide, near Tin Cup Spring. John was used to being lost, confused as we called it. Mary was nice and quiet. She wore big round glasses that contrasted to the smallness of her whole face. Her hair was straight and black. She walked the hardest section of the mountains with us.

"Ha, we are only confused, not lost at all," we would say loudly.

"We like being lost," my sister said to Mary. "It is part of the whole Western experience." More laughter. We had gone away and forgotten our nail brushes and our town manners.

Debbie and I walked into Sandpoint from our pasture-camp on Boyer Road, settling into a booth at the Pastime Cafe. We shared an order of whole wheat toast and sipped our coffee.

The Pastime Sport Shop shared a door with the cafe; boot leather and wool smells combined with the aromas of bacon, hot cakes and sausage. Around a horseshoe counter sat the locals of Sandpoint.

The loggers, with their red "Logger's World" suspenders over plaid wool shirts, sat on one side of the counter.

On the other side, facing the loggers, sat the new pioneers, long-haired homesteaders from places called Rapid Lightening and Upper Pack River.

A see-through plastic pie case sat in the middle of the counter.

An old-timer tapped me on the shoulder and pointed to a ten foot tall cement statue of a jolly looking fisherman, proudly holding up an over-sized trout.

"That's Pend Oreille Pete," he told me proudly. "See that fish? That's the world's record Kamloop Rainbow Trout. It weighed an honest-to-goodness thirty-seven pounds and was more than forty inches long. It was caught right out here in Lake Pend Oreille on November 25, 1947!"

"That fish would feed us for two weeks," I said jokingly to Deb.

Logging trucks, bearing trees five feet in diameter cinched with heavy chains, crept through town, heading South and West with their precious loads.

After a day off in Sandpoint, we had our fill of free coffee refills, cars, and newspapers. We were out of the mountains now, and in the river foothills of the Selkirk Range. When it came time to leave Sandpoint, we were escorted out of town with the help of the local sheriff cars, to block the traffic. The animals' hooves on the long bridge echoed against the blue water far below. We would be to Priest River by nightfall.

We rode all day on a dirt road that follows the river. The river is very wide for about ten miles, as it leaves the lake and heads back for the high country. The huge yellow-leafed cottonwoods were giant flags of autumn, waving to us, silently, from the river's edge. The road was dirt most of the way, an old wagon road, now used mostly by locals who live out in the grassy meadows along the edge of the Pend Oreille River.

As we neared Priest River, great billows of white smoke rose from the mill across the river, and the sound of huge cranes, swinging, heavy with logs, squealed from the mountain tops. No longer were we in Cowboy country. This was chainsaw capital of the West. The whine of the saw as it zipped through the old growth is still etched upon my ear drums. This was the land of the checkered wool hat, the smell of oil and fuel, wood smoke and pine sap.

The woods were grand and mighty in the northern part of Idaho, and from the saddle, it looked to me like every tree would eventually be cut and made into plywood. Logging was the lifeblood of the Northcountry, as were the tourists that dotted the lake in the summer and the ski hill in the winter. The ones that came to see all the standing trees, glistening evergreen by the water's edge.

Newport, Washington

We arrived in the afternoon at four o'clock, and the locals agreed we would be happiest up at the fairgrounds, by the stock pens. We set up camp up there, and headed down to the Mint Cafe, in downtown Newport. The rain was just beginning. It started to pour down onto the street, and I could see people running for their motor home to get the windows up.

This waitress already looked like she was tired of us sitting in the Mint. We were damp and our wool smelled, mixed with the other smells of our life. I had three cups of coffee, a dinner salad with Thousand Island dressing, and about sixteen packages of saltines. The little cellophane wrappers were piled high upon the table, a monument to my ravenous appetite.

The woman in the next booth got up to move, and I wondered if it was because of Gary's huge Bowie knife she noticed, hanging down on the side of his left leg. She wanted to smoke a cigarette, and I watched her strain, placing her big, white, bulging arms perpendicular to the table to lift herself into a standing position. Her polyester shirt was shining in the florescent light. She shuffled away, her bedroom slippers scraping on the linoleum floor of the Mint.

We were able to stay dry and out of the storm in the Mint, which felt like the only place to go in Newport.

It was hunting season and the town was full of men in big pickups with four or five weapons on the gun rack. They were eating huge "Hunter Special" breakfasts on heavy white porcelain plates, and I tried not to stare. The deer must find them ridiculous, the way they dress for the hunt. The ones from out of the area showed up the most. They joked with us about packing out their meat for them.

The waitress was stocky and white. Her straight blonde hair hung limply in her eyes, and she shook her head as she approached us, looking at Gary, and then down at my notebook.

"Writing a book?" she asked, and laughed.

Someone called her from the bar door, which is attached to the cafe. "Hey Kelly, pick up the phone. It's your boyfriend."

She excused herself and ran for the counter. She pulled out a cigarette and lit it, while holding the receiver with her chin. She took a long hard drag of it, and put her fingers to her head, still holding the cigarette. She looked like she was smoking from her forehead. She started to shake her head and I overheard her say, "Don't bring Richard down here with you."

The next person to walk in the door was her boyfriend. She started visually shaking when she heard the bell ring on the greasy glass door, and looked up and saw him, all three hundred pounds of dirty biker man. His black leather vest looked like doll clothes on his massive, hairy frame. The figure of a sad Mermaid peaked through the black hair on his chest. Behind him stood, I assumed, Richard, skinny and white-haired, with a burning cigarette hanging from his mouth. He squeezed through two swinging counter seats, the plastic upholstery squeaking beneath him.

He yelled, "Coffee, now!" and slammed his white porcelain cup on its saucer. She never made eye contact with him. Her "Love" tattoo stood out, black and red on her pale, anemic skin. She served both men a cup of black coffee, and walked away.

I was watching the giant brute as he intentionally spilled his shallow cup all over the grey Formica counter. He smiled up at her with his toothless grin. Yellow stubs, his remaining teeth, showed up for a second, and I shivered.

The storm was brewing outside, and just then the rain started pouring down; sheets of it, faster and harder with each passing second. She cleaned up the coffee with a spaghetti sauce stained terry towel, and he clutched her tiny wrist with his huge hairy hand and held it still, tightly, until she dropped the dirty bar rag. I could see the fear in her face, hidden behind years of rugged survival.

I stood up and started to approach them, just as he let go of her hand and she walked away, quietly and rapidly, and disappeared into the back room. Richard threw back his ugly head and let out a loud, obnoxious sound, like a moose in rut. Smoke seeped from what looked like his whole face, and his ugly laugh filled the room. I looked away. I didn't want to have these people's faces in my mind when I went to sleep.

We read the paper. We drank more of the watery, brown coffee. We watched as Richard and the big boyfriend left the Mint, starting up their bikes and leaving them running in front of the cafe for a good ten minutes, before climbing on and accelerating. The hours passed. It kept raining. Every time I looked at the clock it was an hour later.

Soon darkness came, and the shift changed. The new waitresses were the senior ones, with many years of waitressing behind them. They smoked and drank coffee, and served the meat loaf and mashed potato special to the local old-timers.

I ordered another dinner salad with a basket full of saltines. Hopefully John would show up soon and order spaghetti like he always did. This would allow me more time in the Mint. The storm, the first one of the winter, poured buckets of rain on the earth.

The mules and horses stood, sleeping, with their heads lowered almost to the ground, and their backs to the wind. I knew the wind was icy cold, and I could tell it was cold outside by the breath I could see when a new person entered the Mint. Winter was coming. People came and went; coming from cutting firewood or shooting a deer, they would enter the Mint and report to the old waitresses as if they were their own family. In some cases, I'm sure they were.

The Mint was the only dry place to go. Debbie, Gary and John came and went. I stayed twelve hours, without ever leaving my booth, except to use the restroom.

That next morning, when we packed up and rode out of Newport, we knew the end was upon us. It was hitting twenty degrees in the evenings. The smell of woodsmoke in the valley made us think of the comfort of a home, some home, somewhere. The long summer days of July in Wyoming were way behind us now. I looked back behind me, as we rode out of Newport, and could see the fresh snow that dusted the mountains towards Canada.

B. Shield
©1994

## Short Days and Hard Goodbyes

We headed south, once we made it out of Newport. The storm had left the hills powdery white. The animals kept a good pace. After almost ninety days on the trail, we were all in excellent walking condition.

I could feel the heat coming from Cowboy's nostrils as his breath turned into white clouds of steam. Sarah and Annie were very energetic, as were the horses. I think they knew the end of the road was near. They sensed our anticipation and anguish.

In a week, we would be split up. No longer would we be waking to the smell of the coffee on the fire built by the early riser; looking at each other and smiling, having discovered that the silence of the moment said it all. There were really no words for the golden cottonwoods, the stillness and azure blue of the river, or what it was like to sleep for three months with the heavens as the ceiling of our bedroom.

I rode along in silence, listening to the soft, quiet sound of the hooves on the road. The road from Newport to Spokane was dirt all the way, and wound its way through the meadows, white pine forests and blackberry bushes, taking us through some old stage stops, ghost towns, and by some incredible century-old structures. Still standing since the early days, they remain memorials to the days of the crosscut saw, before the log boom and hauling trucks; back when the trees were substantial and ancient.

I looked back behind me and took one last look at the Selkirks. They were getting further behind us now, and the city of Spokane stained the sky to our south. The farmers were burning the wheat stubble, so the sky was a hazy orange.

We were expected to be at the Lariat Inn, north of town, the next day at three or four. We knew the disc jockey and a news team from the radio station would be there, and maybe a few of my friends from school.

We were riding and walking silently and slowly away from our life on the trail and back to our old lives.

"Just think, Jod," Deb said when we stopped at an old apple tree near Chatteroy, "just think how it would be if we just kept on going. Bear the storms, and keep travelling down through Oregon and Nevada, making it to Arizona by January."

"Deb, you are married, remember?" I reminded her. "Your eager young husband awaits your return." We both laughed.

Like a new swing, we'd had a creaky start, and now the rope that held us together as a band of gypsies was soft and well worn. We had grown to love each other, all of us, even Gary. He had brought many a grouse and sage hen to our campfire, and we found him to be a great partner.

Little Black Beauty, his tiny Lab puppy, was shiny and healthy and was no worse for wear. Neither was my Robin. She was so beautiful, her bright gold stripes drifting across her dark brown coat.

We all knew in our hearts that we would deeply miss life on the road and the slow pace we kept. To ride in a car had become strange to us; I found myself bracing my feet on the floor as if it were one large brake. The speed was frightening at first; I had become so used to seeing every bush I passed, it was difficult to focus on anything from a car window.

I rode down the road, sad and scared. I kept reaching down, giving Cowboy a loving pat on his furry neck. It made me feel safe.

I had grown to love the view from my saddle. I could make sandwiches by simply turning around in the saddle, pulling the materials out of my saddle bags, getting my Swiss Army knife out of my pocket and making lunch — all on Cowboy's delightfully wide rear end.

Robin always kept her third eye on Cowboy; it was in the back of her shiny brown head. She could always see where his dappled feet were landing on the earth and she was always well away from them. Yet they seemed to be walking side by side, peacefully.

This is where I stood. A beautiful white mule from Utah, Cowboy the young gelding, and the best friend of a dog I could've asked for. I was on my own — twenty-two, broke, and at the end of the dream. As we neared Spokane I knew that this three months had changed my future forever.

We were all walking, silent now. We knew they were waiting

for us in Spokane. KGA would be awarding me with the other half of the five hundred they sponsored. In our saddle bags, we carried apples and large vegetables from the gardens of the friends we had made. We carried rolls of film, captured smiles and campfires. We had our journals, and our memories of a long time ago, when we left Park City. It seemed as if it was behind us by years and thousands of miles.

I would miss Debbie, John and Gary, Annie the Mule, and Red. I would miss all of them. My life had become the journey, and I needed to continue on. This I knew. I was three hundred dollars in debt, imagine! It was as if I owed the King of Spain the weight of his kingdom in gold.

We were range riders. We were the sweethearts of the Great Wide Open, all the way from far away Utah. Our friends would look into our faces, asking us, "What was it like?"

It was midafternoon when we saw it, shining flashing neon out in front of the Lariat Inn, north of Spokane. We looked knowingly at each other as we walked, and Gary said, "Thank y'all."

A man with a portable microphone jumped out in front of us. We saw the television cameras, rolling out in front of the entourage.

He said to my sister, smiling, "So how do you feel about arriving in Spokane after twelve hundred miles?"

She answered right into the camera and said, "Broke."

We had waited a long time for this moment, and I found myself wishing the horses and mules would switch into reverse. Nature had been getting the best of us the last few days. And yet I still wanted to go back. Tears poured down my cheeks onto my shirt. Goodbye to our carefree life, picking fruit off the trees. Goodbye!

We tied up our animals to the huge metal sign out in front of the Lariat. Inside, though we couldn't see them through the tinted window, stood my grandmother, my mom and my dad, watching us. We pulled the heavy door open and filed in, into the arms of Mom and Dad and Grandma.

Behind them stood my English professor from Whitworth, Phil Eaton, and three of my friends from school. John Hawkley stood smiling at me, his smile lines accenting his spirit, long blond braids tied with leather hanging down on his dark blue Levi shirt; it was good to see him. Randy Starr and Markas Sloan were there too. I couldn't really concentrate; it was as if I was seeing all these people in a dream.

Mom came running toward me, arms outstretched; she hugged me and I jammed her glasses and they fell to the floor. She wore a blue and gold scarf around her neck, and a gold sweater with a blue Levi skirt. As always, her hair was very short, cut close around her ears, and shiny black. I'm sure we smelled like campfire smoke and horses.

The head of the KGA program was there with the check, and we laughed and couldn't believe Mom and Dad had come all the way from Southern California with Grandma, to get there. We were proud they were our parents. We ordered pizzas and jojos and draft beer. I didn't know what to say to everybody. It felt strange to be inside.

I went outside and stood in front of my horse, facing him. He was sleeping, standing there with his head down low. Red and Annie and Sarah were sleeping too.

We put the animals in a pasture near the campus, and went downtown to the Holiday Inn. The magic of trail disappeared as we stepped up into my father's van, and drove to the motel.

We fumbled about in the white rooms. We looked at ourselves in the clean mirror in the white bathroom under the florescent lights. Our faces were tan and we were both strong and lean. The boys had a separate room; Mom and Dad and Grandma stayed in one.

We drank champagne and ate dinner at a fancy restaurant. Mom and Dad were spoiling us. Our stomachs had shrunk and we were not used to having all this food laid out in front of us. It was John Najar's dream.

After a day of this, we had eaten all we wanted to eat, cleaned up, spread out on the bed, and told a few stories of the trail.

"Don't you think you'd better sell the animals so you can finish school?" Mom asked me.

"Oh no, Mom," I said quietly, "they are with me from now on." She seemed to understand.

I stood there, quietly, and the tears rolled down my cheeks as the truck and trailer disappeared down Division Street in Spokane. Deb's husband, John, borrowed a horse trailer from some friends in Park City and had driven fourteen hours to get there. Our lives were changing faster than we were used to. This parting was hard.

Debbie and I realized that we were, in many ways, the mirror of each other's memories. Things I had forgotten, she would tell a story about. I would remind her of long-ago times. Certain smells would transport us both to a long time before, when we were seven and nine. Deb was off to her new life in the large suburban home in a new subdivision, facing the ski hill at Park City. She would get pregnant that winter, when the snow buried them for weeks on end and they were without a car.

We were sisters, eating apples leisurely from apple trees in abandoned orchards, late in the fall. Once again we would be living states apart. I would miss her.

John Najar was heading back to Park City, to get back to the ski repair shop on the ski hill. He had his horse, Red, and Annie the mule. He had won the second place when we flipped for ownership of the mules, and he was the proud owner of Cadillac Annie, the little mule with the flatulence problem. Also, Red, slow and sure, had gone the distance, and needed a ride back to Utah as well. Gary had Beauty, his sleek black puppy, who had gleefully traced our steps all the way from West Yellowstone, without a yelp of disagreement.

Beauty had a short life. She was killed by a car her first day in Salt Lake. Annie was stolen, from a pasture in Midway, Utah, the second night they were back in Utah. She was gone and not to be found for over a year.

Our adventure had started in a parade in Utah and ended in a brick city called Spokane. The bright yellow and red leaves of the maple and elm trees blanketed the streets, softening the pavement. I had almost forgotten about the pavement. I had viewed the world from hill to hill, water hole to water hole, counting the days by the moon and the last cafe.

I turned and walked up to the corral where Cowboy and Sarah were staying. A neighbor let me keep them there for a week or so, until I could figure out where to go from there.

I climbed up and sat on the fence, and watched the Appaloosa, with his long, honey-colored coat, shimmering in the late autumn sunset and the mule following close behind him, her big white head up in the air. They both cried out their perfect cries. The trailer with their two friends in it had disappeared from view. They would never see Red or Annie again. I sat silently on the fence for a long time, as they ran back and forth along the fence line, spinning at the end, back up on their haunches, gathering speed.

## POEM FOR COWBOY

*He stops and looks around.*
*Brown spotted pony of my youth.*
*He's wild on the hoof and gentle in the hand:*
*Lightly, he dances, his feet land, he's off again.*
*When this snow melts off the mountains,*
*We'll pack up and go off in the woods of Idaho.*
*With a sack of onions and potatoes,*
*We'll head out for the quietest place I know.*
*With the brown Appaloosa and the whitest of mules,*
*Up to the aspen and pine,*
*Far, so far away*
*From the grey city grind.*
       *Jody/Spokane/ 1976*

## *North! To Alaska*

I stayed long enough around Whitworth that Fall to make a genuine nuisance of myself, distracting my friends from their studies with stories of the Great Wide Open, while the horse and mule cropped the greenery around the campus to maximum shortness. I rode Cowboy aimlessly around the suburbs with Sarah in tow, looking for lawns that needed trimming.

I would tie up my horse in front of the local supermarket and go in for a look around. I had nothing to barter with. I became more confused as the days passed. With the chicken coop occupied and no money in my pocket or ample pasture for my horse and mule, I decided to take my friend, Josefa, up on her offer.

"There's a fortune to be made up here, Jod," she had said of Alaska. "I can get you a job at Chilkoot Charlie's anytime you want. And you can live with me."

I called Dad. He agreed to send me money for my ticket to Anchorage. Scott Wilson, a student at Whitworth, called his parents to see if they would watch Cowboy and Sarah for me while I was gone. They had eighty acres of fenced ground with two springs and plenty of pasture, twelve miles from Lapwai, near the Nez Perce Reservation. It overlooked the great, winding Snake River and the golden wheat country of the Palouse. Scott's parents were very kind people, and that winter had to haul water to Cowboy and Sarah when the creeks froze. Of course, Robin would go to Alaska with me.

We flew to Anchorage, but not together. Robin was required to sit in a carrying case in the baggage compartment, which she never got used to. We arrived in the tiny Anchorage airport, were reunited in baggage claim, and I freed Robin from her box and together we waited for Jo.

"Jod, Jod!" she screamed as she came running up in a fur hat, mittens, and parka. I couldn't miss her. She ran up and hugged me, stooping down to pet Rob. "Come on, you have to work tonight."

I felt sick instantly. My stomach remained in a knot for the next seven months, while the Appaloosa and his white mule grazed peacefully in Idaho, overlooking the meandering Snake River.

We raced along Northern Lights Boulevard. Josefa barely touched the brakes the whole ride, to avoid slipping off the road in a tailspin on the ice. I saw the log cabin bar on the right, half buried in snow, smoke pouring from the chimney.

"That's Chilkoot Charlie's!" Josefa yelled in my ear with great enthusiasm as she glided to a stop in the parking lot, packed with muddy trucks with massive tires and equally as dirty smaller vehicles of all sorts, covered with brown muddy snow. "I better take you home first. You look tired. I'll make you some coffee! Coffee will help! And we'll need to get Robin settled in. She'll love our Labrador!" Jo was always enthusiastic.

It was only two in the afternoon and already twilight had come to Anchorage. We pulled up slowly in front of a small suburban home on a side street in this overgrown boomtown. We were there, all of us, to claim our stake in the last of the Great Alaska Pipeline Boom. We were late, in fact we were there four years after the most of it, but Alaska would continue to feel the impact forever.

I may as well have come with a pick and shovel. I was an emigrant from The Lower Forty-Eight, and I'd come looking for pay dirt. This suburban bunkhouse where I would bed down certainly came with more than just my good friend Josefa. Jo had been living with Harlow for the last seven months. Harlow was a towering, black-haired bartender from Boston who looked like he had broken his nose a few times. The two Labradors sniffed each other and became friends almost instantly, as dogs will, but Harlow and I would never warm up to each other.

Josefa and I had met in the bathroom of Hertz Rent a Car in Los Angeles International Airport.

"Do you act?" she asked me, grabbing blonde curls in her perm comb, fluffing her brilliant curly mane in front of the mirror. Before I could answer, she added, "I do!"

We worked together on the graveyard shift at Hertz, renting cars to anyone with a credit card who travelled in the night.

Josefa was in L.A. to become a movie star. She had been successful in some college productions in Cincinnati, and had been attending various auditions, or "cattle calls" as they call them in

Hollywood. Until she was discovered, she would keep her job at Hertz Rent a Car at Los Angeles International Airport. She was a favorite there at Hertz. A good worker and extremely blonde, she wore sheer nylons and short, bright yellow polyester skirts, and was clearly the only woman who looked good in the uniform.

I was fired from Hertz after the police caught up with Ollie May Pleasure in a Pinto, somewhere in the hills by Santa Barbara. I had rented her a car in the middle of the shift, sometime around three in the morning. She had walked all the way from the lock-up ward at General Hospital to the airport and rented a car from me, with a stolen credit card she had reportedly hidden away in her Bible at the hospital. She had escaped and was not going to get caught, and gave the police quite a chase in the little Pinto before she crashed it into a rock wall outside Santa Barbara. Although Ollie May was not hurt, the Pinto was totalled, and I had to go. It was company policy.

I walked outside and removed my little black cloth flats with the embroidery on the toes. They had told me to replace them with something more suitable weeks before. I screamed into the smoggy morning with gusto.

"Yee Ha! I'm outta here!" I called out to the heavens. I left for the Northwest again, shortly after that, leaving the little black shoes in a box with the bright yellow polyester uniform, buried deep in my mom and dad's garage.

Connie was the other person living in this house in Anchorage, up from Ohio to make some money. She was tall, dressed well, and worked as an officer in a local bank, a good job in Anchorage. She wouldn't be caught dead waitressing. After living together for two months in absolute tension with Harlow, Jo and the two dogs, Connie and I grew to dislike each other more than we would have ever dreamed when we first met.

Meanwhile, the two dogs slept next to each other, padded around the white carpet with muddy feet, and waited for us to come home. It was not what you would call a dog's life. They chased snow balls out front in the quiet road, sliding on their haunches on the ice, trying to stop before sliding into the cars parked on each side of the street.

I threw them a few snowballs; it cheered me up. I thought

about Cowboy and Sarah, standing on the bluff above the river in Idaho. I was so used to sharing my days with Cowboy and the gentle Sarah. I was already missing them terribly.

"I bet there isn't one white mule in this whole town," I said to Robin as I threw another snowball. It took her several tries to get moving in the right direction. The road was solid ice, iceberg blue. Jo came out to the street.

"Better get ready to go down there, Jod. A real she-wolf named Grace just quit yesterday after a guy tried to grab her! She's was due on at five."

"What should I wear, Jo?" I asked her. I was faking my enthusiasm. I was scared to death, and Jo knew it.

"Just jeans and a nice shirt. Anything goes. You'll have to join the wet T-shirt contest some night!" she teased me.

I laughed. "Over my dead body," I answered.

We drove down to Chilkoot Charlie's in the pitch blackness of five o' clock in the afternoon. People with day jobs were on their way home after a long day of work. It was a Friday night, and the energy was fast moving and frenetic at five o'clock Anchorage time. The city seemed to be fueled on the hope of making the big buck, beer, margaritas, whatever you wanted. This was my first impression.

The ravens, the biggest ones I had ever seen in my life, hovered around downtown, perching on telephone poles. They flew up the main street of downtown, beating the icy wind with massive black wings. They were there to watch over the Indians who were unfortunate enough to have ended up drunk on Fourth Street. The ravens seemed to keep watch over these Native Alaskans downtown.

We entered the dark entry way of the bar. Jo led the way. I could feel my heart beating hard and fast, and longed for my old life on the  trail.

Inside, I couldn't believe my eyes. There were men of all sizes and shapes, every one sporting a Buck Knife, holding cue sticks and bottles of beer, stuffing peanuts into their faces, throwing the shells on the floor, at least those that didn't stick in their beards; betting over dart games, and weaving in front of three noisy pin ball machines in the back by the bathroom.  Rock music I didn't recognize was about three notches too high.

There was Harlow, behind the bar, straining over the counter to get closer to a barmaid to hear her order. The waitress was up on her tiptoes, leaning forward, and her Levi skirt barely covered her underwear, while several big logger boys watched her from behind with interest. She balanced a round cork tray over her head, spinning around with an order of two pitchers, two margaritas, three Buds, and a basket of the free peanuts she had scooped out of the big box next to the ordering station. She was queen of the upper half of the bar, spinning around with this tray as if it was permanently attached to her hand. She looked serious; worn and peaked under the dim light.

"Jod, meet Jay!"

"Hi Jay," I said. "How do you keep from dumping the drinks?"

They both laughed. "You'll catch on," Jay said, looking at Jo.

I could feel the eyes of a real variety pack of men staring at us momentarily, before they went back to what they were doing when we entered the bar.

There were large, bulky, beer-drinking men in flannel shirts, with long beards and long hair, in every inch of the log cabin bar. There were short, stocky bikers in black leather, tattoos on shiny biceps. The pool cue was used to accentuate the bikers' bulbous muscles. There were tall, lanky, shabby, good-looking, rough men all of all sizes and shapes; too many to mention or remember.

And there were the girls in the bar, "barflies" as some were referred to. They were smoking, blowing the smoke into the air as it circled around their heads. The smoke was slow moving, curling above the drinkers, and spreading out among fifteen tables, all of which were in my area. I tried to breathe deeply, and decided to wait until after my shift.

The band started in. The first three hours were light rock and folk. Two guys had come down from the wilderness to play at Chilkoot's. They looked like the Furry Freak Brothers, and someone told me they planned to compete in the "Last Great Race" — the Alaskan Iditarod, racing sled dogs from Anchorage to Nome.

I cruised the room with Jo. "Just walk around in a circle, Jod, first around the dance floor, then into this room." I stumbled on the ramp leading down into the room next to the dance floor, following her like a toddler.

"Hey Jo, who's your friend?" some young man yelled to her from a table next to the waitress station. He was sipping on a cup of coffee. They called him Coffee Dan.

"You be sweet to her, okay, Dan?" she said to him and winked. She grabbed my hand and led me into the other room of the bar. There were people sipping cold ones everywhere. "Just ask them if they want another," she continued. "You can't write any of this down, Jod, it's a matter of survival. The place gets so packed around midnight, until about three-thirty on the weekends, that the best you can do is remember the orders in your head. Walk up to the bartender, and tell him what you want. First the pitchers, then the shots, the well drinks, the calls and the blenders."

I interrupted her. "The wells? The calls? What are the wells and calls? I don't know what that means, Jo!" Tension gripped my voice.

"You don't know your booze, Jod? You're kidding!" I had spent very little time in bars, and hated the taste of liquor. She laughed and said. "Look, I gotta go. Good luck. Now I'll see you later," and she was gone, a flash of platinum, heading energetically into the opaque smoke of the upper bar. She was off to fight her own service war. I was on my own.

I learned how to be a cocktail waitress in a hurry. I had no choice. I walked, aware of myself, from table to table and started delivering orders. Before long, I could balance seven drinks and six beers on the round cork tray without spilling. Still, the tray was always covered with a little pool of booze, a little bit of every order I had served. The tray was lined with wet dimes and quarters, stuck to the cork, fully submersed in a mixture of alcohol and soft drinks.

At around two in the morning, at the height of a raunchy second set, the band was in a guitar solo frenzy. People had been sitting there since five o'clock and were pretty wound up. Through the light rock and folk hours, and on to the rock 'n roll blast of the Eddie Color Band, they were rocking pretty heavy and I had delivered hundreds of drinks and pitchers.

"Hey, baby, where you come from?" I was asked by a giant mountain man. I was eye level with his belt buckle, straining my neck to see his face.

"Spokane, Washington," I answered. I had only lived in Washington for two and a half years, but California was a dirty word in the Northwest. Washington translated though. Most people in Alaska knew where Washington state was.

Just then, as I looked into the red, white and blue eyes of this giant hairy hunk, a tiny woman, with a bra-like lace top — the only thing containing her giant breasts, ran into the front of my tray as somebody bumped me from behind. As the band reached a barely tolerable crescendo, the dancers swerved recklessly around the dance floor, and the entire floor of the log cabin bar was bouncing up and down. I felt seasick, as if I was in a huge boat, serving drunken sailors.

I could not do anything that moment but stare at this woman's breasts as they were hit by the pitcher of beer, which cascaded down to the floor like water over a dam. The pitcher fell to its side on my round cork tray and emptied into this woman's memorable cleavage. The lace top had disappeared from view and I realized the flood of beer had taken her top with it. She recovered it faster than I could have, and looked at me, from under prohibitive black eye liner.

"Good move! Thanks a lot!" she yelled. The cigarette she had been holding up out of the way of the beer was sizzling, ruined. She watched it wither and start to break, threw it down, stomped on it and walked away, flipping her thin white arms, trying to shake the beer off. Her boyfriend had run for a towel — it would be a good ten minutes before he would make it back through the crowd. She stood there, dripping from the neck down, in a puddle of beer. It soaked into the peanut shells around her feet. I moved on into the crowd, and was surrounded by a smelly hoard of drunks at waist level.

"Michelob! Three screwdrivers, three tequilas and three limes! Six glasses! Two pitchers!" they screamed.

"Can I have change for this hundred?" a quiet man, sitting alone against seven other people, said to me.

"Sure," I said with confidence.

"First night?" he asked.

"Yeah. Can you tell?"

"Yes, I can," he answered. "Now don't make any stops."

"Okay," I said to him, holding a now empty tray with a twenty and his hundred dollar bill between my fingers. I thought he had said "and bring me a pop."

I had to push my way, steadily and firmly, towards the bartender in the little box. I held the hundred dollar bill between my fingers. By the time I got to the waitress station, I had another ten drinks to order. People would grab my arm and scream "Michelob!" in my face, as if they were yelling for their lives.

I looked down in my hand as I started to tell Jeff, the bartender, my order at the bar, and realized right away I had given that hundred dollar bill to another man, mistaking it for a one. I looked over just as this lucky fellow raced for the door, the bottom of his boot was all I saw of him. I was forty dollars in debt to the bar at the end of the night.

"What's a girl like you doing in a place like this?" the bartender had asked me, as I stood there, trying to remember what people had ordered. Was it two Michelobs, or was it "in a minute?" I could think of nothing else, and drink orders spun around in my head like a washing machine on spin cycle.

I caught a ride home with Jo, at five-thirty in the morning. The first rays of the very early morning spilled across the mountains directly behind the city. I yearned for sleep. The sled dogs were training for the Iditarod on a race track close to the bar, and we often stopped to watch them on our way home; their piercing squeals of delight ricocheted off the tall, snowy peaks.

I slept like a lamb, exhausted, with Robin by my side in my tiny bedroom. I had only been off the trail for a few weeks, and in the middle of sleep, I would awake and search the ceiling of the white sheetrocked room for stars, wondering to myself when the cloud cover had come in, before realizing that I was inside, no longer sleeping out under the stars.

I stroked my dog's silky brown head and told her, "Robin, this won't be forever. We'll go back to Cowboy and Sarah in the spring." I couldn't wait to see the horse and mule again. Every day I thought about them, running free in the deep yellow grass, together. I missed them every day I was up there in Alaska. But I was there for the gold, and I had to remember that. I owed my saddle partner, John, three hundred dollars.

When I woke up that following afternoon at two-thirty in the afternoon, it was already getting dark again.

This schedule continued. I would come home in the morning, closing the bar down at five-thirty, and then, sleeping from eight in the morning to the early afternoon, I missed the only few hours of midday light. Anchorage was dark much of the day in the winter.

"I wonder why I feel so tired and run down," I said to Josefa.

"Think about it, Jod! You probably haven't see the sun for three weeks!" Josefa said to me, as she guzzled down a big tall glass of milk.

Every night was wild and chaotic, the waitresses sober and serious in a sea of alcoholic confusion. I worked very hard at cocktail waitressing, and every time anyone ever gave me a tip or bought me a drink, I would save the money, walking my suitcase of bills to the bank every Monday, my suitcase full of hard-earned tips.

My friend Marilyn was looking for a way out of her boyfriend troubles, and thought she wouldn't mind making a little money, too, if she could. Always, Marilyn and I together had meant some serious trouble, and this held true in Alaska, as it always had every other place we'd been together.

She called during a rare time when all of us, all the roommates, were cooking something, their very own something, under the unrelenting florescent lights in the tiny white kitchen.

"Hey, Jod! I'm coming up tomorrow. Meet me at the Anchorage airport at six p.m." Marilyn never wasted words.

"Great, I'll borrow Jo's car, and come on out." I said enthusiastically. "See you tomorrow!"

I loved Marilyn. We needed another waitress at Chilkoot's and she needed to get away from her boyfriend and think things out. You know, relaxing in the quiet, peaceful North Country. Little did she know what Chilkoot Charlie's would be like. She had never been to Alaska, never seen the log cabin bar where I was panning for gold and finding it. Tips were real good. I had cut Marilyn in on the claim.

I saw her instantly, looking for her pack in the baggage area. Amazingly, she had shorts on. She was very tan, her figure slim as it had always been. Aside from the laugh lines around her eyes and smile, she looked seventeen. A huge Mexican basket hung around her neck. It was time for a change, and she chose a real cold one: Alaska in January. It was minus ten degrees.

"You're so white!" she screamed when she saw me.

"You're so tan!" I responded, true to my Southern California roots, if just for a fleeting second. This is a very cherished greeting in Southern California, "You're so tan."

When she walked out of the airport in her thongs, with the rayon Hawaiian print culottes flapping in a wind with a minus thirty degree chill factor, California disappeared from her face. I watched her as she first set eyes on her new world. To me, it was lots of snowy slush, huge mountain men and a little log cabin bar. So far, that was all I had seen of Alaska. The rest of the time I was sleeping in my little white room in the little white house, or walking Robin down to the bank with my tips in the suitcase.

"Oh, Marilyn, get ready for craziness. Are you ready to waitress?" I yelled to her as we closed our eyes against the freezing wind and ran for Jo's car in the parking lot.

"Right now?" She couldn't believe that she was going to be working that night.

"At seven. They'll love you down there, Mare."

So we went to work. After stopping by the house and dropping off her things, we headed for Chilkoot's. Marilyn didn't take any trouble from anybody. She was little, tough, and every man that ever saw her was intrigued by her in a matter of seconds.

When we hitchhiked all over Europe together in the spring of 1973, she had a man on her trail from every country through which we passed, with our thumbs out and "Jesus Lives" stickers on our backpacks. Before that, we had cheered our football players on to victory on the playing fields of La Cañada. The referees would often call a foul, looking up and pointing at Marilyn, who had just yelled something unacceptable in a raspy voice only a cheerleader could muster.

And now I saw her, standing face to face with the tall blond bartender from Oregon, telling him her order. "Four Michelobs, two pitchers, six shots of tequila and a Kahlua and cream." She was a natural.

The night began. I worked one room. She was up in the long bar area. She seemed to be doing okay, and every man in the place was curious about where she had come from; she attracted men like horses attract flies.

At around five o' clock in the morning, only a few really toasted drunks were still standing. Every one else had left. We were picking up ash trays.

That particularly irritating drunk from Oklahoma. Wasn't he a bear to deal with? We both agreed. He had come up to me, swollen red and slobbering and asked me if I wanted to make some extra money after closing time. I turned on my heels and walked away as fast as I could make it through the crowd. He had proposed to Marilyn, bought her a drink, and bragged about the merits of life in Oklahoma for ten minutes straight.

"Oh, if he was here now, I'd break his little neck," Marilyn said as she rubbed her eyes tiredly. She said this to everybody, all the bartenders and waitresses. "Is it like this every night, Jod?"

"Yep. How much did you make? Did you count your tips?" I asked.

"Yeah, I only lost forty dollars. Gave some guy a twenty for a one," she admitted sheepishly.

We walked back into the narrow hallway to the bathroom, beyond the pool tables and pin ball machines. Looking down at the huge steel door, about three feet further, I shuddered. I went into the bathroom with Marilyn, and looked at myself in the tiny steel plate that served as a mirror. I looked oblong and white, like an out of sorts ghost. A certain wily look came to my face as my hand ran across the hundred-plus tips in the pocket of my apron. I smiled into the mirror. I thought about my horse and Sarah. I wondered how they were.

"Let's go clean up," I said to her. She flushed and we walked out as the little wooden door slammed shut loudly behind us.

We walked out into the narrow hall and I grabbed her arm suddenly, as a shiver of fear ran down my back, as if someone was behind me, or the shadow of someone.

"Come on!" I said to her forcefully and led her out of the hallway by her arm. I heard a loud crack behind me, the sound of a gun exploding. The bearded man in the flannel shirt next to us fell to the ground, as the buckshot came blasting into the room from behind us. The two men at the pin ball machines yelled, and Marilyn and I were looking down the barrels of about twenty handguns; every bartender had produced one from under the bar, and everyone left in the bar seemed to have one as well. We froze. I looked out the front door as the door swung open and more people from outside rushed in, and I thought I saw Sarah Jane out in front in the parking lot, her white coat reflecting in the street lights, waiting to take me away, back to the safety of the trail.

I felt a burning sensation on my forehead, pulled out a hunk of hair, and the pain disappeared along with the vision of the angel mule. I had been grazed by the buckshot. I looked at Marilyn. She looked petrified, and angry. It seemed like minutes before anyone moved.

"Welcome to Alaska, Mare," I whispered under my breath.

Later on, the police caught up with the drunk man with a big deer gun, staggering home to his apartment, as the beauty of the white Chugach Range glowed a soft pink, and the day workers started to rise for work.

After we all had lived in the house two weeks longer, with Marilyn refusing to pay for one-fifth of all the meat Harlow was buying, Connie showed up in a frenzy at Chilkoot's in the middle of the shift. It was packed. I had orders for twenty pitchers, twenty shots, twenty wells and calls, and I was sinking fast.

"Jody!" she screamed, walking towards me with exaggerated steps, and then stopping two inches away from me, almost knocking me over with the chilly wind that circled around her from the outside. I could barely see her through the smoke. She smelled like cigarettes and tequila.

She squinted at me and screamed, "I just vacuumed up Marilyn's underwear. She left it on the floor, and now my vacuum is broken. She has got to go! I am sick of cleaning up after you both, your dog jumped up on my silk blouse, the mud is permanently ruining the carpet! Get out! Find another place! I've had it!"

She stomped out, straight across the dance floor and slammed the big wooden door as she went out. Everyone looked at me with different looks, laughed and went back to drinking. I was the color of the red salmon in spawn, and could feel the heat of my face.

There was this fellow in the bar named Michael who seemed harmless enough. He told me that Marilyn and I and Robin could move in with him in his big house in downtown Anchorage. With the giant skyscrapers, built of pipeline gold, dwarfing this house on the railroad tracks, the old three-story house felt like a lone survivor of an older Anchorage. It sat quietly awaiting its fate; the boom would soon come and a parking facility would be built there, overlooking the great expanse of the Cook Inlet, alive with huge shipping liners and tug boats. Until then, it was Michael's castle.

Michael was a young, fresh-faced hippy who carried his mandolin from gathering to gathering. He was a wandering minstrel, a child with a celestial aura. The soft tunes he played on his mandolin were those of an old-time miner. His sister, an active member of society, worried about the wayward, serenading Michael.

He told us the house was free, there would be no more rent, and we could each have our own floor, since there were three floors and three of us. We moved in, driving over with all our thrift store clothes in a huge pile in the back of the old Impala we bought with our tip money. It had the words "Alaska for Alaskans" on the side of it, in big electrical tape letters. We drove it slowly so the muffler wouldn't fall off, and watched the full moon on the water as we headed for our new home.

Months passed, and life was much better. Marilyn had her clothes in three piles on the floor of her room. She had one pile of clothes she would never wear, one for clothes she occasionally would wear, and one pile of the clothes she wore all the time. We shared a steam iron.

The wonder of the North country became evident to us as we watched the light change; shadows cast on the snow by the moonlight, and the sound of the train as it bellowed and chugged slowly by, following the curve of the Inlet. Michael was strange and magical, and, far from the little white house on the other side of town, we lived here peacefully for three months until the landlord showed up.

I answered the door, and a well-dressed old woman said, "Where's Michael! He hasn't paid the rent in five months! He owes me a thousand dollars!"

Right around that time, in early spring, my bartender friend walked into the men's room, entered a stall, looked down and saw a dead man. The man had simply asked the wrong girl to dance, and had two-stepped his way to an untimely end. Luckily, Marilyn and I were not working that night, but friends had seen it all. It was time to start thinking about heading South. Maybe the lucky horseshoe would wear thin. We all started making plans to go.

I put Robin back in her carrying case, and looked at her through the wire screen. "I'll see you in Spokane," I assured her. Her big soft golden eyes looked through at me, full of trust.

I said goodbye to Josefa and Marilyn at the bar and took a cab to the airport, with Robin in her carrying case, next to me on the slippery plastic seat of the cab. I looked behind me, and saw Marilyn, dressed in a parka with a fake fur hood, jumping up and down like a cheerleader, pudgy for the first time in her life.

I don't see how she gained weight on the fortune cookies we had been living on. The smoke from the log cabin bar swirled up and away into the Anchorage evening.

I didn't hear a word the stewardess told us; I had to be asked kindly, as we were taking off, to fasten my seat belt. I had staked my claim, and was returning to the Outside, victorious. I reached in the pocket of my jeans and held close to six thousand dollars in my hand.

I watched the city disappear and blackness took its place. The seat belt light flicked off as we leveled out, and I closed my eyes and fell soundly asleep, my hand wrapped tightly around the money in my pocket.

## Hitchin' With Cowboy, Kathy and Sarah Jane

When I first saw them, they were far away, about a mile it seemed, across a few gullies. The sun was bright and spring grasses were full strength. Cowboy jumped up and kicked his back heels, galloping towards me, as I stood there, holding a bucket of grain. My Levi jacket had an apple in each pocket. Sarah Jane stayed close behind him as they raced down the gullies and back up the hill where I stood waiting.

As they approached me I could see they still were wearing their snow coats. They were both like shaggy dogs, with beautiful soft fur sticking a good four inches out around their bodies to keep them warm in the freezing temperatures. They looked so beautiful, running down the hill. I had pictured them a thousand times that winter in Alaska, but I had forgotten how beautiful they were.

"Cowboy, Sarah!" I yelled, jumping up and down.

They circled around me, saw the grain in my bucket and begged for some immediately. I could tell they were they glad to see me.

I hugged their furry necks and felt their warmth. I had missed them, always dreaming about them as I slept off another shift. They had raced together in my dreams, up and down the gullies, across the high desert land, kicking up their heels as they ran.

We were united again. I buried my face in Sarah's long white coat, and hugged her for a long time. "I missed you girl," I said to her. I put their halters on, and snapped a lead rope to each of them. We walked up the hill. I smiled to myself. "This was it," I thought to myself. "This was my childhood dream."

We walked up to where my friend Kathy was waiting, sitting on the fencepost next to the gate.

"They look great," she said, as she retied her bandanna around her beautiful wavy brown hair.

"They really do," I answered.

"We hitchhiked down to Lapwai to get these guys. Now what do we do?" Kathy asked with a knowing smile on her face.

"We hitchhike back to Spokane," I told her.

I had never hitchhiked with a horse and a mule before. But I had the feeling that since it was so unusual, it just might be easy. Kathy grabbed Sarah's lead rope, and we walked together up the dirt road towards the highway.

"Have you ever tried this before?" she asked me.

"No, this is a first for me. How about you, Kath?"

"I've hitched with the best of them, but never in the company of such a distinguished looking horse," she said to me, laughing.

"Well," I said to her, "just stick out your thumb and smile."

Obviously, the cars wouldn't pick us up, since we were two girls, a large brown horse, a white mule and a dog.

"We'll try it for an hour or so," I said to Kath. "Then let's get on and ride." I hadn't brought a saddle down with me. It would be a long two hundred mile ride back to Spokane, bareback.

The third vehicle to pass was a sixty-six Chevy pickup pulling an empty horse trailer. He slowed the rig down and pulled over. Kathy and I looked at each other and smiled.

"Let's see," Kath said, "that took about five minutes. Not bad!"

"Where you headed?" a tall man wearing a tall cowboy hat asked us, leaning out from the window of the truck.

"Spokane," Kathy and I said in unison.

He carefully removed his huge frame from the cab and came back to us. Cowboy snorted at him and stepped back. Every man looked like a vet or a horseshoer to Cowboy.

"Whoa, easy Boy," I said.

Sarah just stood there and stared right at him, with her dark, intelligent eyes. She knew he had stopped to give us a ride. The horse trailer looked good to her.

"Nice looking mule!" he said, and reached out his hand to Sarah. She cautiously smelled him, the scent of his own horse on his hands. She snorted but not so loud he wouldn't give her that ride she wanted. Mules are survivalists — they think before they do anything. I had a lot to learn from this angel white mule, and I knew it from the very beginning. If I stuck with her, I would be safe. I vowed then and there never to leave her side again.

"Where did you get her?" he continued. He was really handsome when he smiled, if it wasn't for the big wad of chewing tobacco he kept doing his best to enjoy without offending us. Every time he spit at the roadside I found myself shuddering a little. He stood back and put his hands on his hips. His silver rodeo belt buckle was the size of a small frying pan, and it glistened in the hot Palouse sunshine.

"She's from Charleston, Utah. Her mom has been in a few movies. Sarah was born on a big horse ranch up there in the Wasatch Range," I said. "I used to own only a third of Sarah Jane. Then we flipped quarters for her up in a bar on the Clark Fork River, and I flipped six heads in a row. That was one of the luckiest days of my life."

He pulled out a cigarette and offered Kathy and I one. We declined.

"Well," he said, "I guess we'd better get these two loaded up."

He opened the trailer and we loaded Cowboy and Sarah, tying them in.

"Help yourself to the hay, animals!" he said, and the three of us got into the pickup. I moved his Thermos off the seat and tried to avoid the gear shift while Kathy jumped in, bumping me. I jockeyed for my position, he put out his cigarette on the pavement, standing there, looking down at the butt as he methodically moved his foot back and forth over it on the road. Then he hopped in.

"Lucky for you, I'm going all the way to Spokane. I have never picked up hitchhiking horses before," he said thoughtfully. "Or mules." He smiled and tuned in the country radio. Tanya Tucker wailed a sad and lonely love song. I looked over at Kathy and smiled. We watched as the orange sun disappeared into the purple hills above the wheat fields. We listened to the radio, and rode along for a long time in silence, taking in the beauty. The golden rays from the sun were beaming the earth with columns of light.

The cowboy stopped at a greasy spoon on the way up the long highway from Lapwai, and bought us both dinner. The mule and the horse cleaned up the extra alfalfa in the trailer. Everybody was happy.

## A Day Late For Romance

After no more than a day and a half, the horse and mule had eaten all the available pasture around the house. It was time to move on.

I decided to go back down to Utah. I had money in my pocket and high hopes. Maybe the horseshoer just didn't realize he was in love with me yet. What had taken us three months on horseback would be accomplished within a week, hitching rides from the stock yards for Cowboy and Sarah.

I rode out of the familiar Spokane neighborhood, skirting the busy downtown area, reaching the fairgrounds in two hours. I knew the next cattle auction was in the morning. I waited in the dark for Kathy to come down and pick me up in my 1959 Chevrolet pickup truck. It was painted orange, had side racks, and a radio, and didn't burn oil. What more could a girl ask for?

I waited, watching as Cowboy and Sarah settled into the small metal pen in the back of the arena. The cattle moved, groaning softly, crowded in a pen close by. "I'll make sure I get back here at dawn so there's no mix-up," I promised the animals.

The sale started at seven a.m., and I was there with a cup of coffee at six-thirty. It was a beautiful, crisp spring morning in Spokane. I checked on Cowboy and Sarah. They were finishing up a flake of hay when I told them they had better get ready, because in a matter of hours they would be in a stock truck heading towards Missoula.

I walked into the sale area, sliding into the bleachers, as the ranchers bought and sold, answering the call of the auctioneer. I watched as the wide-eyed cows were poked with a stick, to turn them around the dirt floor of the sale corral. Finally I spoke to a cowboy nearby.

"Do you know anyone who is heading back towards Montana empty?" I asked a tall, ruddy faced, white-haired cattleman who seemed centered around his huge belt buckle, the kind that is awarded.

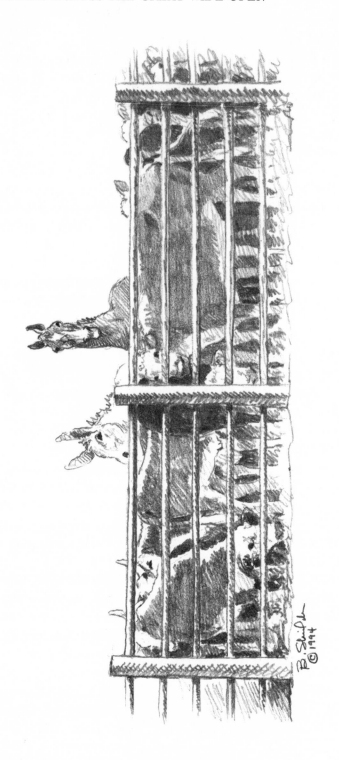

"What ya got?" he asked me.

"An Appaloosa and a white mule. I'm driving my old pickup, but I need to find a ride for the horse and mule down to Utah. Any ride going towards Montana would do!" I explained.

"Why, little lady, you just sit right here and I'll go get Stuart! You just sit right here and don't move! Stuart's going back empty! Now you wait!"

I sat there, in the sale barn, awaiting the cowboy's return, watching these lovely cows being bought and sold, turned and cracked on the rear end with a poker, sending them back out the gate and into the waiting pen. I sipped my coffee. "I will probably be in Montana by tonight," I thought to myself.

In fifteen minutes, my friend had returned with Stuart. He was roly-poly, with big friendly eyes, and a warm, soft handshake. He was about fifty, looked me up and down and said, "No horse trailer, huh? Just the truck."

I nodded. "Yep."

"Sure. I'll carry your animals to Missoula. I'm goin' back empty. They'll ride in comfort in the empty trailer. I'll be over there by ten in the morning." He shifted his cowboy boots around in the well-raked dirt of the sale yard.

"How much do you need for gas?" I asked him.

"I've got all the gas I need, lady," he laughed and added, "You keep your money. You can buy yourself a horse trailer!"

Later, after the sale was over, I watched as he loaded Cowboy and Sarah into the huge stock trailer. As he slid up the ramp, closing them in, I took one last look at my four-legged friends.

"See you in Missoula," I said to the horse and mule, under my breath, like a prayer.

I never let that truck out of my sight, all the way to Missoula. Robin sat next to me on the seat of the pickup, watching the huge stock truck anxiously, as we followed it into the darkness, on Interstate Ninety, cutting our way directly east through the tall evergreens of Idaho; up and over Lookout Pass.

Sarah Jane saw me first. She brayed, and trotted towards me. The driver had unloaded them into a corral behind the old stockyards in Missoula. I sat on the corner fencepost, watching the horse trot around the small pen with the white mule following him close behind, nipping him playfully on the back.

"Hello," an old man said. He was probably at least eighty-five years old.

His white straw hat was pushed back off his forehead. His eyes twinkled, and he squinted in the morning sun. He reached out and gave Robin a pat on her silky head. His white beard was full and bushy, covering up the collar on his grey cowboy shirt. Its pockets sagged, full of chewing tobacco tins and Kleenex. He wore 501 Levis, button down, and the dust of the Missoula stockyards covered the nice leather of his boots. He was a handsome old cowboy.

"Howdy," I answered. I had been staring at him, watching his old rugged hand gently stroking Robin's golden marble coat.

"You sure have a nice looking white mule there, don't ya? She's a beauty!" he said to me, looking towards the corral.

"Thank-you. Do you live near here?"

"No, I'm from Wyoming," he answered. "I have not been to Missoula since 1918, when I was cowboyin', right here at the stockyards."

"That's a long time to be away," I said.

"Good golly, Missoula had changed. It was just cowboys and Indians back in the 'teens. Sure has changed. Sixty years have passed since I've seen this place!" He looked as if he couldn't believe it had been so long.

I looked around. "Where's your truck?" I asked him.

"I'm on foot. They don't let me drive anymore. I had my daughter drop me off here, so I could have a look. You know, just to journey back." He wiped his eyes with the corner of his shirt.

He slowly walked around the edge of the pen, watching the horse and mule eating their hay.

"That is one pretty white mule," he said. "There is no smarter critter in the world than the mule, if you ask me." That was the last thing he said to me. I watched him as he walked away, down the road and out of view.

I bought a bale of hay down at the Lolo Feed and Seed in town, and waited for the next stock sale. Thursday morning, early, the dirt parking area next to the corrals and barns filled with big American pickups. The auctioneer tested out the microphone, and the sale began. I used the same technique that had worked so well in

Spokane.

The horse and mule loaded into the four horse trailer without a hitch.

"See you in Blackfoot, at the stockyards, around five-thirty tonight," the driver yelled from the driver's seat. "Can't miss it. Blackfoot is not much more than them stock pens!"

He laughed at this, shifted into first and started to move forward gently, looking in his rear view mirror. My beloved animals looked out the side of the stock trailer at me as I stood there with Robin. I stood there quietly until the truck was out of sight, and then ran back to the old Chevrolet, jumped in and hit the road for Blackfoot, Idaho.

Robin kept her head out the window, filling her sensitive nose with the wondrous smells of the open country, until she couldn't stand it any longer, and she fell asleep. We crossed the state, heading south towards Idaho, the old pickup truck humming along without a problem.

"Gotta boyfriend?" one of the cowboys asked me.

"I'm not sure. I'm going back to Utah to find out!" I answered.

In Blackfoot, I met a man named Slim.

"He still lives with his mom, and he's got to be forty-four," the waitress had told me, as she poured my coffee without ever looking down at the cup, and still she didn't spill a drop, and knew exactly when to stop.

"Hi, pretty lady," he had said to me the first time I saw him. "I'm Slim, better known as Slim!" He thought this was funny. "Can I buy you dinner?" he continued. "Looks like the horse and mule are settled in for the night, and the night is young! Let's head over to the Blackfoot and have a cold one!"

His tan polyester, western cut slacks were a foot too short. His cowboy shirt was short-sleeved and polyester as well. His hat was shocking white with an American flag emblem pinned to it. It was a summer straw, as they call them in Idaho. He looked about ten percent cowboy and ninety percent used car salesman, as if his car had broken down in Blackfoot, and he didn't have the money to leave. Yet his mother lived in Blackfoot, which made Slim a local.

He had to touch my shoulder as he carefully held the door

open and escorted me into the Blackfoot. The bar was dark, and I looked for the hall that lead to the bathroom. I excused myself as the waitresses looked at Slim with disdain.

"What'll it be, Slim, the usual?" the buxom bartendress asked.

"You guessed it, Sweetie, one cold one!" Slim answered, swirling on the stool at the bar. The beer poster girl stared out from behind the bar, right at Slim. Maybe he had chosen that particular seat, right in front of the poster. He caught a glimpse of himself in the mirror lined with Jack Daniel's bottles.

I looked at myself in the mirror in the bathroom. I had rosy cheeks and long brown hair in braids. My turquoise pendant hung around my neck on an old piece of leather, as it had since my high school boyfriend had given it to me, years before. I was heading towards Utah and the beautiful blond horseshoer, but I was spending the evening with Slim.

"After three more cold ones, we'll go next door to the Blackfoot Cafe. They make their own pies every morning and I can smell them from my house." This was as charming as Slim would get.

After five more cold ones for him and one for me, we walked out of the Blackfoot. From the sidewalk in front of the bar, I could see the whiteness of Sarah Jane, almost glowing, from the stock pens. Cowboy was a dark shadow. Robin had been waiting patiently, as she always did, by the door of the bar.

After meat loaf and mashed potatoes, and lots of white rolls and salad with Ranch dressing, he escorted me out of the Blackfoot.

"If you want to, you can come stay over at my mom's place," he said, sincerely.

"No thanks, Slim. I better sleep out behind the stock pens and keep my eye on the animals."

"Well, how about a little kiss?" he asked shyly. The hairs on the back of my neck stood on end.

"No, sorry Slim." I began to walk away from his car, backwards. "Goodnight!"

I woke up the next morning, rolled up my bag and threw it into the back of the pickup. I walked sleepily over to the stock pen and threw Cowboy and Sarah some oat hay. "Morning guys!" I said to them.

Almost sleepwalking, I headed towards the cafe. Blackfoot was so small, everybody knew everybody. I was sure the locals had already been talking it over. I entered the cafe, pulling the door open with a little too much force, so it hit the newspaper rack, knocking several papers on to the floor.

"It's Slim's new girlfriend," said the big waitress, turning her back as she said it, stuffing her mouth with fries.

I sat down at the counter, wiping up a small puddle of spilled cream with a napkin.

"Coffee?" she asked me, smiling. She was victorious; she had succeeded in embarrassing me. The meat loaf and mashed potatoes were the best thing about my evening with Slim. I kept quiet, wishing I had a horse trailer to attach to my truck so I could leave town.

Slim sneezed right behind me without covering his mouth. I felt the cold spray on the back of my neck, above my collar, and turned around.

"Hi!" he said, smiling like a dog in a chicken coop. "You must've froze yer behind off out there behind that stock pen."

"No, really I was fine."

"Well, today's the big rodeo, and I brought you a free ticket so you'll be sure to go."

"Why thank you, Slim! I'll see you there."

I was glad to have a ticket to the rodeo. It started around four o'clock, as the southern Idaho sun drifted into the western sky.

The bucking broncos gave every cowboy a ride for his money. Slim was always close by, to wink at me every time I looked, even remotely, in his direction. I started to look for him if he wasn't always there; bringing me a Coke or a hot dog.

After the rodeo, he suggested we do the town up right, and head back to the Blackfoot. As I was standing there, with my mouth open, trying to think of something, an older, fatherly cowboy approached me.

"I hear you need a ride to Utah! This is your lucky day! I'm going that way. Do you want me to haul your horse and the mule to Ogden?"

I was saved from another evening with Slim by a cowboy from Preston, Idaho. His old red stock truck sped towards Utah with

Cowboy and Sarah in the back. I watched my rear view mirror until Blackfoot disappeared out of sight, behind the hill south of town.

"Have a good life, Slim," I said to my rear view mirror.

Idaho sort of peters out down in the southern part of the state. The perfect brick farms dot the landscape every mile or so; most people are on their original complete sections. I raced along, with my Willie Nelson cassette wailing out a fine country tune that fit this fruitful land.

I followed the red stock truck down the highway, as the sun set out over Oregon somewhere, and wondered what it would be like to see Dave the horseshoer again after a year and a half. He and I had spent days riding together, up the cottonwood canyons near Park City. He galloped up the well-trodden trail through the young aspen groves.

He always rode bareback, on this beautiful Arab mare, Molly. She was white with a gray shadow and spots on her belly in the summer. Her foal, Moon, was just as beautiful. The young filly would follow behind Molly, racing behind her, leaping forward, trying out her running legs.

David and I would ride up the canyon and into the fir forest to a deep blue lake, a small one, perched there, between a peak and a steep trail down the canyon. We would picket the animals to trees where they could graze in the meadow next to the lake as we swam and roasted in the sun afterwards, and then we would ride back, getting to the corral as the last rays of light disappeared from the aspen grove; riding along without speaking, listening to the sounds of the horses' feet on the soft trail.

He had an old yellow van with feathers and rocks hanging from the mirror and a dashboard that had been a catch all for his paperwork for years. His shoeing forge was in the back of the van.

"I can't wait to see him again," I said to myself. Of course I wouldn't call ahead. I never did. I'd ride up the canyon and surprise him at his little ranch in Peoa.

The cowboy pulled off the road and into the parking lot of the Ogden fairgrounds, awakening me from my daydreams about Dave. The lot was full of single and double horse trailers, with the four horse trailers at the far end. The huge street lights threw a silver-white florescent glow over the trailers. I pulled into the space next to the cowboy and the red stock truck and called out to my horse.

"Cowboy, we're back in Utah, Boy. What do you guys think? Sarah! Hi girl!"

She brayed loudly, and it seemed to me that dead silence followed. I could picture the arena, full of show horses, freezing all movement, ears erect, staring through the arena walls towards the parking lot and the strange sound that had come from outside.

We could hear the voice of the announcer over the loudspeaker. A horse show was in progress. Little girls, not yet teenagers, walked their jumping ponies into the ring and mounted. Older riders were saddling their mounts.

"I don't know how easy it will be to hitch a ride with these folks, since none of 'em are selling nothing. They won't be heading back home empty!" the cowboy said, "and if you want, I'll buy you a motel room so you can have a nice comfortable night sleep. What do you think?"

It was very dark now, and I started to suggest we unload the horse and mule. All of a sudden he walked three steps towards me and I felt the hard metal of his giant cowboy belt as he wrapped his long arms tightly around me and tried to kiss me.

"Hey, cut it out!" I yelled.

"Well now, don't forget I just did you a big favor, sure you don't wanna do me one?" he said, staring at me, with his huge yellow teeth falling over each other like an old stake fence. His face reddened from embarrassment.

I watched as he closed the back of the stock truck and walked back towards the cab. I stood there as he got in the truck and slammed his door slowly.

"Thanks for the ride," I said, glad to see him drive off into the darkness. I stood there for a long time, under the bright light of the fairgrounds parking lot, wondering what to do next.

I looked around and saw an empty corral close by, out beyond the bright glow in the parking lot. I could see the Wasatch Range, ragged and dark against a very starry sky. I knew that the road to Peoa ran right up that canyon, into the folds of the mountains.

I left Cowboy and Sarah Jane in the corral with a flake of hay for each of them.

"You guys eat this, and I'll go find you a ride." I had grown weary of hitchhiking and thought about a horse trailer. I walked with Robin towards an arena, and said to her, "Rob, you go back and stay at the truck. I don't think horse shows like this and dogs like you go together."

She turned around, hung her head and returned to the truck, slinking along the pavement. "Stay girl!" I said under my breath.

I listened as the announcer said, "Thank-you all for coming. Please remember that next weekend we will have the Junior jumping competitions. Thank-you and congratulations to all our young riders. Goodnight."

People started out towards the parking lot. I asked a couple of mothers with their arms full of blankets and trophies if they knew of anyone heading up the canyon on the Interstate, and they said "No."

After a few more cool rejections from the departing Arab enthusiasts, I sat on the board corral and watched as the last trailer loaded up and left the fairgrounds parking lot.

The horse and mule happily ate their hay. The huge lights above the fairgrounds suddenly shut off, and stars covered the heavens above me. I looked up at the front range, dark and towering, the gateway to romance.

I'd figure out what to do in the morning. I wrapped up in my sleeping bag in the cab of my truck and listened to late night talk radio. It was almost like being with people, except they couldn't see me. I closed my eyes and tried to picture people to go with the voices, and woke to the Fairground Security Guard, staring at me through the window of my truck, knocking softly on the glass.

I fed the animals, and drove my truck to a nearby farm. A farmer agreed to keep it for me while I rode the rest of the way. He was friendly and didn't mind at all, saying there was plenty of room for another truck on the farm. They had a thousand acres.

"I promise, I'll bake you some bread," I told him. "I'll get a ride back from my sister to get the truck." He even gave me a ride back to the fairgrounds.

I saddled up Cowboy, and buckled on my saddlebags, filling them with dried fruit, wheat bread, and a jar of peanut butter, coffee, jam and jerky. I put Sarah on the lead rope and buckled Robin's pack to her back; she was carrying her own food. We rode out the fairground gate, through the huge wooden arch that stretched above us, across the entrance.

We reached the Interstate, and I saw instantly that I would have to ride along it to get to the frontage road heading up the canyon. The semi-trucks and trailers flew by, and the young Appaloosa looked at them with eyes wide as saucers, scared to death. After six huge trucks had stirred a wind around us as they passed, a seventh one passed, and the horse jumped straight up in the air and over the metal guard rail along the Interstate with me still in the saddle, waiting for my heart to start beating. Sarah, in true mule form, stood calm and collected on the road side of the barrier, very still, waiting to see what would happen next. I still had the lead rope in my hand.

"Well friends," I said to them, "This is the last freeway riding we will do in our lifetimes."

Sarah jumped over the barrier, onto the safe side. Another huge truck tore by, and I stuck my arms out, waving, with Cowboy's reins in my hand. The truck pulled to a stop, the brakes whining on the tires. Cowboy jumped around a little bit more. He was ready to get off this road as much as I was.

The semi driver got on the C.B. and said, "There's a cowgirl in distress up here on the Interstate, fellas, and she's needin' a stock truck or trailer ride in a big way. We got a horse, a mule, the girl and her big Labrador retriever dog and they all need a lift up the canyon, ten four!"

Within five minutes, two trucks pulling horse trailers stopped, as well as a stock truck with a calf in the back, so I had a choice of three rides up the canyon.

Two cowboys, pulling a two-horse trailer, carried us up to the top of the canyon. I sat in the cab with them, and Robin sat in the back of the pickup. I kept a close watch on her as we raced up the mountain, covering the thirteen miles to the top in twenty minutes. It would have taken me all day to ride. They dropped me off in Wanship, at the junction.

"Thanks so much, you saved us," I said to them and waved as they drove off. I set up camp behind an abandoned house. There was plenty of graze for the animals. I picketed them out on their long ropes and started collecting firewood. It was still light, and I could smell the sage as the wind swept across the hill behind my camp. No one would notice me back there, and I built a small fire and made myself some coffee and two peanut butter sandwiches.

"I can't believe I'll see Dave tomorrow. He will be so surprised!" I said to myself.

I put my saddle blankets down close to the fire and rolled my bag out. Now the lights of the city were far away, down in the great Valley of Salt, and we were in the mountains again. I watched the fire for a long time in a prone position, with Robin curled up next to me on the pad, taking up most of the room. I could hear the white mule sigh, breathing softly. She was laying down close to me, on the grass.

"Goodnight Sarah girl. Does it feel good to be almost home?" She was from a ranch up the road. She looked contended, with a full belly and a nice Appaloosa gelding to keep her company, even though he was a little bit high strung at times. We all fell asleep there, behind the abandoned building, and the fire's last coals were still glowing when I awoke at dawn. It was the dawn of the day of romance!

The sun dawned orange, yellow and gold. The sagebrush started to warm up, and filled the morning air with the smell that sets the high desert apart from any other place on earth. I walked to the edge of the sage and picked off some of the pungent plant, rubbing my fingers together, as the sweet smell of Utah filled the air around me.

Cowboy and Sarah were both standing there on their picket lines, full from the green grass that had been their dinner and their bed. They were half asleep. I smiled as I watched them both sway on their feet, with their eyes closed, the bright sun warming their coats. I reached down to the bottom of the sagebrush and found some dry wood to build a little coffee fire with. I ripped a page out of my notebook, lit a match, and held it against the paper. Within minutes, the sagebrush wood was burning, and I could hear the water boiling in the old coal black coffee pot.

I sat there, sipping my cowboy coffee, and watched the sun rise.

"I can't believe it," I said to Robin, who sat beside me, watching the fire, thinking about that delicious bone Slim had given her in Blackfoot, with all the fat hanging on it. "In about eight hours we'll be in Peoa. It's going to be so great to see David again."

I made myself another peanut butter sandwich on the smashed Home Pride Wheat I had bought in Blackfoot. I poured some creek water over the small fire and listened to the sizzling of the wood. I rolled up my sleeping bag, gave Robin a little food, and saddled up Cowboy. They grazed while they could. We rode off silently, up the bank beside the abandoned house and onto the dirt road that wound it's way up the mountain. No one had seen us back there; we had been invisible from the highway. We started up the road to Peoa, and the sun crossed the Utah sky. The horse and mule travelled fast.

I rode along the edge of the reservoir and watched as a pair of hawks circled over the water's edge. Their cries echoed off the red cliffs. Our reflection, the girl on the horse leading the mule with the big dog walking along in front, shimmered in the still blue water. We looked like we were twenty feet tall, stretched out and wavy, moving forward, pushed along by an occasional ripple. As I watched the reflection, I noticed another image in the water, approaching us. It brought my attention back to the road, and at first I couldn't believe my eyes. I looked back at the reflection to see if I was imagining this, but sure enough, there she was, heading towards us, slowing down. It was Roberta on her ten speed.

I pulled back on Cowboy's reins and said, "Whoa, Boy, Whoa." They both stopped and stood really still, with their ears forward and their eyes on Roberta. She wore cord shorts and a spaghetti strap T-shirt. She smiled at me, tossing her long blond hair back for a better look.

"Jody! I can't believe it. What are you doing up here? I can't believe you are here, and with Cowboy and Sarah and Robin. Where are you going?" She stopped and pulled her perfect, athletic body off the bike. I was speechless, and just sat there on Cowboy, staring at her, smiling.

"Up to David's in Peoa," I said to her, stumbling over the words.

"Me too!" she said, smiling, triumphantly. "Only, I got here yesterday."

After a dinner of homegrown salad greens and fresh corn and some cornbread that Roberta had baked, we three sat around the living room and watched through the windows as the high desert afternoon light disappeared, leaving the land dark red; then night came. Up in the mountains, the stars seem to blanket the entire sky, without the city lights there to steal the darkness. Trampas, David's dog, seemed as comfortable with Roberta as with David.

I had forgotten how Roberta had caught David's eye, down at the old corral; the beautiful blonde who worked at the stable where we boarded the horses and mules before the long trip to Spokane. She and David stood up, looking at each other, and then, taking each other's hand, headed slowly up the steep stairway to David's bedroom.

"Night, Jod!" David said to me as he disappeared out of view.

"Night!" I said, as cheerfully as I could. I went to the back door and opened it, walking out onto the rickety porch. The stars and moon lit up the whole back yard. The moon could not have been any fuller. I stared at the full moon for a long time; I could hear David and Roberta upstairs, laughing and saying sweet secret things to each other. I could see the silhouette of the butte behind the house. The night was magic. The horse and mule were both laying down in the deep pasture, under the trees.

I closed the screen door and went back into the living room, to the couch, my bed for the night. I pulled my sleeping bag over my ears, closed my eyes, and tried to get to sleep. I stayed that way, on the couch in my sleeping bag, wide awake, for hours.

At the first hint of dawn, I sat up straight in my bed on the couch. I looked at the clock, it was four-thirty in the morning. I tip-toed out the back door, grabbed my saddle and went out to catch Cowboy. I saddled him up, and tied him to a tree next to the house. Robin circled around me excitedly.

"Shh, girl," I said to her in a whisper.

I crept silently into the kitchen, the old wood floor creaking with my every step. I grabbed a pen and a piece of note paper from the counter and wrote a short note: "See you soon." I left it there on the table next to the toaster.

"I can literally ride off into the sunrise!" I whispered to myself.

The sun was just coming up over the buttes to the East. I rode up out of the pasture, through the gate and on to the tiny road, heading towards Park City. Cowboy was feeling spunky in the cold morning air and pranced along proudly. Sarah followed with her agile step, and Robin ran circles around us. About fifty cows were out in the middle of the road, and we followed them, riding into the rising sun.

The eighteen-mile ride to Park City took us over the sandy, sage covered hills, and as I rode along, my eyes on a puffy white cloud horizon, I changed the face of Mr. Right from David's face to a blur again.

"I guess if I had called from Ogden, he could've told me on the telephone," I said to myself as Cowboy walked steadily through the sand and sage, with Sarah next to him, and Robin with her nose to the sweet Utah wind. The beauty of the day was overpowering, and even though I lamented the loss of potential love, I was in love with my life, and the moment. I rode the range south to my sister's house. By four o' clock I could see it there on the horizon, Debbie's home at the base of the mountains.

I finally came off the sagebrush and onto the pavement in the subdivision. The sound of the hooves on the pavement echoed off the garage doors of the big, over-built redwood homes. "Stay close, Robin," I said to her as ten different Labradors from ten houses perked up for their approach on the strange dog.

"Hi, Deb!" I yelled. I could see her talking on the phone on the second floor balcony.

"Hey, Jod! Hey, Sarah! Hi Cowboy and Robin!" she yelled out the window, waving. She was six months pregnant. Her long brown hair was shining in the afternoon sun. She was still on the phone. "Put the animals out in the back, but keep them out of the garden," she said to me as I rode onto the driveway.

I went inside. It was good to be in my sister's home. I hugged her. Her large  belly pressed against me.

"So where did you ride from? Spokane?" she asked me, laughing.

"No, from Ogden. I rode up the canyon to Peoa to go visit Gobes, and Roberta was there. They're..." My voice trailed off.

"I could've told you that. They've been together for awhile

now, Jod!" She poured me a glass of apple juice over ice.

Soon she had me laughing, remembering back to the summer before. She was real quiet for a minute, thinking back on that free life; eating plums off the trees across Idaho, sleeping under a trillion stars in Montana, watching the wind blow the cattails along the river bank in the moonlight. She touched her stomach lovingly, and I watched her from behind my apple juice glass. She was a boat safe in the harbor, and I was the sister boat, tossing on a stormy sea, my sails tattered.

Debbie drove me down to the valley to pick up my truck. I took the old man some bread I baked in Debbie's kitchen; his eyes lit up when he saw it, standing on his back porch, looking through the screen.

"So, you really did bake me some bread," the farmer said to me.

"Yep! Thanks for taking care of my truck!"

"How did your ride go? Must've had one heck of a time going up the canyon!" He was concerned, he said, had been since he had seen me last, when I left the truck there, over a week before.

"Well, let's just say I made it," I said, smiling.

I drove down the small dirt road onto the highway heading back for Park City. Debbie had made arrangements for Cowboy and Sarah. A lady down the road from her house had a nice twenty-acre piece. She would let them stay down there for thirty dollars a month. The pasture was good. They ran off, bucking, when we let them free on the acreage. They would enjoy eating the sweet high mountain grasses again. I went to L.A. for two weeks, to see my parents.

B. Shields ©1994

## Cowboy Hits. The Wire

"Jod, for your birthday I'm giving you a trip to the astrologer," my mother said, as if she had said a trip to Disneyland. I was curious.

"Thanks," I said, skepticism dampening my enthusiasm.

"Really, you'll love her," Mom said, as she put on her lipstick, adjusting the makeup mirror.

The wind off the beach blew through the open window in the bedroom. Tomorrow was the appointment with Ms. Eunice Wilson, out in the Valley somewhere, and there was no backing out.

I knocked on the door of a tract house, nothing special, with the kind of cypress bushes that stick you if you get too close to them. The astrologer answered the door. "Hello, come in," she said.

She took an hour to tell me that I retained water and would be divorced.

I thanked her politely, and made it out the door to my car before I started to cry. If I was going to get divorced, why even bother finding Mr. Right in the first place? It was clear he wasn't going to just fall into my lap; the perfect man with the log cabin and the ten acres of pasture. I thought Mr. Right came with a log cabin. Or he would build one.

Back in Hermosa, my mother said, "You had better call Deb. Something has happened to your horse!"

I ran to the telephone and called Debbie in Utah. "What is it?"

"It's Cowboy, Jod. He caught the barbed wire fence in his hock and ran with it, pulled the wire right off the posts. He's pretty bad, Jod. We're putting Golden Seal on it, and giving him antibiotics. He's down in a stall at Mike's. Sarah is fine, she's in with the other horses," she added, to reassure me.

I could feel the heat in my head. I felt sick to think my horse had an accident with the fence and I wasn't there. I flew back in the morning. Mom took me to the airport, and dropped me off in front of the departure gate.

I was back with Cowboy and Sarah that afternoon. He had a huge hole in his hock; the barbed wire had been stuck in the flesh. The Boy would have to take it easy for awhile.

A month passed, in the small paddock where Cowboy was staying. I could be found there, at the old corral, redoing the bandage, taking it off and adding the Golden Seal paste that Debbie had made up. It was a really bad wound, and it was healing slowly from the inside.

"I'll be back, Cowboy!" I hated to leave him lonely, looking out over the bars of the corral. I would put a bridle on Sarah, dust her off, and ride her up the canyon bareback, just like I had the year before. We rode along for hours, crossing the creek ten times before heading up the steep hill to the top. At the top we would stand very still and look back down the hill, amazed at how far we had come. The aspens twinkled like gold coins in the late afternoon sun.

I think I'll just go for the land, and forget the man for now," I said aloud to Sarah, as she struggled up the steep rocky trail.

The land just south of the Canadian line was always on my mind. As soon as Cowboy was well enough, we would head north. The money was diminishing daily, like washwater down the drain.

"Line your pockets with memories," a ninety-year-old woman in Clark Fork had told me.

I would go find a little piece of ground with a low enough down payment and good terms. I was facing the North with anticipation and excitement. I could almost see the smoke, curling up from the chimney in the log cabin of my future, with Cowboy and Sarah standing on the porch, staying out of the snow.

"Jod, Terry and Rick will take Sarah and Cowboy all the way back to Spokane, if you can get them to the fairgrounds in Salt Lake," Debbie told me when I got back to the house. "You should get some land, and when we're old ladies we can live together," Deb said, as the teapot boiled and whistled so loud my ears were ringing.

We sat in the kitchen and quietly drank our tea. The Utah summer was rich, with long, sunny days at eight thousand feet.

"I'm going to miss you, Deb," I told her. "Sometimes I wish we could go back to last summer." She sat there, with the yellow light reflecting in her brown eyes.

She went to the cupboard and pulled out a fresh loaf of bread.

Bread always made us feel better. We were parting again; she'd have a baby in her arms the next time I saw her. We spread fresh apricot preserves across the bread, and ate silently.

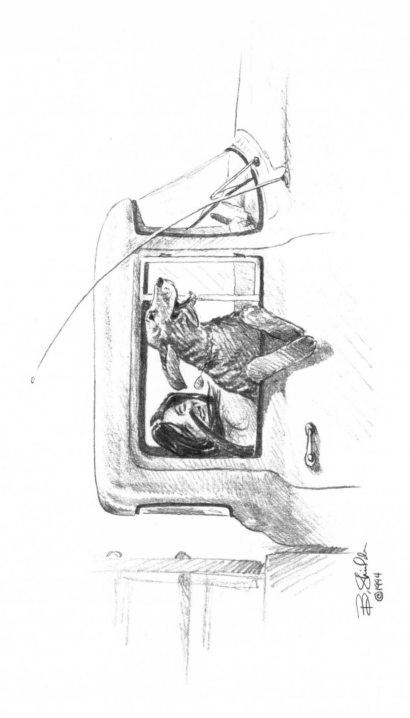

## The Fencepost Farm

I said goodbye to my friends in Park City and headed down to the fairgrounds with Cowboy and Sarah and Robin. A friend from the stable had a horse trailer and gave the animals a ride down, and I followed with Robin in the orange truck, with an Emmy Lou Harris song blasting in our ears through the cheap car speakers.

The fairgrounds were dark. We put Cowboy and Sarah in a pen; their ride to Spokane would not be there until the morning. I would sleep right there next to them in the cab of my truck.

"Hey, what are you doin'!" he yelled at me. I looked up and watched him approach the truck, weaving towards us. He was around sixty, with the red cheeks and swollen eyes of someone too fond of the bottle. He still maintained, even though he was pretty drunk, a gentlemanly manner. His white summer Cowboy straw was in perfect condition; his suit was a white polyester western-style leisure suit, and I could see the square whiskey bottle in his pocket. He had parked his truck at the other end of the fairgrounds parking lot, and was walking slowly but determinedly towards me.

He stopped and looked at Cowboy and Sarah. He stared at Sarah, watching her eat her hay, and he stood there, swaying, trying to light his pipe, swearing under his breath, as I watched him closely to see what would happen next. The fairgrounds were dark, and there were no other people around. He didn't seem threatening to me, but still I had not counted on company down there behind the stock pens. I already missed Deb. Out in the back of the stock pens in the fairgrounds, I could not chose my company.

"Yep, just as I thought. I couldn't believe my eyes at first, but that's her! That's her all right!" He looked at Sarah, shaking his head in disbelief. "I never thought I'd see her again!" he said to me, thoughtfully. "I saw that mule bein' born." He looked at me with eyes full of tenderness. "You should'a seen her mother!" he roared. "She's a beautiful Appaloosa, the prettiest Appaloosa I have ever seen. I bet that's hard for you to believe, but I saw her bein' born, up in Charleston. I swear it!"

He looked at me right in the eye and pulled out a huge bundle of dollars. "I'll give you two thousand for her, right now. Here's the money!" He held up the money for me to see. I looked at the red vessels, broken in his tired eyes. He was telling the truth. He knew Sarah Jane.

"She's not for sale. I could never part with her. I flipped six heads in a row for her, up in a bar in Montana. My sister and my friend John and I owned her together; I guess we each owned a third of her. I flipped six heads in a row, I still can't believe that!" I said to this man who was getting very sentimental about my mule.

He waved the money around again, tried to light his pipe, and offered me two thousand five hundred dollars for Sarah before he finally gave up and walked a crooked path down the alley way between the pens and out of sight behind the big barn. I slept with one eye open, never blinking for too long in case the white mule should disappear.

"The lady's not for sale," I said to Robin. I was using her back as my pillow. I tuned in the country station to keep me company. I slept for twenty minutes or so, then I'd sit up and look out into the pen to make sure Sarah was still there. Somehow, the night ended and morning came.

We were heading north, with a couple thousand dollars and high hopes for the log cabin dream. I just knew there was a pretty little valley up there with my name on it.

I raced along at fifty behind the horse trailer carrying Cowboy and Sarah, and I tried to tune in the radio. The sunshine was pouring in through the windows of the truck. It was really good that Deb's friends could haul the animals back to Spokane for me. They were going anyway, but hadn't been planning on towing a horse trailer. I helped pay for gas, and bought the meals.

"Well, Robin," I said to my dog sitting beside me, "here goes, a whole new adventure. I think we may go back to college. What do you think?" She was looking out the window, watching a herd of sheep shuffling down the barrow ditch. She didn't care what we did, as long as she had my full attention, good food and meadows to play in. She relished Nature, as only a dog can. She always kept her nose to the wind.

Idaho flew by as we raced north, flying along in the orange

truck, going at least fifty-five. The highway stretched out like a ribbon; hill after hill and up into the mountains as we crossed Idaho.

I had rented a room in a house outside of Spokane, in Four Lakes, and had sent the money ahead to my friends from Whitworth, Dave and Carol. Dave was a white-blond California boy, with a big warm smile, a ten speed, and a geology degree in the works. He and Carol had met at school.

Carol was a local girl, from Deer Park, and loved horses as much as I did. She would take care of Cowboy and Sarah for me until school started. I had about ten days to search Montana and Idaho for my piece of the rock.

Once we had Cowboy and Sarah unloaded into the four acres of pasture next to the house, and I had unloaded my belongings, Robin and I drove off in the orange truck, heading for Montana. I played my Emmy Lou tape, and drank a large cup of coffee in a styrofoam cup.

I flew  towards Montana, with my dog riding shotgun, her long silky ears flapping and her nose out the window, upwind. We drove along that way for a long time, as the old truck flew down the Interstate, along Lake Coeur d'Alene, a big blue lake stretching across the Panhandle. Before nightfall, I was in a little town outside of Kalispell, eating an oversized cinnamon roll, reading the Real Estate Gazette, at a little cafe called the Park Inn. It is famous for its huge cinnamon rolls the size of hub caps.

"This sounds good," I said to myself, as I circled an ad for twenty acres, part pasture, part timber, a thousand dollars down and a hundred a month for the rest of my life. The waitress came by and brought me more coffee. I sat there, in that little cafe with the huge cinnamon rolls for a long time before I finally packed it up and took Robin her share. She gobbled it up in no time. We drove down to the river and slept in the cab of my truck.

I drove north on the highway, forty miles or so, and found a pay phone. There was an antique shop there, and I went in and looked around, and then headed back out to the phone and called the number in the ad for the twenty acres.

"Why sure, come on out, this afternoon at two, if you like, and we'll show you YOUR NEW RANCH!" the man on the phone said to me.

"My new ranch?" I said to myself as I jumped back in the truck. I drove down the highway a little further, out of town and towards Canada. As the crow flies, Canada was only a few miles from there, through the trees. It was Big Sky Country. It was summertime, and everything looked so good to me. Maybe it was just the land I was looking for.

I turned off at the mailbox with "two thousand and six" written on the side, just as the man on the telephone had told me to. I saw the airstrip, as I drove slowly down the long driveway, parking next to a house that looked like one you'd see on a cul-de-sac in some suburb, not in the wilds of northern Montana. There were six Cadillac Sevilles in the driveway, but I didn't see any people around.

I got out of the truck, slamming the door before Robin could get out. "You stay here, girl. I'll go find out what this is all about."

Before I even made it through the door, a short man with dark glasses and a permanent grabbed my arm and escorted me to a chair. "Here, little lady, wait until you see your RANCH! We'll be going out there, soon as Shorty gets back," he said to me in a real friendly voice; too friendly.

"Shorty?" I said to myself. They all walked in at once, six men in suits. They were dressed to the tee, and all had the same type of sunglasses on. Was this the real estate company? I shifted nervously on the parlor seat.

We all packed into two of the Cadillac Sevilles, with Robin watching us leave from the cab of my truck. All of the men smelled good; like expensive aftershave. I was almost afraid to get out and walk around the woods with these guys, all of them looking like they just stepped out of a gangster movie. They left their sunglasses on the whole time, as we walked the boundaries of "my" twenty acres.

"You can start a fencepost company, with all the lodgepole pines you have on this piece!" He talked as if I had already bought the place. The land was beautiful, and sure there were lots of poles, but it was a nice piece, and would be even nicer when the road came all the way to the property. They promised me this would happen by the following summer. The men in the suits escorted me through the woods as if we were looking at used cars on a lot in Chicago. They stepped over the downed trees in their path with the finesse of businessmen on an escalator. These men were not from Montana, I was sure about that.

We loaded into the Seville and headed back towards the house.

Before I left that day, the sunglassed men with the perms had convinced me that the land was going fast, and I had better put some earnest money down, just in case someone else wanted that particular piece. It could be sold by the morning!

I drove slowly back to town, the bundle of money in my pocket feeling lighter already. I had given them a hundred and fifty dollars in earnest money, and I already had buyer's remorse, and had completely changed my mind by the time I got back to the little one-street town nestled in the endless pine trees. I parked the truck, fed Robin her dinner on the truck seat, and went into the bar.

I walked in and every single person stopped talking and turned around and stared at me. The smoke burned my eyes as I made my way up to the bar and sat down. New girl in town. This was a big deal up here; the land was rich in trees and big brown bears and rivers, but not ladies. I ordered a cup of coffee with cream from the bartender, who was wiping his hands on his apron; the keg had just exploded.

"So, what's a pretty girl like you doin' in a place like this." A big logger was breathing down my neck, and he smelled like chainsaw oil, pine sap and diesel fuel. And on top of it all, he reeked of cigarettes and beer. But underneath, the fuel smell was always with him. He was one of those men who apparently never bothered to get his hands clean, since he'd just get them dirty again.

"I'm going to buy some land up the road from here, on the flat."

"Oh, yeah? What are you gonna do, raise fenceposts?" This brought a peal of laughter from the bartender and the other drinking men.

The bartender walked slowly down the bar and approached me with concern, saying, "You didn't give the old man any money, did you?"

I swallowed hard. The logger heard him say this to me and bellowed, at the top of his lungs, "You bought a fencepost farm from them! Are you crazy?" His face was about three inches from mine, and he looked right at me, his eyes on fire. "Them guys are the mob."

I felt the hair on the back of my neck stand on end. What had I done? I had given money to the Mafia.

"So, what are you doing?" A boy, about nineteen, slid in next to me at the bar.

"Well, I came up here, looking for land, and found twenty acres today, the first twenty acres I looked at! The price is right," I said defensively.

He was looking at me very seriously, from behind his matchbook, as he lit a cigarette. "That guy's the mob."

I sat there, quietly, drinking my coffee, wondering how I would get my money back. Maybe buying that twenty wasn't such a hot idea. I had let them push me into giving them that earnest money.

I looked at this kid next to me. His young skin was bright red, in the neon glow from the Bud sign behind the bar. He smiled, revealing a missing front tooth. He had a NRA hat on, and a vest that looked like he had hunted in it; there was dirt and dried blood ground into the quilted fabric. He was a local. He knew the country.

He lit another cigarette, and blew the smoke out slowly,

watching it drift down the bar. "I know where there's some land for sale. It's my dad's land. It's forty acres up on top."

"Up on top?" I said to him. "What's up on top?" I took a quick, nervous drink of my lukewarm coffee. He smiled at me; yep, the gap was still there, right in the middle of his big friendly grin.

"Up on the ridge. My dad is selling some acreage, real cheap. You don't want to buy the land from those other guys. I'm sorry you didn't run into me first." He ordered us each a beer.

We both turned away from each other, and I went back to feeling bad about giving that earnest money away for the twenty acres of fenceposts. It was not what I wanted. I had to slow down, and remember what my parents' friends had told me: "Location, location, location."

The bar was picking up by this time. A very tall, skinny cowboy, looking out of place in this logger bar, sauntered up to the pool table with the cue tucked under his arm. He pulled the brim of his cowboy hat down over his eyes, and set up the game, gathering the balls together in the black plastic triangle. He moved slowly, methodically. Beer ran through his veins like blood, I could tell. He was very aware of himself as he pulled the cue stick back into position for the first shot of the game. "Take this job and shove it, I ain't working here no more" rang out the song, loud and clear, over the jukebox. Everyone in the bar joined in. Most of these men worked at the mill north of town. They all sang, "Take This Job and Shove it" at the top of their lungs, with gusto.

The bartender paced back and forth, wiping his hands on his apron when he could, occasionally looking out onto the street where the big pickup trucks with the fuel tanks on the back were lined up in front of the bar. He looked worried, like he had been there too long, and he was wondering to himself if this was it for him; he'd be there forever, serving beer to the loggers, over and over again.

My young friend sitting next to me spun around on his stool and said, "I'll take you up there right now to see it if you want."

"It's pretty dark, don't you think?"

"Nah, the moon is full. Let's go take a look!"

"Oh, why not, let's go take a look," I said to him. "I have a big dog, you know. She's got to come with us."

"Okay, let's go." We walked out onto the street of the tiny, silent Montana town. The only noise in the whole valley was generating from that little bar, out in the middle of nowhere, just south of Canada, where the valleys widen and the mountains reach to the heavens. The moon was full. I jumped in his truck, a new pickup, and put Robin on the seat between us.

"The dog has to sit in the back." He was serious.

"Okay, girl, get in the back," I said to Robin. She jumped out of the cab and into the back of the pickup. He started forward slowly and I slammed my door.

He drove to the top of a mountain on the paved road, and then took off on a dirt road, heading down into a meadow. We drove along on a bumpy road for about twenty minutes, circling around the mountain. He stopped in an open meadow. The moon dashed bright light across the grasses, as they swayed in the breeze coming off the top of the mountain.

"Well, here's the land my dad is selling," he said as he popped the top off a beer. He lit a cigarette. We both sat there for at least ten minutes, until he had finished his smoke.

"Come here, baby," he said to me in a baby talk voice. He reached over and started to slide himself onto my side of the cab. Robin was looking through the glass at me.

"What are you doing? Let's head back to the bar. I want to go back." I pushed against him as he tried to kiss me. He smelled like a cigarette.

"No. Forget it! Take me back!" I yelled at him.

"Get out of my truck. Get out!" he screamed at me. He started up the motor. I looked up and realized that Robin was still in the back of the truck.

"Robin! Robin, girl! Come on!" I screamed to her.

He stepped on the gas and took off, just as Robin jumped off the bed of the truck onto the dirt road. It was a long walk back to town.

I listened as the sound of his engine was overtaken by the night sounds of the woods. The crickets were singing in harmony, like one voice. The moon lit up the whole valley. I could hear the river now, laughing its way through the night. I was alone with my dog, out in the middle of nowhere. I walked down the dirt road towards town. Four hours later, in the early hours of morning, Robin and I made it back. We had walked most of the night.

"Let's go get our money back," I said to Robin.

The coffee shop wasn't even open yet. The town was quiet. Everyone was still asleep. The sun was pushing over the top of the cedar covered mountainside. It made its way with its golden shadow across the morning darkness, and the whole world came alive.

The door on the coffee shop jingled as the waitress unlocked the door and turned around the CLOSED sign. I could smell the coffee. I walked into the Chain Saw cafe and was the first customer. I watched the coffee as it rolled into my white porcelain cup. I was tired, but elated. I had walked off the mountain with the full moon lighting my path, my dog beside me.

I wrapped my hands around my coffee cup and ordered breakfast. The eggs tasted like the griddle; a combination of hamburger, pancakes and bacon. The hashbrowns looked like they had been smashed with a twenty pound spatula, then deep fried. The toast was wet and warm, with the margarine melted into the center. I was gathering myself for my morning with the mob, and hoped to get back my hundred and fifty dollars.

I walked out onto the still empty street and reached down to give Robin a piece of toast. She gobbled it up and smiled at me. We walked slowly towards the old orange pickup and drove out of the one coffee-pot town, to "two thousand and six" Highway North.

"They have their own air strip, Robin, can you believe this?" I drove slowly up the long driveway to the suburban house and parked the truck.

The shorter man with the permanent came out and said, "How did you sleep, little lady? Did you dream about your new homestead?" He took one hand and laid it flat against his permanent, to see if the waves were in place. He smiled at me, his silver tooth glittering in the Montana morning.

"Is the boss here?" I asked him.

"No, he went to Missoula in the plane. Should be back by this afternoon. Why?" His Doberman came out of the house, tapping his claws on the pavement; the entire yard was paved. Robin growled at the dog; she was sitting in the cab of my truck.

"I've changed my mind about the twenty acres, and I want my earnest money back," I said to him. I looked deep into his eyes, or at least I stared hard at the center of his sunglasses. I hoped I was making some serious eye contact, but I couldn't be sure.

The Doberman was running around my truck, then standing on his haunches with his big runny nose pressed to the window. Robin growled. Luckily, the glass was between them.

"Down, boy!" He yelled at the dog. He looked down and realized he had stepped in some gum. He leaned his body against the Seville and tried to peel it off his shoe with a pocketknife.

"Now why would you go and do a thing like change your mind about the land. You are making a big mistake, that's all I'm gonna tell you!"

"Can you give me my money back? I really need to get going."

"Where are you going?" he asked me.

"Down the road, I don't know for sure."

He smiled at me and said, "Big Sky Country is going fast. You are walking away from the chance of a lifetime. Maybe you had better stay here and wait."

He turned and started towards the house.

"No! Please! I really need to get going. Can't you give me my earnest money back?" I was not going to back down and sit around all afternoon waiting for Mr. Big.

He looked a little irritated. He stood there in the driveway with the Doberman running small, neurotic circles around him. He shook his head, pulled a huge wad of money out of his pocket, and peeled off a hundred and fifty dollars. He pushed at the center of his glasses and shuffled towards me, his head down.

"Here, now get out of here!" he said, as he pressed the bills into my hand.

I drove down the long driveway, and turned right, shifting into third and then fourth, heading back down the highway. I wrapped a bandanna around my forehead and tied it in the back as the day warmed up. It kept my hair from blowing in my face.

I was holding on to the remaining few coins of my treasure. I would go back to dinner salads with lots of saltines and coffee. Robin had a new sack of dog food, so she was set. The longer it took to find the homestead, the less money there would be to give to the Realtor.

"Robin, I don't know where we're going, but we're on our way," I said to the dog riding shotgun. We pulled into a turn-off next to Thompson Falls. The waterfall was crashing down into the roaring river.

Standing there, next to a rock, was a tall man in buckskin clothing. This character was a regular old Daniel Boone, complete with fringe and laces. He was standing still, with his head up and his hand balancing on the top of a walking stick. His Chihuahua huddled close by, his back hunched up, tiptoeing around the parking lot, looking miserable.

"Interested in poetry? This is my book of poetry, 'Firewater and Gas.' What do you think? Would you like to buy a copy?"

He leaned over and handed me the book. I flipped through it and could see that it was full of rhyming Western poetry; poems about Sacajawea, the bears, and the cowboys that found themselves in all sorts of predicaments. The sound of the river roaring below the falls made conversation a yelling match.

"This looks good," I said to him. "I'd like to buy one."

"Thanks, little lady. Two dollars and fifty cents will buy you one. This is the way I feed me and Skeeter, here. And lucky for me, I still have my wife cookin' it up for me. We are retired, and the poetry is my livin'. This is my backyard, sweetie pie!" He yelled, motioning with his free arm, beyond the waterfall to the high cedars and the mountain tops. The Chihuahua huddled against his legs, looking for any amount of warmth he could find.

"Looks like your dog needs a little sweater or something!" I said to him, pointing down at Skeeter.

"Oh, we have one. The wife knitted Skeeter a little sweater, you should see the darn thing!" He walked over and opened the trunk of his mid-Sixties two-door Impala. It creaked open, with rust popping off around the edges. He slammed it closed, and walked over, his buckskin fringes blowing in the wind, his long white hair blowing off his narrow shoulders. Years of hard life filled his face, and yet he had such a child-like love for the wilderness.

In his big hand he had a tiny, blue, knitted dog sweater. He leaned down and pulled the sweater over the shivering legs of the tiny pup, its nails catching in the neck hole.

"Here you go, Skeeter, little fellow," he said to the

Chihuahua who skittered off in the little blue sweater. "Isn't that the cutest little sweater you have ever seen?" he asked me, as he pulled some tobacco out of a pouch and started stuffing his pipe. "It's kinnickinick, have you ever heard of it? The Kootenai Indians gave it to me. They are all friends of mine."

He lit the pipe, and looked out over the waterfall. "This is what I call my home." We both were quiet, listening to the waterfall, watching the white spray rising towards us. "So what brings you to the Northland, little lady? I can see by your plates you're from Washington state. Spokane? I used to go to Spokane and sell poetry down there, but then people thought I was a bum, so I came back out here, closer to home. The wife and I have a little trailer just outside of Libby, beyond the mill. It's on a little crick." He stopped and laughed, watching the dog try to walk with dignity in the little blue sweater.

"Oh, I went to Alaska last winter and saved up enough money to buy a little piece of land," I told him. "Since I have a horse and a mule back in Spokane, I need to find a place with a little pasture, a nice watering pond, and lots of trees for building."

He stopped me. "Down in the Bull River is nice, same with the Clark Fork. Both of the valleys have rivers runnin' right down the middle of them, and lots of nice pasture land on the side. What are you gonna do, settle down and raise a family with your husband?" He could see my immediate embarrassment.

"I don't have one," I said to him softly. "It's just me and the dog and the horse and the mule."

"What's your mule's name?" he asked me.

"Sarah Jane," I said. "She is a beautiful white mule, smart as a tack. You should see her. She's really something."

"Do you ride her?"

"Oh yeah, we ride her," I told him. "Last summer we were on the trail for three months, and rode all the way from Utah to Spokane. That is when I first saw the Clark Fork River and Lake Pend Oreille. I fell in love with this country."

"Just remember, little lady," he said to me, dead serious now. "Just remember, the only true home you have, you carry with you, in your heart. That way, you are always home. Don't forget that. Sometimes you buy the land, and you work hard to pay for it, and sometimes, you know what? It ends up owning you."

He stopped and looked quietly at the river. The Chihuahua and Robin were sniffing each other, walking in circles, nose to tail. The Chihuahua's front feet were barely on the ground as he circled around trying to get a good whiff of my dog. Who was she, and where had she been? We listened to the river.

"Thanks for the book. I'll enjoy it," I said to him. He smiled. I started heading for the truck. It was getting on in the afternoon, and I had not slept at all last night. "Goodbye, and thanks again," I said.

"Goodbye, little lady. Remember what I told you," he said, as he waved his pipe in front of me, slowly, "home is really right here," he patted his chest, "in the heart."

I watched him approach another car full of people who had just pulled into the parking pull-out for the waterfall view. He had his poetry books in a bundle, underneath his arm, the buckskin fringe on his jacket waving at me as I drove off and lost sight of him in my rear view mirror.

I plastered my outhouse walls with the poems from "Firewater and Gas", and read them over and over again, as I sat on the wooden seat, looking out at the pasture that ended up owning me. The man in the buckskin suit was right about a lot of things.

## A Piece of the Rock

The orange truck glided along the small two-lane highway heading down the Bull River. This valley, edged between mountains, is the definition of natural beauty. The lake's reflection was the light, yellow face of Cabinet Mountain, rising thousands of feet above the valley. As I drove slowly south, the sun was this certain way, this certain golden light, that lit up the mountain face and the cottonwoods along the river, grazing ground for the elk and the whitetail deer.

I walked into the Bull River Inn, and three men were slumped over draft beers, trying to keep from slipping off the tiny, spinning bar stools. They all spun around, stopping themselves from a complete spin by lowering their cowboy boots onto the linoleum floor all at once, scraping them along the red floor tile.

"I'll have a cup of coffee with cream and sugar please," I said to the bartender.

"Sure. You are one of our only customers today. Where is everybody?" he asked me.

"I don't know. I'm just passing through the valley for the first time. Never seen this place before; it sure is beautiful."

"Beautiful it is, he said. "But you should check it out in February. Now, that is what I call beautiful. Where are you going?"

"Back to Spokane, eventually," I told him. I could see Robin, sitting up straight as an arrow in the cab of the truck. "I'm looking to buy some land."

"Oh really, do you have any money on ya?" This made the three drunk men start to laugh between themselves.

"Well, not much. I only have about a thousand dollars left now. I have been looking around for a few months, and you know what?"

"What?" He poured himself a draft.

"I spent almost all the money I saved in Alaska, first looking for Mr. Right, and now looking for the right land."

He laughed. "Shoulda come seen me months ago. I've got

land! Wanna get married, and solve all your problems at once!" This really got the three spinners at the end of the bar going; they were laughing, spinning back and forth on the tiny bar stools.

I headed out into the clear, sunny afternoon. "Where's our dream ranch, Robin?" I yelled to her.

I opened the door of the orange truck and let her out so she could take a quick sniff around. I had left her in the cab because there were so many dogs around, more dogs than people in Bull River.

We drove south as the sun slipped behind Cabinet Mountain, down the highway, past the ancient cedar grove, crossing the Bull River twice. It was a big, clean, powerful river full of fish, that flowed into the Clark Fork River, on its way to Lake Pend Oreille.

"We're back in Clark Fork, Rob. Remember this town?" I said to her as we pulled into the dirt parking lot in front of the Real Estate Office. Land was still cheap over there. Still far from Sandpoint and the real desirable waterfront acreage, it was a good hour's drive from town.

Last fall, I had arrived on a dirt road on the other side of the river. We had approached Clark Fork at three and a half miles an hour, not fifty. We were broke and hungry, and the name of the cafe then was the "Broke and Hungry Cafe".

I got out of the truck and told Robin to stay. I went into the cafe for a quick cup of coffee before I talked to the Realtor. I sat at a small red stool at the counter. An older woman brought me a cup of coffee. She was round, with a flowered apron over her dress and her hair was put up in silver curls wound tightly to her head.

"I remember you, from last fall," she said. "Didn't you ride through here on an Appaloosa with a bunch of horses and mules?" She was standing there, looking at me, smiling.

"Yep, that was me."

"Where's that big dog you had with you last year. Is she still with you?"

"Yes, she's out in the truck."

"Oh, so you're not on horseback this time. Well, I'll be!" she said as she refilled my coffee cup.

"I bet she's looking for her little piece of the rock," the Realtor said to his secretary, as he watched me leave "The Cedars

Cafe and Saloon", heading across the street towards his office. The air smelled like lilacs and pine sap, wood smoke and freshly milled lumber.

The Clark Fork River was right down the street. It was big and slow moving, making its way to the slough before opening up into the deep, blue Lake Pend Oreille, jewel of the Panhandle.

I entered the office, the screen door swinging open in the wind, and shook the warm hand of a friendly man named Dave.

"Hi, I'm Jody. I'm looking for some land." I looked at the aerial view photo of the area. The photograph was criss-crossed with property boundaries. He offered me a cup of coffee.

"Well, you've come to the right place, Jody. How much do you want to put down, so I know what to show you?"

"Oh, I have a thousand to put down," I told him.

"Oh." He looked a little disappointed. "Well, do you want to go look at land with me, out in the valley? I have some parcels for sale out there that you might like. They are twenty acres, with some nice trees, a potential pond, a good view of the Cabinets. No developed water but a lot of surface water and a place that looks like a spring."

"I remember you from last summer. You rode through here with your sister, heading towards Spokane. Did you make it over there before the big storm hit in October?" he asked.

"Yes, we did," I told him. We arrived in Spokane two days before the big rain."

"That must've been quite a trip. I wish I could just take off like that sometime." He motioned me towards his truck and he let Robin ride along with us in the cab, once he moved all his paperwork off the seat. He pointed towards the Cedars. "It was the Broke and Hungry when you were here last year, wasn't it? They went broke."

We drove out across the bridge, and I looked down into the clear, slow moving river. I remembered what I had felt like that night, when we camped by the river, and I sat on the bridge for hours, watching the water below me. We drove along in his new pickup, heading backs towards the Montana line. "The road turns to dirt at the Montana line," he said to me.

I looked out the window as we sped down the county road. I smiled to myself, and thought about last summer, riding Cowboy down the same road, remembering how we were then. We ate berries off the bushes, apples off the overladen trees and fish given to us by men that fished the lakes and rivers. We were so free, packing our mules across the West without a worry in the world.

We walked around the entire twenty acres. Robin raced around, sticking her nose in the rotting logs that lay scattered around the property. The view of the Cabinet mountains was magnificent. There was lots of pasture, even a big pond that was half full.

"You can make your own bricks out of the mud in this pond," the Realtor told me. "Or, dredge it out and raise ducks."

I looked around at the big cottonwoods and white pines and ponderosas and cedars growing on the place. I pictured a big log cabin, with the smoke curling from the chimney. I could see Cowboy and Sarah grazing peacefully, and Robin, digging holes until she could dig no more. The Clark Fork River was right below the land, down a rugged dirt road that dropped to the water.

"It's almost riverfront, except for the thousand foot drop to the river," he said, smiling. Before the hour was up, I would sign on the dotted line and give my last thousand dollars to the Realtor.

We walked up the little seasonal creek. It was a trickle, but had promise.

# About the Author

Charlie Parker

Jody Foss lives in Northern California with her five mules:
Mavis, Sarah Jane, Brighty, Reba and Nadine; her true
love Charlie Parker, seven cats and a dog named Mate.
Since 1976, the author and her mules have travelled over
6,000 miles on the back roads and trails of the West. Jody
is working on her second book, about her homesteading
days in northern Idaho and a six hundred mile solo mule
trip from her cabin in Clark Fork, Idaho to Newport, Oregon.
Her mule-ti-media program, *Mules Across America,* has
been a favorite of audiences at schools and libraries all
over the West and in Japan.

# About the Artist

*Rebecca Holland*

It's not easy bein' a mule artist these days. Your subjects won't stand still and your critiks are legion —but, *somebody's* got to do it!

Born and raised in southern Indiana, I was not around mules until I moved to middle Tennessee in 1965. When the mule and I first met, it was like a blow from the fist of fate and neither one of us has been "right" since. On *my* part, the blow went straight to the heart. Don't ask the mule where the blow hit *him*! I've been drawing and painting all my life (none of your business) starting my career at the age of four on grandma's kitchen wall. Since then my education has been in dibs and dabs on the formal side, but blipps and blapps on the practical side. All grist for my particular mill, I ass-shure you.

Speaking of such, I met Jody Foss (and Sarah and many of these other characters) when I moved to the wilds of Sandpoint, Idaho in 1980. It's been fun keeping up with each other's adventures through the years and comparing mule stories. Oh, yes. I have several mules up here on the Brass Ass, our little "spread."

I also have several mule type art prints, bronzes, and assorted stuff available. If you're interested, just write me at: *The Tennessee Mule Artist,* 3450 Gold Creek Rd., Sandpoint, Idaho, 83864. I'd love to hear from you. Meantime, like my hero mule, Leroy says—keep your traces tight.

*Bonnie*

# Order Page

For copies of *Mules Across the Great Wide Open*

Send check or money order to:

Mules Across America

Box 225, Tomales, California  94971

For credit card orders:

Call or fax us at 707-878-2095

Please include name, address, Visa or Mastercard

number, and expiration date.

Softcover: $14.95

Hardcover: $19.95

In California add 7.25% tax to price of book.

Please add $3.00 per book for first class shipping.

Discounts for wholesale orders.

Delivery by mule is a little extra.